Praise for *Fundamentals of Psycholinguistics*

"*Fundamentals of Psycholinguistics* contains an astonishing amount of information about speech and language use, all presented so deftly that reading is a pleasure."

Janet Dean Fodor, Graduate Center, City University of New York

"What most shines through is the authors' great enthusiasm for elucidating the ideas that drive contemporary research in psycholinguistics. The wealth of their experience has produced a fresh, modern, and above all appealing introduction to this interdisciplinary field."

Dianne Bradley, Graduate Center, City University of New York

"Fernandez and Cairns expose the mysteries of the human language ability by weaving together the insights gained from fifty years of psycholinguistic research into a highly readable introductory text."

Lyn Frazier, University of Massachusetts, Amherst

"The coverage of this textbook is exactly right for an introductory-level course. It offers clear and up-to-date information in every area without overwhelming the reader. The thread on multilingualism is unique."

Dana McDaniel, University of Southern Maine

"The authors have done a masterful job of reviewing current and long-standing issues in Psycholinguistics in a balanced, engaging fashion. An excellent introduction to the field!"

Janet Nicol, University of Arizona

Fundamentals of Linguistics

Each book in the Fundamentals of Linguistics series is a concise and critical introduction to the major issues in a subfield of linguistics, including morphology, semantics, and syntax. The books presuppose little knowledge of linguistics, are authored by well-known scholars, and are useful for beginning students, specialists in other subfields of linguistics, and interested non-linguists.

What is Morphology?
Mark Aronoff and Kirsten Fudeman

What is Meaning? Fundamentals of Formal Semantics
Paul H. Portner

Fundamentals of Psycholinguistics
Eva M. Fernández and Helen Smith Cairns

Fundamentals of Psycholinguistics

Eva M. Fernández
and Helen Smith Cairns

WILEY-BLACKWELL

A John Wiley & Sons, Ltd., Publication

This edition first published 2011
© 2011 Eva M. Fernández and Helen Smith Cairns
Adapted from *Psycholinguistics: an introduction*, Helen Smith Cairns (1999)

Blackwell Publishing was acquired by John Wiley & Sons in February 2007. Blackwell's publishing program has been merged with Wiley's global Scientific, Technical, and Medical business to form Wiley-Blackwell.

Registered Office
John Wiley & Sons Ltd, The Atrium, Southern Gate, Chichester, West Sussex, PO19 8SQ, United Kingdom

Editorial Offices
350 Main Street, Malden, MA 02148-5020, USA
9600 Garsington Road, Oxford, OX4 2DQ, UK
The Atrium, Southern Gate, Chichester, West Sussex, PO19 8SQ, UK

For details of our global editorial offices, for customer services, and for information about how to apply for permission to reuse the copyright material in this book please see our website at www.wiley.com/wiley-blackwell.

The right of Eva M. Fernández and Helen Smith Cairns to be identified as the authors of this work has been asserted in accordance with the UK Copyright, Designs and Patents Act 1988.

Library of Congress Cataloging-in-Publication Data

Fernández, Eva M.
    Fundamentals of psycholinguistics / Eva M. Fernández and Helen Smith Cairns.
        p.   cm. — (Fundamentals of linguistics)
    Includes bibliographical references and index.
    ISBN 978-1-4051-9152-4 (hardcover : alk. paper) — ISBN 978-1-4051-9147-0 (pbk. : alk. paper)   1. Psycholinguistics.   I. Cairns, Helen Smith.   II. Title.
    P37.F47 2010
    401'.9—dc22

                                        2010003120

A catalogue record for this book is available from the British Library.

Set in 10/12pt Palatino by SPi Publisher Services, Pondicherry, India

1   2011

*This book is dedicated to the students
in Introduction to Psycholinguistics at
Queens College: past, present, and future.*

Contents

List of Figures

Tables

Prologue

For almost 40 years we (first Helen, then Eva) have been teaching 'Introduction to Psycholinguistics' to undergraduate students at Queens College of the City University of New York (CUNY). This book is dedicated to those students and others who come after them.

In 1999 Helen Cairns wrote *Psycholinguistics: An Introduction* (1999, now out of print), which was informed by years of figuring out which pedagogical strategies work and which don't when introducing students to the study of language acquisition and use. Both of us experienced great success teaching with that book, so we have adopted its focus and organization for *Fundamentals of Psycholinguistics*. The present volume offers updated content, given the empirical developments in the field of psycholinguistics in the past decade. We have also incorporated a new orientation triggered in part by our experience of teaching this material to the diverse student body at Queens College: we have woven multilingualism into the basic narrative.

We begin our story by asking what it means to know a language, a question whose answer necessarily includes an exploration of the biological underpinnings of language and its representation in the brain. We then explore the acquisition of language in children and adults. The book then focuses on the production and comprehension of sentences, describing the steps that intervene from the time an idea is born in the mind of a speaker to the moment it is understood in the mind of a hearer. We conclude with an overview of how language is used in discourse.

We have many people to thank for their assistance in the writing of this book. Danielle Descoteaux of Wiley-Blackwell has given us both enthusiastic support and helpful suggestions from the beginning of this project, and we received invaluable assistance from the editorial and production team. A number of anonymous reviewers provided invaluable suggestions for improvement of the original manuscript. Dianne Bradley, Chuck Cairns, Dana McDaniel, Lucia Pozzan, and Irina Sekerina have provided guidance in a number of areas. We have also benefited from being part of the psycholinguistics community in and around the CUNY Graduate Center and Queens College.

We are fortunate to have students and colleagues with expertise in some of the languages we have used in examples throughout the book. For their help with these, we thank Yukiko Koizumi, Ping Li, Shukhan Ng, Irina Sekerina, Amit Shaked, Iglika Stoyneshka, and F. Scott Walters.

Our primary goal is not to provide our readers with a great many facts about language acquisition and use. As in all healthy empirical fields, data change with ongoing investigations. Instead, we hope to convey to our readers the amazing story of the unconscious processes that take place as humans use language.

Eva Fernández
Helen Cairns

1 Beginning Concepts

Psycholinguistics is an interdisciplinary field of study in which the goals are to understand how people acquire language, how people use language to speak and understand one another, and how language is represented and processed in the brain. Psycholinguistics is primarily a sub-discipline of psychology and linguistics, but it is also related to developmental psychology, cognitive psychology, neurolinguistics, and speech science. The purpose of this book is to introduce the reader to some of the central ideas, problems, and discoveries in contemporary psycholinguistics. In this chapter, we explore key concepts about language that serve to distinguish it from related aspects of human behavior and cognition, and we identify the basic characteristics of language as a system. We also provide a brief account of how psycholinguistics emerged as a field of inquiry.

■ The Creativity of Human Language

A good place to begin is by thinking about some of the unique features of human language. Language is a system that allows people immense **creativity**. This is not the same creativity of people who write essays, fiction, or poetry. Instead, this is the linguistic creativity that is commonplace to every person who knows a language. The creativity of human language is different from the communication system of any other animal in a number of respects. For one, speakers of a language can create and understand novel sentences for an entire lifetime. Consider the fact that almost every sentence that a person hears every day is a brand new event not previously experienced, but which can be understood with little difficulty. Similarly, when speaking, people constantly produce novel sentences with no conscious effort. This is true for every person who speaks or has ever spoken a language. We can extend this observation to every person who uses a signed language to produce and comprehend novel sentences.

This remarkable ability to deal with novelty in language is possible because every language consists of a set of principles by which arbitrary elements (the sounds of speech, the gestures of sign language) are combined into words, which in turn are combined into sentences. Everyone who knows a language knows a relatively small number of principles, a small number of sounds put together to create words, and a large but finite vocabulary. This finite knowledge provides the person who knows a language with infinite creativity. The set of possible sentences for a given language is infinite. Everyone who has ever lived and known a particular language has produced and heard a miniscule subset of that infinite set. Knowledge of language confers upon every person the creativity to produce an infinite number of novel sentences. When that knowledge is shared with others in a given language community, speakers and hearers are able to produce and understand an indefinitely large number of novel sentences.

A second important kind of creativity humans possess is that we can use language to communicate anything we can think of. No other animal communication system affords its users such an unlimited range of topics. Many mammals have complex sets of calls and cries, but they can communicate only certain kinds of information, such as whether danger is coming from the ground or the air, who is ready to mate, where food is located, and so forth. The philosopher Bertrand Russell once said, "No matter how eloquently a dog may bark, he cannot tell you his parents were poor but honest" (Gleason and Ratner 1993: 9). Language is so flexible that it not only allows people to say anything they can think of; it also allows people to use language for a vast array of purposes. Language is used to communicate, to interact socially, to entertain, and to inform. All cultural institutions – schools, communities, governments – depend upon language to function. Written and audio-recorded language allows people to communicate and convey information – as well as interact and entertain – across vast spans of space and time. It is probably the case that human dominance of the planet has been possible because of the power of human language as a medium for transmitting knowledge (Dennett 2009).

Language as Distinct from Speech, Thought, and Communication

Language is the primary communication system for the human species. In ordinary circumstances it is used to convey thoughts through speech. It is a special system, however, that functions independently of speech, thought, and communication. Because one of the main themes of this book is to identify the unique aspects of the human linguistic system, it might be helpful to distinguish between language and the other systems with which it usually interacts: speech, thought, and communication.

Before we discuss those other systems, let us emphasize that here and throughout this book our discussion of human language includes the signed languages of the deaf, unless explicitly noted. Sign languages are just as structured as any spoken language and are just as capable of conveying an unlimited range of topics (as discussed in the previous section). Sign languages also operate under principles distinct from thought and communication. What differs between signed and spoken languages is the transmission mode: gestural for the former and articulatory-phonetic (speech) for the latter.

Speech ought not to be confused with language, though speech is indeed the most frequent mode for transmitting linguistic information. Other modes for transmission include the gestures used in sign language and the graphic representations used in writing. Later in this chapter (and later in the book), we will address the differences between the signal (speech, signs, written symbols) and the abstract information carried by that signal, and we will demonstrate that producing or perceiving a speech signal is possible and efficient because of knowledge of language. For now, consider the "linguistic" abilities of parrots and computers. Both can produce speech that might sound very human-like (promising new technologies are also able to create gestural sequences, using computer-animated figures, in sign language). But animal or computer-generated speech (or signing) differs from true human language production in one crucial respect: it is not based on knowledge of language as a finite system that yields an infinite set of possible sentences. Notice in particular that parrot and computer speech will fail to be creative in the senses described above.

Another mode for transmitting linguistic information is **writing**, but writing is markedly different from both speaking and signing. Writing systems are invented by people who already use language, so the central difference is that writing is a cultural artifact, while speaking and signing are biological; we will examine this point in more detail in Chapter 3. Writing is always dependent on spoken language, though the connection differs from language to language. In some languages, like English, the written symbols – also called **graphemes** – are linked to the language's sound system (consonants, vowels); in other languages, like Chinese, the symbols represent words. Writing has had a very different historical trajectory than speech: humans have been using spoken language to communicate for tens of thousands of years, while writing is a relatively new development, with the earliest examples dating back to only about 5,000 years ago. Children learn to speak spontaneously and without explicit instruction, yet require hours and hours of teaching and practice when they are learning to read and write. While all human communities have some form of spoken (or gestural) language, in the majority of the world's languages a writing system has not been invented. It is important to remember that languages without a writing system are no less complex than their counterparts with standardized writing systems. The complexity and sophistication of all human languages is independent of whether speakers have developed a way to write the languages down.

It is tempting to confuse **thought** and language, because we verbalize our thoughts using language. The distinction between language and thought (or general intelligence) becomes clear when one considers the many kinds of individuals who can think but cannot communicate through language. Among these kinds of individuals are infants and people who suffer from neurological pathologies that have impaired their language ability. Moreover, many animals can think but cannot communicate using language. In the language pathologies, we observe pronounced mismatches between level of intellectual development and linguistic ability. Specific language impairment (SLI) is not a rare disorder in children without any neurological or motor pathology. In children with SLI, language development lags far behind that of their peers. While there are numerous cognitive deficits associated with children with SLI, their non-verbal intelligence is within normal range and their cognitive deficits are not sufficient to account for their language disorder (Leonard 1998). The flip side of SLI is Williams Syndrome, a genetically based disorder causing severe retardation. Children with Williams Syndrome are deficient in many other aspects of cognition. While some aspects of their language are impaired (Jacobson and Cairns 2009), these children have surprisingly good language skills, in both vocabulary and in the ability to form grammatical sentences (Lenhoff et al. 1997). Pathologies such as SLI and Williams Syndrome, that demonstrate a dissociation of language and general intelligence, are of interest because they demonstrate the independence of language and thought.

The thoughts that people have are distinct from the language (or languages) in which they encode them. Bilinguals can use either of their languages to transmit the thoughts they want to convey. It may be that one of the languages of a given bilingual will have a richer vocabulary for conveying certain thoughts, as in the person who prefers to speak about art in English and about soccer in Portuguese. Perhaps it is more convenient to convey information in one of the two languages; for example, memorizing word lists in one language will facilitate recall in that same language (Cabeza and Lennartson 2005). But neither of these phenomena alters the basic point: when required to, bilinguals are able to convey any thought in either of their languages, or in both. This observation can be extended to all human languages, of which there are close to 7,000 (Ladefoged, Ladefoged, and Everett 1997; Gordon 2005): any thought can be conveyed in any human language. A corollary of this is that any sentence in any human language can be translated into any other, even by ordinary bilinguals, as opposed to experienced translators or trained interpreters. It may take more than one sentence to do the job, and the translation may not be as elegant as the original, but all languages possess an ability to formulate equivalent meanings with precision. Thus, one can think of general intelligence as the system responsible for generating the "language of thought" (Fodor 1975), and this in turn is translated into speech by our linguistic system, which we describe in the following section and, in more detail, in Chapter 2.

Language is the primary communication system for human beings, but it is not the only way to communicate, so language can be distinguished from **communication** in general. Many forms of communication are not linguistic; these include non-verbal, mathematical, and aesthetic communication through music or the visual arts. Frequently, language is not used to communicate or transfer information; language can be used aesthetically (consider poetry or song lyrics) or as a means to negotiate social interactions (consider how *Yo, whassup!* might be the preferred greeting in some contexts but quite inappropriate in others). One of the wonderful things about language is that it can be studied in many different ways. Its social, cultural, and aesthetic characteristics can be analyzed independently of one another. In psycholinguistics, however, researchers are primarily concerned with the underlying structure of language as a biologically based characteristic of humans, derived from the human neurological organization and function; we come back to this topic in greater detail in Chapter 3. Human language is unique to human beings and its general structure is universal to our species. All and only humans have human language. These facts have profound implications for the way language is acquired by infants (see Chapter 4) and for the way that language is produced (Chapter 5) and perceived (Chapters 6, 7, and 8).

Some Characteristics of the Linguistic System

Language is a formal system for pairing signals with meanings (see Figure 1.1). This pairing can go either way. When people produce a sentence, they use language to encode the meaning that they wish to convey into a sequence of speech sounds. When people understand a spoken sentence, language allows them to reverse the process and decode a speaker's speech to recover the intended meaning. Obviously, these activities depend upon the speaker and hearer sharing a common language: both must have the same linguistic system for pairing sound and meaning.

The linguistic system that enables sound and meaning to be paired contains a complex and highly organized set of principles and rules. These rules are ultimately the source for the infinite creativity of language because they describe (or generate) any one of an infinite set of sentences. The set of rules that creates sentences in a language is a language's **grammar**, and the words of a language are its **lexicon**. Notice that this way of defining language is very specific about what it means to know a language. Knowing a language involves knowing its

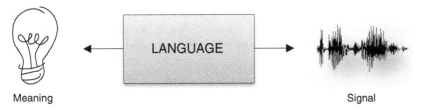

Meaning   Signal

Figure 1.1 Language is a system that connects signals (the sound wave on the right, symbolizing speech) and meanings (the light bulb on the left, symbolizing an idea). In the figure, the signal is acoustic, a speech sound. The signal could take on other forms (it could be written, it could be gestural).

grammar and lexicon. Knowledge of such a system will give a speaker the ability to organize ideas into words and sentences, and sentences into sequences of sounds. This special kind of knowledge is called *tacit* (or *implicit*) *knowledge*, to distinguish it from explicit knowledge, such as your knowledge of a friend's telephone number. Tacit knowledge is represented in the brain and is put to use, in this case, in the production and comprehension of sentences, but is not consciously available to the individual who possesses it.

The Distinction between Descriptive and Prescriptive Grammar

The term *grammar* means something different to linguists than what it means to language teachers. People who teach language are interested in teaching a standardized use of language, the form of a language that is accepted in academic and business circles. We can refer to this type of language as conforming to **prescriptive grammar**. Knowing how to adapt to the standard (*prescribed*) way of speaking or writing is very useful for people conducting a job interview or producing a formal piece of writing. People who study language, in contrast, are interested in what is called **descriptive grammar**, that is, the language system that underlies ordinary use. This is not an easy concept to grasp, so some examples are in order. Many people who speak English – especially young people or people talking in informal contexts – will say sentences like the following:

(1) Me and Mary went to the movies.

(2) Mary and me went to the movies.

These sentences are generated by a person's internalized grammar of English, which licenses those constructions, but which would not generate an **ungrammatical** sentence like the following:

(3)   *Me went to the movies.

(The asterisk, *, indicates that the sentence is badly formed.) The use of *me* in subject position is possible in English only with a compound subject (*me and Mary* or *Mary and me*), not with a singular one. A person who can say (1) and (2) but not (3) has a particular kind of grammar that a linguist would want to be able to describe.

English teachers are not interested in describing the properties of people's underlying grammars; they want instead to make sure that their students know that certain ways of saying things are not considered "correct English." The prescriptive rules of English grammar require that *I* be used in subject position, whether it is singular (*I went to the movies*) or compound (*Mary and I went to the movies*). (English teachers would further object to (1) because it is considered impolite to place oneself before others.) Similarly, students are told that they should say *It is I* and *This is she* rather than *It's me* or *This is her*. However, most people – including the occasional English teacher, in casual speech – say *It's me* and *This is her*. The grammar that people develop during language acquisition is the (colloquial) grammar of other members of their language community. In fact, when people are acquiring the bulk of their linguistic ability in their first language (or languages) – a process that lasts from birth until a child is around 5 or 6 years of age – they have not even heard of linguistic correctness. There can be many differences between the sentences generated by that colloquial grammar and those sentences dictated by prescriptive grammar. For example, many people will answer the telephone with *It's me* or *This is her*, rather than *It is I* or *This is she*. It is interesting to note that learning the prescribed rules of usage for a particular language is often a tedious and difficult process, and one that requires a great deal of conscious attention as well as explicit instruction, in contrast to the ease with which children acquire (implicitly and without instruction) the rules for the language or languages they acquire early on in life.

The issue of correctness also arises when one considers dialectal variation. English, like most languages, takes on many different forms; the language varies geographically, by class, and by ethnicity. People from different English-speaking countries, from different areas within these countries, and from different racial and ethnic groups not only pronounce words differently, but also have profound and highly systematic lexical and syntactic differences from the transnational standard version of English, or from regional standards, like Standard American English or Standard British English. For instance, people from the south of the United States use the word *purse*, whereas people from the north use the word *pocketbook* to refer to the same thing. A feature of Southern American Vernacular English is "modal stacking," such that it is perfectly grammatical to say the sentence in (4), in which the two modal verbs *might* and *should* are stacked.

(4)   We might should pay our bills tonight.

Different dialects – their distinguishing properties, their origins, and their development over time – are of great interest to linguists. So-called "standard" English, spoken by people like network newscasters who have been trained to use it, is considered to be the ideal form of the language, but it is actually spoken by very few people. The fact is that most people speak some sort of non-standard variety of English, some coming closer than others to the idealized standard form. Linguists do not take a position on whether there should be a standard version of a language or on what form the prescriptive rules of the grammar should take. Yet language with prescriptive grammar guiding usage in formal contexts is a fact of life in modern society. Since business and professional communities ascribe to the ideal, most people would be well advised to become consciously aware of the differences between the colloquial version of English acquired naturally by children (the language that linguists are interested in describing) and the standardized form of the language that will get someone a good job or an A+ on an essay exam. It is a mistake, however, to believe that there is anything inherently better about the set of sentences acceptable based on the prescriptive grammar of a language compared to those sentences generated by the grammar acquired naturally and unconsciously. Unfortunately, non-standard varieties of English are generally stigmatized, even by the very people who speak those varieties (Preston 1998), and are often mistakenly seen as reflecting lack of intelligence or education. Yet all human languages have variations that extend across their speakers, so if one considers a naturally occurring linguistic characteristic to be good, any deviations from the linguistic norm are wonderful – or at the very least, normal. The point is that linguists are interested in describing people's grammars and dialects, and psycholinguists are interested in understanding how those grammars are put to use in the production and comprehension of sentences. Psycholinguists are not concerned with correctness or standard forms.

The Universality of Human Language

Linguists tend to refer to human language as a single entity, despite the fact that there are many different versions spoken by the thousands of different language communities around the world. The fact is that all human languages are cut from the same mold: they are highly similar in their organization and in the abilities they confer on the people who know them. All human languages have a grammar and a lexicon, which together allow the creation of an infinite set of sentences to convey any possible thought. The fact that all humans have languages of similar organization and function strongly suggests that language is part of the human biological endowment, as the communication systems of animals are specific to their species. The **universality of human language** has profound consequences for the way psycholinguists analyze the human use of language.

At the same time, linguists are interested in understanding what is specific and what is universal, not only about knowledge of language but also about the mechanisms that put that knowledge of language to use. The majority of the world's population is bilingual or multilingual, and most of the world's children grow up in environments that expose them to multiple languages (Romaine 1995). These facts indicate that the mechanisms for representing and processing language can handle efficiently more than one linguistic code.

Implications for the Acquisition of Language

An important area of psycholinguistics is **language acquisition**. Just as every human culture has at least one language, children in every culture acquire the grammar and lexicon of the language or languages in their environment and develop the ability to employ that linguistic knowledge in the production and comprehension of speech. Children do this without effort and without being taught. Just as there are profound similarities among human languages, there are profound similarities in the way children everywhere acquire their native language or languages. Language acquisition is more similar to the acquisition of other skills that develop in early childhood, such as walking, than it is to skills that are learned later in life, such as riding a bicycle or writing. If a person does not know how to ride a bicycle, one does not assume there is anything wrong with this person, only that the person has not been taught how to ride a bicycle. If a person is unable to talk or a child is unable to acquire language, then one assumes a basic pathology and seeks professional advice. The rapid, effortless, and natural acquisition of language by children is likely a result of the fact that language is a faculty of the human brain. As the brain develops, it organizes the language the child is exposed to in ways that are common to all humans.

This picture is complicated somewhat by second language acquisition after early childhood, because learning a language as a teenager or as an adult is perceived as being very difficult, especially compared to the ease with which we learned our first language. Indeed, learning a second language is a great deal of work, particularly when the learner lives in an environment in which the language is not spoken regularly. Certain aspects of a second language are quite difficult to master, pronunciation in particular. And when learning a second language, one's first language sometimes seems to get in the way. Yet (adult) second language learners go through similar developmental stages as do (child) first language learners. Furthermore, many people acquire high levels of competence in a second language without having been taught explicitly. Underlying these abilities, therefore, is a system for acquiring human language that is engaged fully during first language acquisition and again at least partially with exposure to a second language, at any time within the lifespan of an individual. To account for the perceived differences between first and second language acquisition, research has pointed to variable amounts of exposure – usually vastly more extensive for first language learners – as well as to factors that include the learner's psycho-social proximity to the target language culture. Also, some recent proposals link age effects in second language acquisition to the decline in memory abilities observed with aging (Birdsong 2005).

How Language Pairs Sound and Meaning

In any human language, the principles and rules of the grammar organize words from the lexicon into sentences used to convey meaning. Three kinds of rule systems make up a grammar. **Phonological rules** describe the sound patterns of the language; they are used to create individual words and are responsible for the rhythm and intonation of speech. **Morphological rules** and **syntactic rules** are involved in creating the structural organization of words and sentences, that is, the relationships between words and phrases in sentences. (Chapter 2 describes the basic operations of these various rule systems, as well as the organization of the lexicon.) It is a fundamental concept in psycholinguistics that the meaning of a sentence is a function of the meaning of individual words and how those words are organized structurally. People are consciously aware of many elements of language – like consonants or vowels, syllables, and words – but they tend not to be aware of sentence structure. When one reads in the popular press that some subculture, like teenagers or video gamers, has a different "language," it usually turns out that this "language" differs from English only in that it has some special vocabulary items or some specialized pronunciation features. People are probably not as aware of sentence structure as they are of sounds and words, because sentence structure is abstract in a way that sounds and words are not. The acoustic signal of a recorded sentence has properties that reflect the consonants and vowels it carries (more on this phenomenon in Chapter 5). Also, though they are not usually pronounced in isolation, words are generally written with spaces around them in most of the world's writing systems. In contrast to sounds and words, syntactic structure is not represented in the spoken or written signal. At the same time, sentence structure is a central aspect of every sentence. Though it has no physical reality, sentence structure has psychological reality: it must be represented by the speaker and recovered by the hearer in order for the meaning of a sentence to be conveyed. In other words, the meaning of a sentence depends on the structural organization of the sentence's words.

When a person sets out to learn a new language, something usually done in school, the task is frequently conceptualized as memorizing new vocabulary. Language learners quickly realize, though, that structure is just as important a feature of a new language as is its vocabulary. Indeed, bilinguals usually have a better sense of language structure than monolinguals, because they are accustomed to noticing that ambiguities in one language are not parallel in the other, for example, and that word-by-word translations usually do not work. All of this makes bilinguals more consciously aware of sentence structure than are monolinguals.

We can appreciate the importance of sentence structure by looking at examples within a single language. For instance, in English, the same set of words can convey different meanings if they are arranged in different ways. Consider the following:

(5)   The senators objected to the plans proposed by the generals.

(6)   The senators proposed the plans objected to by the generals.

The meaning of the sentence in (5) is quite different from that of (6), even though the only difference is the position of the words *objected to* and *proposed*. Although both sentences contain exactly the same words, the words are structurally related to each other differently; it is those differences in structure that account for the difference in meaning. The same ten words could be combined in such a way that they would have no structure and no meaning:

(7)   The to plans senators objected proposed the by generals the.

An unstructured collection of words does not convey meaning, and the same collection of words can mean different things depending upon their organization. A person who knew only a lexicon, without a principled system to combine the words into sentences, could get some ideas across, but would lack a system of sufficient precision to convey more than just some simple thoughts.

Another way to get a sense of how meaning depends upon sentence structure is to see how the same string of words in the same linear order can convey two different meanings, depending upon the abstract structure assigned to them. Consider the structurally ambiguous sentence in (8):

(8)   The man saw the boy with the binoculars.

The sentence can mean either that the man saw the boy by means of the binoculars or that the man saw a boy who had the binoculars. Thus, *with the binoculars* is associated either with the verb *saw* or with the noun *boy*.

Figure 1.2 illustrates the structural differences associated with each of the two meanings of (8), using tree diagrams to spell out the structural (hierarchical) relationships between the words for the two meanings of the sentence. In the top tree in Figure 1.2, *with the binoculars* is a prepositional phrase (PP) completely separate from the noun phrase (NP) that contains the noun *boy*. In contrast, in the bottom tree, the PP *with the binoculars* is grouped inside the NP that contains *boy*. The structures illustrated in Figure 1.2 reflect the difference in meaning that distinguishes the two interpretations of the sentence, namely, *with the binoculars* tells us the instrument used by the man to see the boy (top tree),

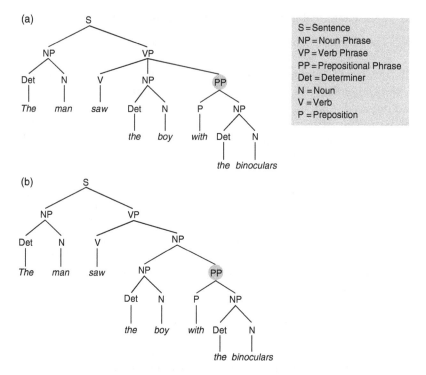

Figure 1.2   Abstract structures associated with the two meanings of the structurally ambiguous sentence *The man saw the boy with the binoculars*. Focus on the different location for the prepositional phrase (the shaded node labeled PP), *with the binoculars*, in each of the two structures.

or conveys information about which boy was seen, namely the one with binoculars (bottom tree). The crucial difference is that the node labeled PP (which dominates the prepositional phrase, *with the binoculars*) attaches directly to the VP node in the top tree, but to the NP node in the bottom tree.

The structures in Figure 1.2, like the ones that will appear elsewhere in this book, are not constructed with the type of detail a linguist would use. When linguists draw representations of the structures of a sentence, such theoretical objects take on a level of detail – like a drawing of a molecular structure by a biochemist – that goes well beyond our needs in this book. We will use simplified graphic representations, illustrating only the particular aspects of sentence structure that need to be focused on. The structural elements in Figure 1.2 will be described in more detail in Chapter 2.

◼ Linguistic Competence and Linguistic Performance

A grammar and a lexicon are those components of language that allow sounds and meanings to be paired. When people know a language, they know its grammar and its lexicon. This knowledge is called **linguistic competence**. Linguistic competence is a technical term, different from the usual meaning of the word *competence*. Being competent at something usually means that a person has adequate abilities to perform an action with skill, but that is not what is meant by linguistic competence. Linguistic competence has no evaluative connotation; it simply refers to the knowledge of language that is in a person's brain (or mind), knowledge that provides a system for pairing sound and meaning. **Linguistic performance**, in contrast, is the use of such knowledge in the actual processing of sentences, by which we mean their production and comprehension. Typically, linguists are concerned with describing linguistic competence and psycholinguists are concerned with describing linguistic performance. Beyond basic sentence processing, psycholinguists are also concerned with the actual use of language. After a sentence is processed, it is stored in memory and combined with other sentences to form conversations and narratives. The description of how language is actually used is called **pragmatics**, a topic we address in Chapter 8. It is important to distinguish between the grammatical and pragmatic aspects of a particular linguistic event. For example, let us return to the structurally ambiguous sentence in (8). The sentence can have two distinct meanings, each of which is described by a different structural representation, like those shown in Figure 1.2. These two structures are made available by the grammar and conform to a number of syntactic rules. If this sentence is actually used by a speaker and understood by a hearer, only one of the two meanings will be the one intended by the speaker and only one of the two meanings (hopefully the same one!) will be recovered by the hearer. Which meaning is intended or recovered will be a purely pragmatic issue, determined by the situation, the participants in the conversation, the function of the communicative exchange, and so on. The grammar is completely indifferent to the speaker's intent or to the hearer's recovery of the message. The grammar simply provides structures that are available for the encoding of meaning in sentences. The actual use of those sentences in conversation is a function of encoding and decoding processes and pragmatics.

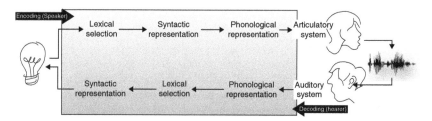

Figure 1.3   Steps involved in encoding by the speaker (left to right) and decoding by the hearer (right to left).

There are several actual processes that must take place when people use language to exchange ideas, processes for the **production** and **perception** of sentences. Figure 1.3 illustrates these operations, by expanding on the gray box of Figure 1.1. The speaker begins (top right of the figure) with an idea or a thought she wants to convey to the hearer. In order to do this, she first must translate her thought into a semantic representation (a representation of meaning) for a sentence in her language. Then she must select the words from her lexicon and use her grammar to construct the **syntactic representation** (representation of sentence **structure**) that will convey the meaning she has selected. The words must then be represented as sounds, that is, as a **phonological representation**, since they are eventually going to be pronounced. Finally, the phonological representation is sent to the motor areas of the speaker's brain and instructions are sent to the articulatory organs that are used to produce speech. The speech signal is the result of a precisely timed and exquisitely organized interaction of hundreds of muscles, including those of the jaw, lips, tongue, vocal folds, and respiratory system. Speech sounds reach the auditory system of the hearer, and he begins the process of reconstruction that is necessary to decode the speaker's message. First, he must reconstruct the phonological representation in order to recover the speaker's words and their meanings. Then, using the grammatical and lexical knowledge that he shares with the speaker, he must reconstruct the words' structural organization. He then has sufficient information to recover the basic meaning for the speaker's sentence that will ultimately lead to her idea or thought. (We have arbitrarily chosen to refer to the speaker as a woman, and to the hearer as a man. This is a convention we will follow throughout the book.)

Exchanging ideas using speech is so commonplace that people never think about the complex cognitive processes that underlie that experience.

Like the complex processes underlying most of the activities of living – walking, breathing, sleeping – the activities involved in the production and perception of sentences are completely unconscious. It is not possible to introspect and experience a piece of the process, like the retrieval of words from the lexicon or the use of one's grammar to create a structural representation of a sentence. As we will see – particularly in Chapters 5, 6, and 7 – psycholinguists have developed experimental procedures that have led to an understanding of a great deal about these unconscious processes, which are quite remarkable in their speed and complexity.

In the **encoding** process, an abstract object – an idea – is translated into a physical object – a speech signal. When we say that an idea is abstract, we mean that it does not have an observable physical reality. Certainly, an idea must have a physical representation deep in the neurological connections of the brain, but it has no such physical representation for the hearer nor is that neurological representation measurable with ordinary instruments. Speech, on the other hand, is concrete; it is part of observable physical reality. Not only does it have an effect on the auditory system; it can also be recorded and its physical properties measured. When the hearer **decodes** the physical signal, he recovers the same abstract object – the idea – that was encoded by the speaker. Let us take this a step further by pointing out that, since the idea and the physical signal are not part of the linguistic system, neither is directly reflected in the (also abstract) representations built by the linguistic system during the encoding or decoding processes. (We come back to the nature of these abstract representations – the gray box of Figure 1.1 – in Chapter 2 and in Chapters 5, 6, and 7.) The linguistic system is the system that bridges the idea and the speech, allowing them to be related. The linguistic system represents sounds and words, and creates the structures that organize those sounds and words into sentences.

The Speech Signal and Linguistic Perception

The fact that the signal is the only physical link between speaker and hearer is a critical psycholinguistic point. The speech signal must contain enough information for the hearer to reconstruct the abstract structures that eventually convey the abstract ideas, and that reconstruction is essential to the decoding process. To fully appreciate the complexity of this task, it is necessary to understand the relationship between speech and the linguistic representations that it encodes.

Figure 1.4 Waveform for the sentence *Linda loves the melody*, illustrating graphically the continuous nature of the speech signal. The superimposed vertical lines mark the approximate locations for word boundaries. The word boundaries are not particularly salient, and neither are the boundaries between the consonants and vowels that make up the words.

In fact, even the phonological representation of a sentence is far removed from the properties of the acoustic signal. The phonological representation can be thought of as an idealization of the physical speech sounds. The abstract representation is made up of discrete phonological units (consonants and vowels, syllables, and higher-order rhythmic units, like prosodic words and intonational phrases). The physical signal itself is very different, however. The portions that correspond to abstract phonological units overlap, and the words run together; this is illustrated in Figure 1.4, which shows that the waveform for an utterance is continuous. The speaker may be speaking rapidly and with an unfamiliar accent, with chewing gum in her mouth and with a radio playing in the background, all of which will affect the signal, making it measurably different from a signal for the same sentence produced slowly by a native speaker with no gum in her mouth and in a quiet room. The relationship between the continuous (and perhaps very noisy) physical signal the hearer receives and the neatly structured units of the idealized phonological representation he must reconstruct is not at all direct. A complex set of mental processing mechanisms must consult the hearer's grammar and lexicon in order to reconstruct a series of linguistic representations, resulting in the recovery of the speaker's meaning. Researchers think that those mental processes are executed by neurophysiological operations that are specialized for the perception of speech as a linguistic object.

In every modality people make the distinction between the actual stimulus (the physical signal) that impinges on our eyes or ears and the percept that the brain constructs when we interpret that stimulus.

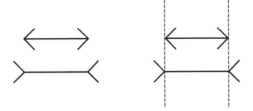

Figure 1.5   Müller-Lyer illusion. In the figure on the left, two horizontal lines appear to be different lengths, the one on the bottom seeming longer than the one on the top. On the right, the exact copy of that figure demonstrates that the two horizontal lines are in fact of identical length.

A stimulus is never consciously available to us; what we are aware of is the mental percept that the stimulus gives rise to. An example of this process can be illustrated by viewing optical illusions, like that shown in Figure 1.5. With the Müller-Lyer illusion (Müller-Lyer 1889), in the left panel of the figure, the stimulus that actually falls on our retinas contains two horizontal lines of equal length, but we perceive the bottom line to be longer than the line on the top. The percept of relative length depends not just on the actual length of the lines, but also on the context in which they occur. The fact that these lines are adjoined by angles pointing in different directions affects our perceptual interpretation of their length.

Perceiving a linguistic representation based on the stimulus of a speech signal requires the hearer to have linguistic competence. Knowledge of language is necessary for a person to reconstruct, and therefore perceive, the phonological representation for the speech signal, which then unlocks the sequence of words and in turn gives way to building the syntactic structure for the sentence. Without linguistic knowledge, a hearer would be unable to perceive anything other than a jumble of disorganized sounds. For example, dogs can be excellent communicators, but they have no knowledge of language, so when they hear speech, they may recognize the acoustic signal associated with their names and a number of familiar commands, but that is all. Animals "understand" what we say to them through our tone of voice, body language, and gaze. For humans, understanding a sentence involves very different processes: the organization of sounds, words, and ultimately sentences derives from human knowledge of language and takes on the form of mental representations reconstructed, quite indirectly, from the physical speech signal.

■ Origins of Contemporary Psycholinguistics

Contemporary psycholinguistics is an interdisciplinary field combining the two disciplines of linguistics and experimental cognitive psychology. Obviously, this union will be successful only to the extent that the two subfields have compatible views of language. When the field of psycholinguistics was first developed, this compatibility was indeed the case, just as it is now. What is interesting is that those views have changed dramatically over the last few decades.

The inception of the field of psycholinguistics occurred in the summer of 1951 when, at a meeting of the Social Science Research Council at Cornell University, a committee on Linguistics and Psychology was formed, with Charles Osgood as its chairman (Kess 1992). Subsequently, in the summer of 1953, a seminar was held at Indiana University in conjunction with the Linguistic Institute. This seminar formed the basis of the first book with psycholinguistics in its title, *Psycholinguistics: A Survey of Theory and Research Problems* (Osgood and Sebeok 1954). At that time linguists focused on a *taxonomic* analysis of languages, which meant that they had as their primary goal the classification of observable aspects of language. When linguists of that era approached a new language, their method of analysis was to listen to the speakers of the language, figure out what the phonological units were, and then classify them further into higher-level categories. This method fit in well with the view of language held by psychologists, which was that speech was simply a type of motor behavior exhibited by people. The **behaviorist psychology** of that day took the domain of psychology to be behavior (of people or animals), rather than mental operations of any kind. They believed that all behaviors could be explained as associated (linked) chains of smaller behaviors. Thus, speech was regarded as behavioral units of sound combined into words, which were then associated to form phrases, and so on. Acquisition in the child was thought to be the process by which correctly associated speech behaviors were built up by rewarding the desired ones and failing to reward the undesired sequences. Behaviorists believed that this system of learning, known as conditioning, was common to all organisms, and that all organisms learned everything the same way. All learning consisted of the acquisition of behavioral routines, and all behavioral routines were acquired by the same principles of learning. The common thread that bound linguistics and psychology at the middle of the twentieth century, then, was the view that everything interesting about language is directly observable in the physical speech signal. This view of language was later determined to be fundamentally flawed, and is diametrically opposed to the view of language presented in this book.

There were, of course, linguists and psychologists who saw difficulties with the traditional view. The famous linguist Edward Sapir wrote a paper entitled "The psychological reality of phonemes," suggesting that the mental representation of language should be addressed rather than focus exclusively on its physical representation (Sapir 1949). The psychologist Karl Lashley wrote the now-classic paper "The problem of serial order in behavior," questioning the explanatory power of associative chaining (Lashley 1951). The general view of linguists and psychologists at this time, however, was of language as a system of discrete behaviors that could be observed, classified, and understood in the individual as chains of associated behaviors, created by conditioning in childhood. These principles of conditioning were taken to be general principles of learning for all organisms.

This view of language was challenged, beginning in the late 1950s, by Massachusetts Institute of Technology professor Noam Chomsky, who proposed an entirely new way to think of human language, an approach that has been adopted by contemporary linguists and psychologists, and scholars in related fields, and is essentially the view adopted in this book. Chomsky (1959) said that speech should not be the object of study for those who want to understand human language. Instead, the object of study should be the set of rules – in the mind (which is really an abstract term to refer to the brain) – that create sentences and underlie observable speech. This is the grammatical system, and it is not observable in the same way that speech is observable (Chomsky 1975). Nonetheless, it is possible to test hypotheses about the properties of the grammatical system and thereby discover the set of rules that constitute people's knowledge of their language. Children acquire language as effortlessly as they do, not because there are any general principles of learning that apply to all organisms (as argued by behaviorist psychologists), but because this internal system of rules is biologically based in the human species (Chomsky 1975).

Obviously, the Chomskyan conception of language was totally incompatible with the behaviorist view. A few psychologists, including George Miller (1965), were instantly aware of the implications of Chomsky's ideas to the psychological study of language and its acquisition. These psychologists were primarily responsible for bringing those ideas to the attention of the psychological community. In 1961, the linguist Sol Saporta published a volume sponsored by the Social

Science Research Council's Committee on Psychology and Linguistics (just 8 years after the first), titled *Psycholinguistics: A Book of Readings;* the volume (Saporta 1961) included papers by Chomsky and Miller, as well as by more traditional linguists and psychologists. This publication ignited an intellectual battle that raged for more than a decade. In the end, an entirely different view of language became accepted, one different from the view that had united linguistics and psychology in the middle of the century. Now, at the onset of the twenty-first century, both fields predominantly accept the Chomskyan view of language as an abstract system represented in the mind or brain that is unique to the human species, develops in the maturing infant, and underlies but is only indirectly related to physical speech. This is not to say that controversies have disappeared within the fields of linguistics and psychology regarding the best way to characterize linguistic knowledge and investigate its use by adults and acquisition by children. Healthy fields always contain controversy. However, the controversy exists among people who have the same basic view of language as an object of study.

How This Book Is Organized

This book is structured around the issues presented in this chapter. The next chapter describes the rules and principles that constitute linguistic competence and the information contained in the lexicon. Chapter 3 presents arguments for the biological basis of language and describes its neurological representation. Chapter 4 discusses the process of language acquisition in the child within the context of a nativist view of language. Chapters 5, 6, and 7 describe the encoding and decoding processes of the speaker and the hearer. Finally, Chapter 8 deals with the use of language in memory and discourse.

Every chapter has a list of **new concepts** corresponding to terms in boldface in the body of the text. Every chapter also has a set of **study questions** designed to help you read with focus. All references cited in the chapters are listed together at the end of the book.

Throughout the book, we describe a broad range of empirical evidence on how language is acquired and processed. We have tried to be explicit in our descriptions of experimental methods when they come up. In recognition that much of this may be new to you, we have also included an appendix that explains in some detail how psycholinguistic experiments are designed and gives some examples of techniques that are commonly in use.

New Concepts

behaviorist psychology
communication
creativity of human language
decoding
descriptive grammar
encoding
grammar
grapheme
language
language acquisition
lexicon
linguistic competence
linguistic performance
morphological rules

perception
phonological representation
phonological rules
pragmatics
prescriptive grammar
production
speech
syntactic (structural) representation
syntactic rules
thought
ungrammatical
universality of human language
writing

Study Questions

1. What are the two types of linguistic creativity that give us insight into the nature of human language?

2. Why is it important to distinguish between language and general intelligence? Between language and communication? Identify specific examples.

3. Why are linguists interested in describing rather than prescribing grammar?

4. Why might some people think that one speech style or dialect is better than another? Is this a psycholinguistic issue or a social issue? Why?

5. What determines the meaning of a sentence?

6. What does it mean to say that structure is psychologically real, though abstract?

7. What is the distinction between linguistic competence and linguistic performance?

8. What is meant by encoding and decoding in reference to sentence processing? What must the speaker and the hearer share in order for these processes to take place?

9. How do the views of contemporary psycholinguists differ from the views of the behaviorists from the first half of the twentieth century?

2   The Nature of Linguistic Competence

Knowledge of the grammar and lexicon of a language constitutes a person's *linguistic competence*. In Chapter 1 we distinguished competence from *linguistic performance* – the language processing mechanisms responsible for both acquiring and using knowledge of language. Performance is the focus of this book, but a solid understanding of how language is acquired, produced, and perceived is not possible without at least a basic grasp of what exists in the competence repositories. This chapter provides, then, a necessary overview of the components of linguistic competence, the modules responsible for determining the well-formedness of combinations of sounds, words, and phrases. The chapter also addresses the question of how consciously accessible this knowledge of language is. Finally, we will examine the contents and organization of the lexicon.

What follows is by no means a comprehensive review of linguistic representations. Our goal is to explain the manner in which grammars and lexicons are organized, and what their organizational units are, so that you will have sufficient linguistic knowledge in preparation for the psycholinguistic information in the remainder of the book. Many examples presented in this chapter will come up again in subsequent chapters. This chapter excludes discussion of *semantics* – rules governing meaning inside sentences – because this area of knowledge of language will not come up in much detail in the upcoming chapters; some aspects of lexical semantics are discussed in this chapter, in the section on lexical knowledge. *Pragmatics* – rules governing use of sentences in particular contexts, and thus part of *communicative competence* – will be discussed in detail in Chapter 8.

The Universality of Human Language

Chapter 1 made the point that all human languages seem to be cut from the same mold. All languages are profoundly similar, even though thousands of languages are spoken in the world now, thousands have been spoken in the past, and still thousands more will be spoken in the future. If you have struggled trying to learn a new language, you may be quite skeptical of this similarity; if you already speak two or more languages, you may feel that their differences are far more numerous than their similarities. It is true that every language has language-specific ways to combine sounds into words, words into phrases, and phrases into sentences. Even the structure of words can differ among languages. As an example, consider the fact that the five-digit append-age at the end of your arm is called a *hand* in English and a *mano* in Spanish. The two nouns have very different properties. *Mano* is gram-matically feminine, and therefore takes the feminine determiners *la* or *una*, and adjectives modifying it must be in their feminine form; *hand* has no grammatical gender. Also, the syllable structure of *hand*, per-fectly common in English, is not possible in Spanish. Indeed, languages appear to have many differences when viewed like this, differences that are quite obvious to second language learners and to speakers of more than one language.

However, what is meant by saying that human language is univer-sal is something very different. Languages are all similar in their organization and in their function. Every human language has a lexi-con and a grammar, components which contain the building blocks used to create a potentially infinite set of sentences. Furthermore, the organization of lexicons and the formal properties of grammatical sys-tems are similar in all human languages. This is what psycholinguists mean by the statement that all languages are cut from the same mold. To see how this similarity of organization works, it is necessary to explore the kinds of principles and rules that are included in gram-mars, and the kinds of information contained in lexicons. Before we begin, we remind you that the words "rule" and "grammar" have dif-ferent meanings in linguistics than they do in ordinary language. A grammar is a formal description of a language, internalized as lin-guistic competence in language users. A rule in a grammar is simply a statement that captures a regularity of the language. (Recall that lin-guists think of grammar in very different terms than do teachers of writing, for whom grammar has to do with the prescriptive conven-tions followed in standard writing practices: rules of usage, orthogra-phy, and punctuation.)

All languages have a grammar consisting of a phonological compo-nent with rules related to regularities of the sound system of the lan-guage; a morphological component with rules governing word forms; and a syntactic component with rules governing sentence structure. The details of the subsystems of the grammar differ from language to language, but the existence of these independent components, the kinds of information they incorporate, and the form and properties of their grammars are the same in all languages. This is equally true for languages with long literary traditions, and for languages without a writing system; for languages with millions of speakers scattered around the world, and for languages with only a handful of speakers in a very small location; for languages that use speech as the main medium for transmission and for languages that instead use hand and face gestures (signed languages). The general form, subsystems, organization, and function of grammar are all universal and therefore common to all human languages.

Another universal feature of human language is that language-specific grammars are restricted by something called **Universal Grammar**, or UG. UG consists of general principles, which are the same for all languages, and specifies the ways languages can differ. The properties of specific languages vary in very few ways, and these variations create large classes of languages that are similar on a particular characteristic. For example, some languages mark grammatical functions in sentences (subject, verb, and object) primarily by morphology – by changing the form of the words. In German, for example, a noun phrase meaning 'the man' is *der Mann* if it is the subject of the sentence, *den Mann* if it is the direct object, *dem Mann* if it is the indirect object. Other languages identify grammatical functions by ordering them differently, something that is informally referred to as *word order*. The **canonical word order** (default or preferred word order) differs from language to language. English, for instance, is among a large class of languages that employs a subject–verb–object (SVO) ordering for grammatical functions, as illustrated by the example in (1a), while Japanese is among a large class that uses subject–object–verb (SOV) ordering, as in (1b):

(1)   a.   Mary eats cherries.
       b.   メアリーはサクランボを食べる
            Mearii-wa sakuranbo-wo taberu.
            'Mary cherries eats.'

These major differences among large classes of languages are called *parameters of variation*. How does this fit in with the notion of UG? Universal Grammar supplies a collection of characteristics that have to be the same in all languages, general principles of organization and operation – e.g., all languages have syllables with vowels; all languages have sentences with subjects, verbs, and objects. And the Universal Grammar also specifies the range of different settings that are permissible, the possible **parametric variations** – e.g., languages permit simple or complex syllable final consonant clusters; languages mark grammatical functions by morphology or word order. Accordingly, all human languages must obey the general principles of organization given by UG and can vary only in the types of variation UG specifies.

A third universal characteristic of human languages is that they each have a lexicon. A lexicon is the collection of words for a given language, and it is in the lexicon that most language specificity exists. Yet lexical entries in all languages contain the same kind of information (e.g., pronunciation, meaning, grammatical function, etc.), and lexical entries are organized with respect to each other in similar ways. We will come back to the lexicon and its organization at the end of this chapter, after we identify some of the key characteristics of the phonological, morphological, and syntactic components of the grammar.

■ The Speech Signal

In Chapter 1 we distinguished between language and the signal into which it is encoded – speech, writing, gestures. This section takes a brief detour from our objective of examining the grammar and lexicon of natural languages and provides an introduction to some of the properties of speech sounds. We concentrate on speech here, to give you sufficient background for many of the points to come later in this chapter and elsewhere in the book. In principle, if we had no space restrictions, we could have also provided similar introductions to the properties of gestural systems and of writing systems. Importantly, both gestural systems and speech are rooted in human biology, while writing systems are cultural artifacts. We will come back to this in Chapter 3.

The human vocal tract, diagrammed in Figure 2.1, can articulate a great many sounds, only a subset of which is used across the world's languages. It is those sounds associated with speech – also called **phones** – that are the object of study for phoneticians. Speech sounds are studied from two different general perspectives: *articulatory phonetics* is concerned with how the vocal tract is configured when a particular speech sound is made; *acoustic phonetics* is the study of the characteristics of the sound wave associated with a particular speech sound.

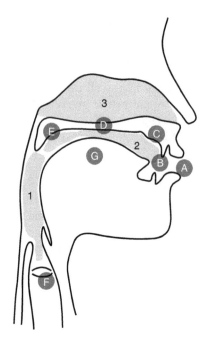

Articulators:

A. Lips (bilabial sounds)

B. Teeth (labiodental and dental sounds)

C. Alveolar ridge (alveolar sounds)

D. Hard palate (palatal sounds)

E. Velum, soft palate (velar sounds, and nasal/oral distinction)

F. Larynx, vocal folds, glottis (glottal sounds)

G. Tongue

Cavities:

1. Pharyngeal

2. Oral

3. Nasal

Figure 2.1   Diagram of the vocal tract, identifying the organs involved in producing speech (*articulators*) and the spaces in which speech sounds resonate (*cavities*). For examples of some of these sounds, see Table 2.1.

A specific human language – say, English or Spanish or Xhosa – has an inventory of speech sounds that is itself a subset of the many sounds used by all the world's languages. For example, not all languages have mid-central vowels like in the English word *hut*, [hʌt]; or trills like in the Spanish word for 'river', *río*, [r̃io]; or clicks like in the Xhosa word for 'perfume', [ukuk!ʰola] (the symbol [!] represents a postalveolar click consonant). The inventory of speech sounds for a given language is the language's **phonetic inventory**.

It is likely that you share the intuition of most English speakers that speech in English consists of sequences of discrete speech sounds. An important distinction between these sounds, probably familiar to you, is between *consonants* and *vowels*. Phoneticians group speech sounds into two large classes: *obstruents* are sounds produced with a major obstruction somewhere in the vocal tract; *sonorants* are sounds made with no such major obstruction. All vowels are sonorants, but some consonants are obstruents and others are sonorants. Table 2.1 provides some examples of English consonants and vowels, indicating for each whether it belongs to the category of obstruent or sonorant.

Table 2.1 organizes the phonetic inventory of English based on the *articulatory* characteristics for the sounds, that is, based on how they are produced (articulated) by the vocal tract. (In Chapter 5, we will come back to these sounds and describe some of their *acoustic* characteristics, that is, the properties that serve to identify them in the speech signal itself.) Table 2.1 also introduces the symbols of the International Phonetic Alphabet that we will use throughout this chapter and elsewhere in the book, when a phonetic or phonemic transcription is called for.

The diagram in Figure 2.1 identifies the key organs in the vocal tract involved in the production of speech sounds. To classify speech sounds based on their articulatory properties, the first characteristic to consider is **voicing** (also called *phonation*). An important organ in the production of speech sounds is the *larynx*, which houses the *vocal folds*, two folds of flesh around an opening called the *glottis*. When the vocal folds are brought together and air is forced through them, they come apart and back together ("vibrate") very rapidly, creating a sound. Sounds produced with vibration of the vocal folds are *voiced*, compared to *voiceless* sounds, which involve no such vibration and are produced by drawing apart the vocal folds. Notice that when you whisper, you are actually de-voicing all sounds by separating your vocal folds to prevent them from vibrating. Compare the final sounds in the words *hiss* and *his*, or the beginning sounds in *sue* and *zoo*. The first in each pair is voiceless, the second is voiced.

A second dimension for classifying speech sounds is **manner of articulation**. We have already mentioned the distinction between obstruents and sonorants. Within the category of obstruents, there are sounds produced with a full closure somewhere in the vocal tract, followed by a release; these sounds are called *stops*. There are also obstruent sounds for which there is a partial closure somewhere in the vocal tract, through which air is forced, creating noisy and sustained turbulence; these sounds are called *fricatives*. A third type of obstruent consonants, *affricates*, includes sounds that are a combination of a stop and a fricative: complete closure followed by turbulence. Examples of stops, fricatives, and affricates are all in Table 2.1.

Obstruent consonants can be articulated at several **places of articulation**. For example, the lips are brought together in the articulation of *bilabial* stops. *Labiodental* fricatives involve the upper teeth and lower lip. The tongue and the velum come together in the articulation of *velar* stops.

Table 2.1 English phonetic inventory (based on Standard American English). Voiceless sounds are listed first, followed by one or two example words containing the sound, written in standard orthography (the underlined letters correspond to the sound).

Consonants

Place of articulation

Manner of articulation		Bilabial	Labiodental	Dental	Alveolar	Postalveolar	Palatal	Velar	Glottal
Obstruents	Oral stops	p p<u>i</u>n b <u>b</u>in			t <u>t</u>in d <u>d</u>in			k <u>k</u>in g <u>g</u>un	ʔ sa<u>t</u>in
	Fricatives		f <u>f</u>in v <u>v</u>in	θ <u>th</u>in ð <u>th</u>en	s <u>s</u>in z <u>Z</u>en	ʃ <u>sh</u>in ʒ vi<u>s</u>ion			h <u>h</u>en
	Affricates					ʧ <u>ch</u>in ʤ <u>g</u>in			
Sonorants	Nasal stops	m Pa<u>m</u>			n pa<u>n</u>			ŋ pa<u>ng</u>	
	Approximants	w <u>w</u>ind			r <u>r</u>iver l <u>l</u>iver		j <u>y</u>en		
	Flap				ɾ ci<u>t</u>y				

Vowels

Vowel height	Front	Central	Back
High	i h<u>ea</u>t ɪ h<u>i</u>t		u h<u>oo</u>t, wh<u>o'</u>d ʊ h<u>oo</u>d
Mid	eɪ h<u>a</u>te ɛ h<u>ea</u>d	ʌ h<u>u</u>t ə <u>a</u>head, sof<u>a</u> ɝ h<u>ea</u>rd ɚ h<u>ea</u>ter	oʊ h<u>o</u>pe ɔ h<u>aw</u>
Low	æ h<u>a</u>t		ɑ h<u>o</u>t
Diphthongs	ju beau<u>t</u>, c<u>u</u>te	aɪ b<u>i</u>te aʊ b<u>ough</u>	ɔɪ b<u>oy</u>

Most sounds in the English phonetic inventory are *oral*, and all involve resonance in both the pharyngeal cavity and the oral cavity. There is a special category of stop consonants called *nasals*, which are produced with the *velum* (or *soft palate*) lowered. Lowering the velum allows the sound to resonate in the nasal cavity. The three nasal consonants in English – [m], [n], and [ŋ] – are characterized as stops, because they involve a full closure somewhere in the vocal tract. Notice, though, that since air is flowing through the nasal cavity and out through the nose, there is no major obstruction to the airflow, so nasals are classified as *sonorants*.

Other sonorant consonants in English include the class of *approximants*, which includes *liquids* like [l] and [r], and *glides* like [j] and [w]. Liquids have a "flowing" character (hence their name). Notice that [l] and [r] both involve positioning the tip of the tongue on or near the alveolar ridge, but the air flows over the center (or middle) of the tongue for [r] (also called a *central approximant*), and around the sides of the tongue for [l] (also called a *lateral approximant*). The glides [j] and [w] (also called semivowels) are characterized by the movement that is involved in their articulation. The [r] of American English is a rare sound among the world's languages; not listed in the table, since it is not part of the American English inventory, is the trill [r̃], which you might have heard in Scottish and some other dialects of English. This sound also exists in Spanish (at the beginning of words like *río* 'river' and in the middle of words like *perro* 'dog') and many other languages.

There are two additional consonant sounds in American English worth pointing out. One is the flap [ɾ], in the middle of words like *city* and *seedy*. It is produced by flapping or tapping the tongue against the alveolar ridge. The other is the glottal stop [ʔ], which appears – in some dialects – in the middle of words like *satin* and *cotton*, and sometimes preceding vowel-initial words like *ape* and *otter*. The glottal stop involves complete closure at the vocal folds, followed by a release.

The final class of sounds for us to consider is vowels, which are sounds that involve no obstruction in the vocal tract. This permits a sound generated by the vocal folds to resonate unobstructed in the pharyngeal and oral cavities. (We will describe in greater detail how vowels are produced in Chapter 5.) Different vowels are articulated by configuring the tongue such that its body is higher or lower in the mouth (**vowel height**) and more front or more back in the mouth (a dimension that loosely corresponds to the places of articulation for consonants). Compare the vowels in *heat* [i], *hoot* [u], and *hot* [ɑ]. Your tongue is high in your mouth for the first two, compared to the third, and further in the front for the first than for the last two. These two dimensions in the articulation of vowels (vertical and horizontal position) turn out to be the key not only to vowel production but also to vowel perception. There are additional characteristics of vowels we will not describe here: rounding, lengthening, nasalization, rhoticity (*r*-coloring), tenseness. Another distinction we will not discuss is that between monophthong and diphthong vowels, though Table 2.1 lists both types of vowels, to provide a sense of the complexity of the vowel inventory of English. Monophthong vowels are single speech sounds, while diphthongs are a blend of two speech sounds.

The Phonological Component

The genius of all human languages is that they take meaningless sound units and combine them in regular ways to produce meaningful units like words and sentences. (There is a parallel to this in signed languages: the gestures that when combined make up meaningful sign language words and sentences are by themselves essentially meaningless. Even signed languages have something very much like a phonological component, guiding the rhythm and intensity of gestures and providing cues to the information structure of a sentence – like whether the sentence is a question or a statement.) The phonology of a language is the component of the grammar that specifies what sound units the language uses to make words, and how those sound units are combined into syllables, words, and intonational phrases. The phonological component plays four key roles:

- it specifies the language's phonemic inventory;
- it adds predictable phonetic details by the application of phonological rules;
- it specifies the language's phonotactic constraints; and
- it supplies prosody.

The phonemic inventory

The phonemic inventory for a given language is the set of sound units that are distinctive for that language. These units are called **phonemes**, and they are abstract, mental representations of sounds. Phonemes are linked only indirectly to the actual sounds articulated by a speaker (or to the symbols that might represent them in the writing system). We will describe phonemes by alluding to the speech sounds they are related to. We will also write out phonemes using the symbols from the International Phonetic Alphabet introduced in Table 2.1. Some of those symbols are familiar to you, since they come from the alphabet we use to write Standard English. But it is important for you to remember that phonemes are abstract, mental representations that must not be confused with speech sounds or letters of the alphabet. Linguists distinguish between the mental units (phonemic representations) and the actual speech sounds (phonetic forms) by transcribing phonemic representations inside slashes, and phonetic forms in square brackets, like this, for the word *pink*: /pɪŋk/, [pʰĩŋk]. We will follow this convention in this chapter, and throughout the rest of the book. (We will also explain any additional transcription notations – e.g., the superscript *h* and the tilde above the vowel – as they come up.) But not every sound in a language has the same status with respect to other sounds: some sounds serve to distinguish words from one another, while others seem to be variable ways of uttering the same underlying abstract unit. The **phonemic inventory** for a language is the set of phonemes that are distinctive for that language, that is, the phonemes that serve to distinguish words from one another. And phonemes, you will recall, are abstract units of sound. Let us illustrate these concepts with some examples.

For a particular language, a pair of phonemes will be in **contrastive** (or **overlapping**) **distribution** if exchanging one phoneme for the other will create a contrast in meaning. Pairs of words that illustrate such contrasts are called **minimal pairs**. A sound's *distribution* is the set of positions in which it is allowed to occur; when two sounds are different phonemes in a particular language, their distribution is said to overlap. In English the words *big* and *pig* differ only in their first phonemes, so /b/ and /p/ are both different phonemes. A pair of words can differ minimally in many ways. The minimal difference could be a word-initial consonant (as in the *big–pig* example), or a word-final consonant (as in *bid* and *bit*, where the contrast is between /d/ and /t/); it could be a contrast tucked inside the beginning consonants of a syllable (as in *sprint–splint*, /r/–/l/), or a contrast between consonants with vowels on either side (as in *ether–either*, /θ/–/ð/). All those examples are of contrasts between two consonants, but we can create minimal pairs with vowels as well (as in *heed–hid*, whose contrastive phonemes are /i/ and /ɪ/).

There are differences between speech sounds (phones) that are not phonemic. For example, in English the phoneme /p/ in *pin* is pronounced with a slight puff of air (noticeable if you place the back of your hand in front of your mouth as you utter the word), while the /p/ in *spin* has no such puff. That puff of air is called aspiration, and is written as a superscript letter *h* in phonetic transcription, like this: [p^hɪn]. These two varieties of /p/ are called **allophones** of the phoneme /p/. Notice that [p^h] and [p] in English are not in contrastive distribution, because they do not serve to distinguish words from one another. Incidentally, English orthography does not distinguish between [p^h] and [p], using the letter *p* to represent both. There are languages, however, such as Korean and Thai, which use aspiration to distinguish words from one another. In such languages, aspirated /p^h/ and unaspirated /p/ are separate phonemes, in contrastive distribution. For example, the Korean word for 'fire', 불, is pronounced [pul], and the word for 'grass', 풀, is pronounced [p^hul]; the two words are a minimal pair. Notice that the two words are written differently: ㅂ represents the unaspirated /p/, and ㅍ represents the aspirated /p^h/.

Korean has a phonemic distinction that in English is allophonic (aspirated and unaspirated voiceless stop consonants). Let's examine an example of a phonemic distinction in English that is allophonic in another language. In English, /r/ and /l/ are different phonemes in contrastive distribution, as indicated by minimal pairs like *peer* and *peel*. In Korean, however, there is no pair of words distinguished by [r] and [l]. In Korean, [l] may only occur at the end of a word (as in the words for 'fire' and 'grass'), a position that may never be occupied by [r]. The [r] sound – which is actually articulated much like a flap [ɾ] – appears in word-initial position in the Korean word 루비, [rupi], which means 'ruby'. Korean [r] and [l] are allophones of a Korean phoneme we will call /L/ (the capital L stands for "liquid").

When two sounds cannot appear in the same position in words, they are in **complementary distribution**. This is the case for the consonants [r] and [l] in Korean: [l] is word-final, [r] is word-initial. This is also the case for aspirated and unaspirated /p/ in English: [p^h] must be the first consonant in a stressed syllable, [p] appears in consonant clusters that begin with /s/. In both languages, we have an example of a pair of allophones linked to the same phoneme. Incidentally, both languages write the different sounds using the same symbol, ㄹ for Korean [r] or [l], and the letter *p* for English [p^h] or [p].

The phonemic inventory of a language has a profound effect on a speaker's perception of speech sounds. Phonemically distinct sounds

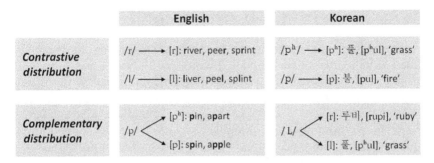

Figure 2.2 Distribution of [r], [1], [pʰ], and [p] in English and Korean. Both languages have the four sounds in their phonetic inventory, but their phonemic inventories treat these four sounds very differently.

(sounds in contrastive distribution) are perceived as being very different, while allophonic variants of the same phoneme are difficult to distinguish. This is the case even when the difference between two sounds is articulatorily or acoustically clear (e.g., the presence or absence of a puff of air for [pʰ] versus [p], or the different manner of articulation for [r] versus [l]). Figure 2.2 summarizes the facts described above for English and Korean. For speakers of English, the difference between [pʰ] and [p] goes unnoticed, and so an English speaker learning Korean will struggle distinguishing between the words for 'fire' and 'grass'. For speakers of Korean, in comparison, [r] and [l] sound as similar as [pʰ] and [p] do to speakers of English, and Korean learners of English have great difficulty distinguishing between words like *river* and *liver* or *peer* and *peel*; they will also have difficulty producing [l]-initial and [r]-final words. In Chapters 4 and 6 we return to the effect that the phonemic inventory has on the perceptual system.

Phonological rules

An important function of the phonological component of the grammar is to supply predictable phonetic details to phonemic representations. One way to understand how this works is to think of the phonology as subjecting words to a set of rules that transform sequences of phonemes (stored abstractly and lacking in detail) into representations with all the details necessary to specify how speech is articulated. For example, a phonological rule for English requires aspiration for /p/ phonemes appearing in the initial position of stressed syllables. By this rule, the /p/ phonemes in *apart* and *important* are produced with aspiration, but not the /p/ phonemes in *apple* and *spin*. A phonological rule for Korean ensures that the phoneme for the [r]–[l] allophone pair is articulated as [r] word-initially, and as [l] word-finally. Notice that this gives us one way to think about what might be ungrammatical (with respect to phonology) in a language: representations that violate the phonological principles of a language are ungrammatical. The sequence *[ˈæpʰəl] is ungrammatical in English, because it violates a phonological rule of English; /p/ may not be aspirated when it appears in an unstressed syllable (the symbol [ˈ] is used in phonetic transcription to indicate that the following syllable is stressed; the symbol [ə], called a "schwa," is used to transcribe the vowel in the unstressed syllable). Ungrammaticality is marked by placing an asterisk, *, in front of the ungrammatical sequence.

There are many phonetic details that are predictable in English, and are thus controlled by phonological rules. For example, /t/ and /d/ are pronounced similarly in many words, like *writing* and *riding*, or *matter* and *madder*, all of which in American English are pronounced with a flap, [ɾ]. The rule describing when the phonemes /t/ or /d/ can be flapped in American English must handle some rather complicated facts: /t/ or /d/ is pronounced as [ɾ] when appearing between two vowels and also in the onset of an unstressed syllable. This explains why, for American English speakers, there is a [ɾ] in *fatter*, where it is between two vowels and begins an unstressed syllable (don't let the double letter *t* throw you off) but not in *captain*, where it begins an unstressed syllable but is not between two vowels; this also explains why there is a [ɾ] in *city*, where it begins an unstressed syllable, but not in *baton*, where it begins a stressed syllable, and in the second but not in the first /t/ of *potato*. Another phonological rule in English causes vowels to lengthen when they precede a voiced consonant. For example, *pad* and *pat* have the same vowel, but the vowel in *pad* [æ:] is longer than the one in *pat* [æ]. (Vowel lengthening is transcribed with the symbol [:] following a lengthened vowel.) Vowels in English are also subject to a nasalization rule. When preceding a nasal consonant, vowels become nasalized, as in the following words: *Pam* [pʰæ̃:m], *pan* [pʰæ̃:n], *pang* [pʰæ̃:ŋ]. (Nasalization is transcribed by using a tilde [˜] over a nasalized vowel. Since nasal consonants are voiced, vowels preceding them are lengthened, as the transcriptions indicate.)

A final example of a phonological rule for English applies to the phoneme /l/, which is pronounced differently when it begins than when it ends a word. This difference can be observed when one compares the two /l/ sounds at the beginning of *leap* and at the end of *peal*. The one that begins a word is called a *light-l* (transcribed like this: [l]); the one that ends a word, a *dark-l* (transcribed like this: [ɫ]), is produced with a slight hump in the back of the tongue. Both are allophones of the phoneme /l/.

Phonotactic constraints

All the details of pronunciation that are part of the phonological pattern of the language and are, therefore, predictable, are described by the phonological rules of the language. Another role of the phonological component is to set constraints on what sequences of phonemes are possible in the language. These are the **phonotactic constraints** of the language. Phonotactic constraints are really constraints on the way syllables can be created in a particular language. A **syllable** is a group of sounds which must contain a *nucleus* (usually a vowel), and may have an *onset* (one or more syllable-initial consonants) and a *coda* (one or more syllable-final consonants). Together, the nucleus and the coda are the syllable's *rhyme*. The structure of a syllable is diagrammed in Figure 2.3.

Certain phonotactic constraints – that is, constraints on syllable structure – are thought to be universal: all languages have syllables with vowels, and all languages have syllables that consist of a consonant

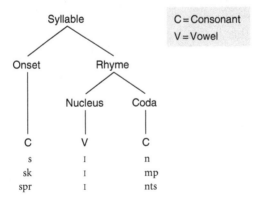

Figure 2.3   Schematic diagram of the structure of a syllable, and examples of three monosyllabic words with different onsets and codas: *sin*, *skimp*, and *sprints*. The number of consonants permitted in onset and coda position is controlled by phonotactic constraints.

followed by a vowel. But there is also a great deal of language specificity in phonotactic constraints. A language like English allows just about any type of consonant to appear in the coda (syllable-final) position – try it yourself, by coming up with as many words as you can that add only one consonant to the sequence /kɪ_ /, like *kit*. You will find there are many. In contrast, languages like Spanish and Japanese have strict constraints about syllable-final consonants. Spanish permits only the following phonemes syllable-finally, and only one at a time: /l/, /r/, /n/, /ð/, /s/, and (for the dialects that have it) /θ/. Japanese is even more restrictive, permitting only syllable-final nasals and the first half of a geminate consonant. (*Geminates* are formed when the same consonant appears in the coda of one syllable and the onset of the next syllable. Consider the difference between the English words *holy* and *wholly*, when spoken slowly; the latter has a geminate /l/. The difference between non-geminate /n/ in *unattractive* and geminate /n/ in *unnatural* is another example.)

One language may *borrow* a word from another. This means that the word from one language is incorporated into the lexicon of the other. (We will discuss language borrowing again in Chapter 5.) When this happens, the word may be transformed to conform to the phonotactic constraints of the language doing the borrowing. For example, when Japanese speakers borrow words from English, Japanese phonotactic constraints apply. *Beer* in Japanese is ビール, pronounced [biiru]; and *bus* is バス, pronounced [basu] – notice the extra syllable in each, added to conform to the syllable-final phonotactic constraints of the language. Neither /r/ nor /s/ can appear as syllable-final in Japanese. Therefore, in order for the Japanese speaker to pronounce the /r/ in *beer*, the /r/ has to be pronounced as the onset of a syllable, which means that it must immediately precede a vowel. There is no vowel in the correct position of the English word *beer*, so the Japanese speaker inserts one, /u/, which puts the /r/ into the onset of a syllable. Similarly, the /s/ in English *bus* must also be made into the onset of a syllable for the Japanese speaker, a syllable with the nuclear vowel /u/.

Consider how English has many words beginning with /bl/ (*blight*), /pl/ (*plight*), /kl/ (*class*), and /gl/ (*glass*), but no words beginning */dl/ or */tl/. Such ungrammatical syllable-initial sequences violate the phonotactic constraints of English. Words that do not actually occur in the language but adhere to the phonotactic constraints are *possible non-words*, so a made-up word like *blick* is a possible non-word in English, while a made-up word like *tlick* is an impossible non-word. This is not because /tl/ is impossible or even difficult to pronounce. In fact, this initial sequence occurs in languages like Nahuatl, a language spoken in central Mexico, where place names like *Tlalpan* and *Tenochtitlan* reflect the Nahuatl linguistic heritage. Having tacit knowledge of the phonotactic constraints of one's language has important psycholinguistic implications, which we will discuss in Chapter 6. People can judge which words are possible and which are impossible in their language, because people have tacit knowledge of phonotactic constraints, and know when these are violated. Knowledge of phonotactic constraints has an effect on the lexical retrieval system, as well. If you hear an impossible word, your lexical processor will not even attempt to locate it in your internal lexicon. There is even some evidence that possible and impossible words activate different parts of the brain; we will return to this in Chapter 3.

Prosody

An aspect of language controlled by the phonological component is **prosody**, which could roughly be defined as the rhythm and intonation of speech. With prosody, signed languages and spoken languages are similar in that both have rules to capture regular prosodic characteristics, like the insertion of pauses in sentences, or the grouping of words into rhythmic phrases. Prosodic rules apply to units such as *syllables, prosodic words*, and *intonational (prosodic) phrases*. Because these units extend over more than one segment at a time, they are called *suprasegmentals*.

Languages have been categorized into classes based on their general rhythmic tendencies. Languages like English and Dutch are often described as **stress-timed** languages, because of the role that stressed syllables appear to play in organizing the rhythm of an utterance. Languages like Spanish, French, and Italian, in contrast, are categorized as **syllable-timed**, and languages like Japanese are categorized as **mora-timed**. (A **mora** is a unit of prosodic weight. It is smaller than a syllable; consonants or vowels in the syllable's rhyme – its nucleus and coda – contribute moras.) The basic idea behind this categorization is that languages have *isochronous* rhythm: the amount of time will be regular, stress to stress (in English), or syllable to syllable (in Spanish) or mora to mora (in Japanese).

The distinction between these three broad rhythmic classes is not very clear cut. For example, some languages, like Brazilian Portuguese, have been demonstrated to have properties of both stress- and syllable-timed languages. Also, the difference between these rhythmic classes may really be based on differences in syllable structure constraints rather than rhythm: stress-timed languages tend to tolerate complex rhymes; syllable-timed and mora-timed languages tend to have simpler rhymes. In addition, stress-timed languages tend to change vowels in unstressed syllables to vowels that are more central, a process known as *vowel reduction*. In English, for example, many unstressed syllables contain [ə]; compare the pronunciation of the underlined vowels in the second syllable of *harmonic* and *harmony*, which are a full [ɑ] and a reduced [ə] vowel, respectively. This process of vowel reduction is rare in syllable- or mora-timed languages.

One suprasegmental feature that many languages use phonemically is *tone*. Mandarin Chinese, for example, has four tones, which serve to distinguish words from each other. The word 搭, pronounced [dā] with a high and level tone, means 'to hang over something'; the word 答, [dá] with a rising tone, means 'to answer'; 打, [dǎ] with a tone that falls and rises, means 'to hit'; and 大, [dà] with a neutral (falling) tone, means 'big'. (The diacritics above the vowels in the transcriptions are the symbols used to transcribe the different tones.)

We have already alluded to prosody, in discussing phonological regularities that depend on syllables, such as phonotactic constraints that apply to syllable onsets or codas. Stress is also a suprasegmental feature. In every word in English, different syllables have different amounts of *prominence*, and the most prominent syllable is said to have main stress. Prosodic prominence is manifested acoustically in a variety of ways. Stressed syllables can be produced more loudly, or with longer duration, or with a higher pitch than unstressed syllables. In the word *elephant* the first syllable is stressed, while in the word *giraffe* the second syllable is. Stress can distinguish between some verbs and nouns in English. Though there are many counter-examples, bisyllabic nouns in English typically have a trochaic stress pattern, meaning primary stress falls on the first syllable like *table* or *paper*. In contrast, bisyllabic verbs typically have an iambic stress pattern, meaning that primary stress falls on the second syllable, like *reflect* or *admire*. Compare the stress difference between the noun *forest* and the verb *arrest*. There are even minimal pairs, like *permit* (a noun referring to a document that allows you to do something) and *permit* (a verb indicating that permission is granted), for which the contrast is location of stress.

Some aspects of prosody extend well beyond syllables and words. Entire sentences have patterns of intonation that are reflected in the way pitch rises and falls and in the way words are grouped together in intonational phrases. Consider the following two sentences, which are segmentally identical (they have the same consonants and vowels) but intonationally are very different:

(2)   a.   My computer has wireless.
        b.   My computer has wireless?

Declaratives, like (2a), tend to be uttered with falling intonation, from the beginning to the end of the sentence; in contrast, interrogatives, like (2b), are pronounced with rising intonation at the end of the sentence.

Consider now how you might utter a sentence like the following, without any other sentence as context:

(3)   Tony disconnected the modem.

It's probable that the only prominent word in your utterance was *modem*. (We use prominence here as we did in discussing syllable stress: a prosodically prominent word is a little longer, a little higher in pitch, and a little louder than other words in the sentence.) In a declarative English sentence, the last word tends to get a little bit of prominence, by a prosodic rule that requires prominence at the end of intonational phrases; this type of prominence is called a *pitch accent*. Suppose now that you are uttering (3) as an answer to *Who disconnected the modem?* In this case the word *Tony* receives more prominence because it is in focus: Tony is the new information; it is the answer to the question, so it is more prominent prosodically. This kind of prosodic prominence is called *focus accent*, and it is realized by making the word even more prosodically prominent than when it bears just a pitch accent. In contrast, as an answer to *What did Tony disconnect?* you would probably place focus accent on *the modem*, and as an answer to *What did Tony do to the modem?* you would probably place a focus accent on *disconnected*.

Prosody can also reflect the syntactic structure of sentences, by marking where important syntactic boundaries are placed. Say the following two sentences out loud, making a small pause at the location of the comma:

(4)   a.   They invited Sue and Jim, and Amanda got rejected.
        b.   They invited Sue, and Jim and Amanda got rejected.

You probably understood (4a) to mean that only one person was rejected (Amanda), while in (4b) two people were rejected

(Jim and Amanda). The prosody you produced suggested how you should group those words syntactically.

Summary: Phonology

The phonological component of the grammar provides information about the inventory of phonemes in a language and the principles that govern their combination into words. It also provides details of the pronunciation of sentences, including both allophonic variation and the prosodic characteristics of words and sentences.

The Morphological Component

Phonemes are completely meaningless by themselves, yet they combine to form **morphemes**, the smallest units of meaning or grammatical function in a language. Morphemes can be divided into two classes, **bound** and **free**. Free morphemes are individual words, like *dog* or *bite*, that can appear alone or with other morphemes. In contrast, bound morphemes – like the *–s* in *plays* or the *re–* in *rewrite* – must be affixed to other words. Bound morphemes are called *affixes* in general – or, more specifically, *prefixes* (*dis–* in *disbelief*) or *suffixes* (*–sion* in *suspension*), depending on how they attach to the *stem* (or *root*) of the word. Some languages have *circumfixes*, which affix around the stem, like the German past participle morpheme *ge–…–t*, which added to the verb *spielen* ('to play') gives us *gespielt* ('played'). And some languages have *infixes*, in which a morpheme is inserted into the stem. For instance, in Tagalog (a language of the Philippines) the word for *write* is /sulat/. The morpheme /um/ is infixed before the first vowel to create /sumulat/, meaning 'one who writes', and /in/ is infixed to create /sinulat/, meaning 'that which is written'. Affixes attach to the stem, which can be a free morpheme (like *dare* in *daring*) or not (like *fer–* in *refer*). In English, stems are very frequently free morphemes, but in some languages stems never stand on their own; they must have one or more bound morphemes attached.

Some morphemes change based on the phonological environment in which they occur. These regularities are expressed as **morphophonological rules**. An example of such a rule applies to indefinite articles (also called determiners) in English. Words like the definite article *the* are used to specify a noun (e.g., *the book* specifies a particular book), while the indefinite article *a* is less specific (e.g., *a cat* refers to some cat, any cat). The pronunciation of the indefinite article varies depending on the phoneme that follows: we say *an apple* and *a cat*. More examples of morphophonological rules are in the sections below.

Inflectional morphemes

Bound morphemes belong to one of two classes which perform very different functions: *derivational morphemes* (which we will discuss below) and *inflectional morphemes*. **Inflectional morphemes** mark features like tense, number, gender, and case. The meaning of the stem to which an inflectional morpheme is attached does not change, nor does its **grammatical category** (also known as **part of speech**, such as noun, verb, adverb, or adjective). The inflection simply adds to the stem *grammatical features* like tense, number, gender, and case (we will discuss each of these below). *Race* is a verb that refers to a particular kind of locomotion; adding *–ing* does not change the part of speech nor the meaning of *race*, but it changes the verb's aspect to progressive: *racing* in *It was racing down the street* performs a different grammatical function than does *raced* in *It raced down the street*. Of course, there is another use of the bound morpheme *–ing*; it can change a verb to a noun, as in *Racing can be lots of fun*.

The morpheme *–ed* is used in English to mark past **tense**, so the entire sentence in which a verb with *–ed* appears must indicate past action. It is therefore ungrammatical to say **Tomorrow the boy walked*, because the word *tomorrow* indicates future action. The past tense morpheme actually has three different pronunciations, determined by a morphophonological rule that refers to the final phoneme of the verb stem *–ed* is affixed to: *–ed* is voiceless [t] if it is attached to a verb ending in a voiceless phoneme, like *walk*; it is voiced [d] if affixed to a verb ending in a voiced phoneme, like *buzz* or *show*; and it is syllabic [əd] if the verb stem ends with /t/ or /d/, like *hate* or *pad*.

The inflectional morpheme *–ed* actually has two functions in English. It marks the simple past tense, like in the example in (5a). It also marks past participles, which are verb forms used in passive sentences, like (5b), and in verbal constructions that use auxiliary verbs, like in (5c). **Auxiliary verbs** (also called **helping verbs**), like *be*, *have*, and *do*, in English, are verbs that accompany the main (lexical) verb in a verb phrase and carry agreement features. Notice that in example (5d) *raced* is a past participle in a *reduced relative clause*, a construction we will discuss briefly later in this chapter and at length in Chapter 7.

(5) a. The Corvette raced down the street.
     b. The Corvette was raced at the Daytona Speedway by a driver named McMurray.
     c. McMurray has raced in Talladega and Indianapolis.
     d. Danielle emailed me a photograph of the Corvette raced at the Daytona Speedway.

Other inflections in English are those required to satisfy a requirement that subjects and verbs must agree in **number**. By this principle, *They laugh* is grammatical, but not **He laugh* or **They laughs*. English marks plurality on nouns with an *–s* morpheme (*one boy, two boys*), and singularity on verbs also with an *–s* morpheme (*they laugh, he laughs*). (A third *–'s* morpheme, which has nothing to do with number agreement, is used to mark possession, as in *Beth's mother*.)

The three *–s* morphemes also follow a morphophonological rule that changes their pronunciation based on the final phoneme of the stem they affix to. A voiceless form [s] is produced following a voiceless phoneme (*fights, cats, Beth's*), a voiced form [z] following a voiced phoneme (*finds, dogs, Bob's*), and a syllabic form [ɪz] following phonemes like /s/ or /z/ (*freezes, passes, Max's*), /ʃ/ or /ʒ/ (*brushes, garages, Raj's*), or /tʃ/ or /dʒ/ (*judges, peaches, Marge's*).

In some languages, inflectional morphemes mark **gender** and **case**. In Spanish, for example, articles and adjectives must agree in gender with the noun they modify. So the adjective meaning 'tall' takes a different ending (*–o* or *–a*) depending on whether it modifies a masculine or feminine noun: *niño alto* ('tall boy'), *niña alta* ('tall girl'). Finally, inflectional morphemes are used to mark case. In Russian, the noun that means 'sister' takes a different case ending depending on what grammatical function it serves in the sentence: if it is the subject of the sentence, it is *сестра*, pronounced [sestra]; as direct object it is *сестру*, [sestru]; with some prepositions it is *сестре*, [sestre], and with other prepositions it is *сестры*, [sestrə].

Derivational morphemes

The second class of bound morphemes, **derivational morphemes**, includes morphemes that can change the meaning or the grammatical category of the stem to which they are affixed. For instance, adding *–er* to a verb changes it into a noun (*make, maker*); adding *–ness* to an adjective changes it into a noun (*kind, kindness*); adding *–ly* to an adjective changes it into an adverb (*interesting, interestingly*).

Some derivational morphemes change the meaning of a word without changing the part of speech. For example, *un–* is a prefix that can be added to adjectives to create an adjective with the opposite meaning, as in *unkind* and *uninteresting*. Another such derivational morpheme is *re–*, which is prefixed to a verb to indicate repetition of the action of the stem, as in *rewash* or *reconsider*.

Some derivational morphemes alter the pronunciation of the stem, by morphophonological rules. The derivational morpheme *–ity* often causes its stem to change phonologically. When *–ity* is added to *stupid* and *specific*, the position of the stress shifts to the right: *stupidity* and *specificity* (note the final /k/ in *specific* also changes to /s/ in *specificity*). Also, when *–ity* is added to *sane*, the vowel in the stem changes: *sanity*.

▨ Summary: Morphology

The morphological component of the grammar includes both inflectional and derivational morphemes that create new words for a variety of syntactic and semantic functions. Many are associated with morphophonological rules that provide information about the pronunciation of the word that results when the morpheme is attached to a stem.

▨ The Syntactic Component

The syntax of a language creates the structures of its sentences, which, along with the words in them, determine meaning. Syntax carries out three fundamental kinds of operations:

- it creates basic structures for sentences;
- it combines simple sentences to form complex ones; and
- it moves (or reorders) elements of sentences.

These three operations of the syntax give people the ability to create sentences with great precision of meaning. These operations – the second one in particular – also give human language its most readily observable creativity. The syntax of every human language consists of a finite set of rules which, coupled with a finite lexicon, generates an unlimited number of different sentences, allowing each speaker to experience a lifetime of novel utterances. Every sentence you will produce or hear today is likely to be a sentence you have never produced or heard before.

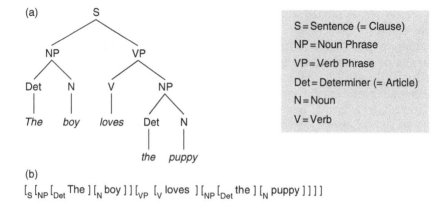

(b)
$[_S [_{NP} [_{Det} \text{The}] [_N \text{boy}]] [_{VP} [_V \text{loves}] [_{NP} [_{Det} \text{the}] [_N \text{puppy}]]]]$

Figure 2.4 Two ways to represent the constituents in the simple sentence, *The boy loves the puppy*. We will use the tree diagram notation in (a); the bracket notation in (b) contains identical information and resembles notation used in mathematics.

Simple structure

The basic meaning of a sentence is determined by its words and their structural organization. Syntax provides that structure. Sentence structure consists of hierarchically organized constituents. Constituents are the components of a sentence that form a unit. Figure 2.4 illustrates constituents by diagramming the structure of the simple sentence, consisting of a single **clause**, *The boy loves the puppy*. A clause, then, is a constituent consisting of an NP (the subject of the sentence) and a VP (the sentence's *predicate*). (Remember, the figures in this book do not contain all the information that a linguist would specify for the structure of a sentence. Only those aspects of structure that are necessary to illustrate points in the text are included.)

To get a good sense of what is meant by the term *constituent*, try the substitution test. A set of words is a constituent of the sentence if it is possible to substitute a single word for those words and still have a sentence of the same type (in this case, an active, declarative sentence) – although, of course, the sentence will have a different meaning. One can substitute *John* for *the boy* and have the perfectly fine sentence *John loves the puppy*. Thus, the **noun phrase (NP)** *the boy* is a constituent. Similarly, one can substitute *Spot* for *the puppy* and have the sentence *The boy loves Spot*. Finally, one can substitute a single verb *sleeps* for the **verb phrase (VP)** and have *The boy sleeps*. The substitution test demonstrates that *the boy, the puppy*, and *loves the puppy* are all constituents of this sentence. By this same test, we know that *boy loves* is not a constituent of the sentence. There is no single word that one could substitute that would make *The ____ the puppy* an acceptable sentence.

Syntactic constituents are said to be hierarchically organized because they are embedded in one another. For example, the NP *the puppy* is part of the larger VP. We say that the second NP is embedded in the VP or that it is dominated by the VP. These simple facts illustrate a fundamental point about the organization of a sentence. Words in sentences are not related to each other in a simple linear way, as beads on a string. Even though words end up being produced one after another, their structural organization is not predictable from their linear order. Instead, their structure is a result of the hierarchical organization of the constituents that form them. Thus, a verb that follows the first NP in a sentence could be the main verb of the sentence or not, depending on how it is structurally related to that NP.

Note that the phrases we have discussed take their names from the main lexical item in the phrase, which is called its **head**. The phrasal head of an NP is a noun, the head of a VP is a verb, the head of a prepositional phrase (PP) is a preposition, and so on.

It is now possible to make a more precise statement about the ambiguity of a sentence discussed (and diagrammed) in Chapter 1.

(6)   The man saw the boy with the binoculars.

In Figure 1.2(a) the PP *with the binoculars* is a constituent of VP, while in Figure 1.2(b) the PP and *the boy* are constituents of the same NP. These represent the two meanings of the sentence. In Figure 1.2(a) the PP is semantically related to the verb *saw*, while in Figure 1.2(b) the PP is semantically affiliated with the NP *the boy*.

One task of the syntax, then, is to create basic sentence structure, which consists of hierarchically organized constituents. A basic sentence consists of a single verb and the grammatical elements required by the verb's **subcategorization frame**; these grammatical elements are called **arguments** of the verb. Figure 2.5 provides diagrams for sentences containing verbs that take different types of arguments.

All verbs require at least one argument, a subject. In some languages, like Italian or Spanish, the subject position can be empty (e.g., *canto* means 'I sing' in both Italian and Spanish; the stem is *cant–*, and the suffix *–o* indicates the verb is first person singular); these are called **null subject languages**. In a sentence with a null subject, even though the

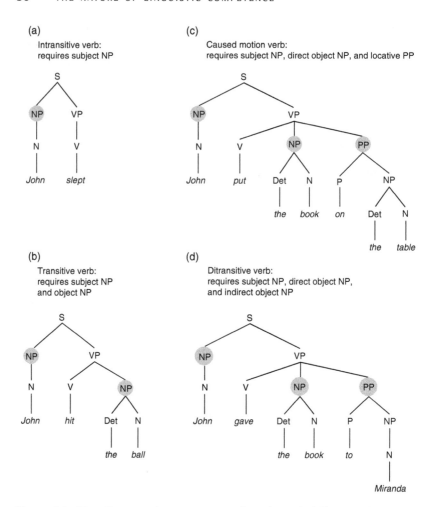

Figure 2.5   Tree diagrams for sentences with verbs with different subcategorization frames. The shaded nodes are arguments of the verb.

subject is not explicit, the structural position is assumed to be there, filled by a null subject pronoun, called *pro*.

In addition to structural relations, verbs and their arguments have *thematic relations* between them. Two such thematic relations are *agent* and *patient*. The agent of a sentence performs the action of a verb, while the patient (also called the *theme*) undergoes the action of the verb. We can use thematic relations to define the difference between *active* sentences, like the example in (7a) and *passive* sentences – like (5b), earlier, and the example in (7b), below.

(7) a. John hit the ball.
     b. The ball was hit by John.

In both sentences, *John* is the agent and *ball* is the patient. Notice, however, that the agent and patient occupy different structural positions. In
passive sentences in English, the subject is the patient, and the agent
appears in a PP whose head is the preposition *by*.

Intransitive verbs, like *sleep* or *snore*, require only a subject. **Transitive
verbs**, like *hit* or *include*, require two arguments: a subject and a direct
object. Other verbs require three arguments. The verb *put*, for example,
requires a subject, a direct object, and an argument indicating location;
in fact, if one of the three arguments of *put* is missing, the sentence is
ungrammatical, as with **John put the book*. *Give* also requires three arguments: a subject, a direct object, and an indirect object.

Each argument of a verb is a distinct constituent of the sentence and
can be substituted by a constituent of the same category. Thus, the sentence *The respected politician gave the rare old book to his local public library*
contains the same three arguments as *John gave the book to Miranda*, but
those arguments are represented by longer and more complex constituents. This is another example of how the structure of a sentence is composed of constituents that are defined in terms of their grammatical
function, not in terms of their length.

One final remark concerning simple structure is in order. We now
have a structural way to define the concepts of **subject** and **direct
object**. The subjects in the four examples in Figure 2.5 are the NP nodes
directly dominated by S. The direct objects are the NP nodes directly
dominated by VP.

Complex structure

The second function of the syntax is to allow simple sentences to be combined into complex ones. One way to create complex sentences is to
embed a simple sentence into another, as an argument of the verb. The
main sentence is called the **matrix** or **independent** or **main clause**, and
the embedded sentence is called the **subordinate** or **dependent
(embedded) clause**. Here is an example, in which the simple clause *Ian
is brilliant* is embedded inside the simple clause *They claimed [something]*:

(8) They claimed that Ian is brilliant.

The structure for this sentence is diagrammed in Figure 2.6. This particular type of embedded clause is called a **sentential complement**.

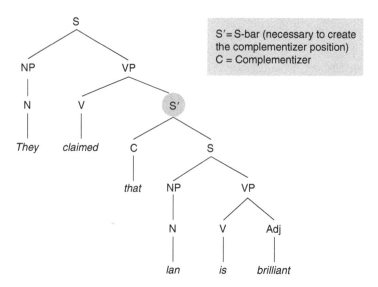

Figure 2.6   Tree diagram for a sentence with a sentential complement (the constituents dominated by the shaded S′-node).

Sentential complements are clauses that are embedded in a VP and introduced by *that*, a *complementizer*. The complementizer is optional in English (though it is obligatory in some languages). The sentence in (8) is perfectly grammatical and has the same structure and meaning if *that* is omitted.

There is no limit to how many such embeddings the grammar will allow in a single sentence, a property of syntax known as *recursion*. The sentence *Mary speculated that they claimed that Ian is brilliant* is grammatical. Too many embeddings, however, might make a sentence difficult to understand (consider *Bob denied that Mary speculated that they claimed that Ian is brilliant*), but the grammatical process of embedding is not limited in the number of times it can apply. In Chapter 1 the distinction between linguistic competence and linguistic performance was discussed. Competence is the knowledge of the grammar and lexicon of one's language; performance is the act of putting that knowledge to use in the production and comprehension of sentences. Competence places no limit on the number of embeddings in a sentence, but performance factors make it difficult for people to either produce or understand a sentence with too many embedded clauses.

Another common type of complex sentence is one containing a **relative clause**. Relative clauses are simple sentences embedded into a noun phrase. Consider the following three simple sentences:

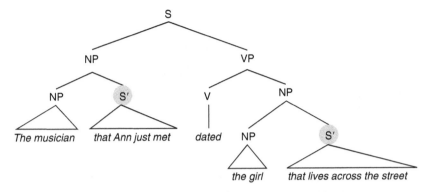

Figure 2.7   Tree diagram for a sentence with two relative clauses (the constituents dominated by the shaded S'-nodes). The triangles indicate that the internal structure of those constituents has been omitted from the diagram.

(9) a. The musician dated the girl.
    b. Ann just met the musician.
    c. The girl lives across the street.

We can take the three sentences and combine them into a complex sentence containing two relative clauses:

(10) The musician that Ann just met dated the girl that lives across the street.

This sentence is diagrammed in Figure 2.7. The relative clauses modify the two nouns in the matrix clause: *musician* and *girl*.

    Notice that relative clauses can be introduced by the complementizer *that* (just like sentential complements). Relative clauses can also be introduced by relative pronouns, like *who*. (In fact, you can substitute *who* for *that* in (10), without consequences.) There is no important difference between a relative clause beginning with a complementizer and one beginning with a relative pronoun, so it is convenient to refer to the word that begins a relative clause as a *relativizer*. The relativizer may be omitted entirely from a relative clause, to create a *reduced relative clause*, but only when the element of the sentence that the relativizer refers to is not the subject of the relative clause. In (10), above, the first *that* (which refers to the object of *dated*) may be omitted, but not the second one (which refers to the subject of *lives*).

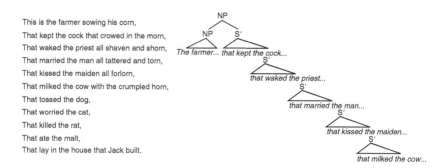

This is the farmer sowing his corn,
That kept the cock that crowed in the morn,
That waked the priest all shaven and shorn,
That married the man all tattered and torn,
That kissed the maiden all forlorn,
That milked the cow with the crumpled horn,
That tossed the dog,
That worried the cat,
That killed the rat,
That ate the malt,
That lay in the house that Jack built.

Figure 2.8   Excerpt from the children's poem, "The House that Jack Built," and a diagram illustrating its recursive structure.

Embedding sentential complements and relative clauses inside matrix clauses is one way that language is **recursive**, a property of all human languages that we will come back to in Chapter 3. The children's poem "The House that Jack Built" exploits the recursive ability of English syntax (see Figure 2.8). The poem begins with the sentence *This is the house that Jack built*, a sentence with only one relative clause. The poem continues with *This is the malt / That lay in the house that Jack built*. The story gets progressively more complicated as the basic sentence is lengthened by embedding it inside another sentence.

Chapter 7 will discuss the fact that in order to recover the meaning of a complex sentence, the structural processor must decompose it into its simple sentences. This is because the meaning of a complex sentence is the combination of the meanings of all the simple sentences that are its constituents. There are many kinds of complex sentences other than those containing sentential complements and relative clauses. There are, for instance, **infinitive clauses** like *to run for President* in (11), and **adverbial clauses** introduced by subordinating conjunctions, like the clause introduced by *while* in (12).

(11)   Jane decided to run for President.

(12)   While she was preparing her speech Jane's computer crashed.

We will not describe the syntax for these types of sentences, but by now you should have developed a better sense for how to find the clausal constituents of complex sentences, by looking for verbs and their arguments.

Movement

The third fundamental operation of the syntax is moving constituents around. Movement operations have applied when the grammatical elements in a sentence are ordered differently from their basic (canonical) order. The dative (indirect object) alternation illustrates one type of movement:

(13) a. Robert gave a cashmere sweater to his girlfriend.
     b. Robert gave his girlfriend a cashmere sweater.

In (13a), the direct object (*a cashmere sweater*) and the indirect object (*his girlfriend*) are in their expected positions. In (13b), those two constituents have switched positions. This example helps us make an important point: movement rules in syntax are structure dependent, a universal property of grammar that is of paramount importance to a description of syntactic processes. Structure dependency means that constituents of sentences, rather than individual words, are involved in syntactic processes. In this example, the constituents involved are the direct and indirect objects.

We can observe structure dependency by looking at the formation of questions that can be answered *yes* or *no*. To create *yes/no* questions, the element of the VP that agrees with the subject (the element that carries tense and agreement features) moves to the front of the sentence; in the following examples, *is* and *has* move:

(14) a. The girl is petting the cat.
     b. Is the girl ___ petting the cat?

(15) a. The girl has eaten at the restaurant.
     b. Has the girl ___ eaten at the restaurant?

(The underlined space shows the original location of the moved element.)

This movement rule doesn't apply to just any VP: it has to be the VP in the matrix clause. The sentence in (16a) contains two VPs: one in the relative clause (*is dating*) and one in the matrix clause (*is petting the cat*). To make a *yes/no* question from this sentence, in (16b), we have moved *is* from the matrix clause, and the question turns out to be grammatical. In (16c), in contrast, we have moved *is* from the embedded relative clause, and the result is ungrammatical. Notice that this movement rule specifically makes reference to the structure of the sentence, i.e., the matrix clause as opposed to the relative clause. Thus, it is a structure dependent rule.

(16) a. The girl who my brother is dating is petting the cat.
      b. Is the girl who my brother is dating ___ petting the cat?
      c. *Is the girl who my brother ___ dating is petting the cat?

The examples in (14)–(16) contain complex verbs, in which the tensed element is the auxiliary *be* or *have*. But many sentences in English have simple verbs, in which the tense and agreement markers are part of the main verb, like in (17a). In such sentences, an operation called ***do-support*** applies: the tense and agreement features are taken off the verb, and incorporated into a "dummy" auxiliary, *do*, that gets inserted into the VP and moved to the front of the sentence, as illustrated in (17b). Without *do*-support, a *yes/no* question created from a sentence with a simple verb will be ungrammatical (17c).

(17) a. The girl fell on the frozen pond.
      b. Did the girl ___ fall on the frozen pond?
      c. *Fell the girl ___ on the frozen pond?

In negated sentences, the negative marker *not* is inserted following the auxiliary, as in (18a) and (18b) below. Negation in a sentence with a simple verb, which has no auxiliary, is formed with *do*-support, as in (18c).

(18) a. The girl is not petting the cat.
      b. The girl has not eaten at this restaurant.
      c. The girl did not fall on the frozen pond.

Another type of movement – ***wh*-movement** – is illustrated by the following examples, all of which are variations on the structure of a sentence like *The soprano delighted the audience with a double encore*. In each example, one of the constituents has been replaced by a *wh*-expression (containing *who* or *what*) and has been moved to the front of the sentence:

(19) a. Who did the soprano delight ___ with a double encore?
      b. With what did the soprano delight the audience ___?
      c. What did the soprano delight the audience with ___?

Who in (19a) is really the direct object of the sentence, only it has moved up from its regular position after the verb, and left behind a gap (also called a *trace*). It is not a literal gap: there is no pause when you say the sentence. The gap is structural, as Figure 2.9 illustrates. Psycholinguists

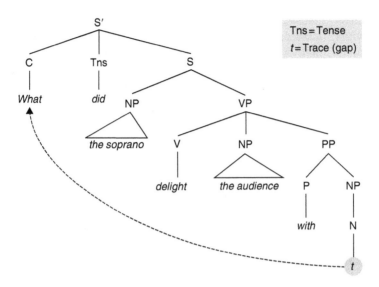

Figure 2.9 Illustration of *wh*-movement, for the sentence *What did the soprano delight the audience with?* The *wh*-word that has moved, *what*, has left a gap, *t*, in the NP embedded inside the PP.

use the term *filler* to refer to *wh*-expressions that have moved, and the term *gap* to refer to the structural slot left behind by movement. In (19b) and (19c), the gap is at the very end of the sentence. (Note that since there is no auxiliary, *do*-support has applied.)

(You might be wondering whether *who* in (19a) shouldn't be *whom*, and whether the sentence-final *with* (19c) isn't ungrammatical. Remember that our objective is to describe the grammar that people use to create sentences – like those in all the examples used in this chapter – rather than to prescribe the way that people ought to speak or write. Indeed, in formal English *whom* is preferred in (19a), and many English teachers might find (19c) to be objectionable, but most speakers of American English, including the most erudite of speakers, produce sentences like those on a regular basis.)

We will see in Chapter 7 that matching fillers and gaps is an important task during sentence comprehension. Just as there is no grammatical limit to recursive embedding, there is no grammatical limit to the distance a *wh*-word can move; in the following example, *who* has moved from a clause embedded two clauses down from the main clause:

(20)   Who did Betty say that Don thought that the soprano delighted
       ——?

Relative clauses and *wh*-questions are very similar, in that the relativizer (*wh*-word) that introduces each is a filler that must be matched up with a gap. Consider the following sentence:

(21)   They videotaped the double encore that the soprano delighted the audience with ___.

The relative clause introduced by *that* is very similar in structure to (19c): the relativizer has moved from a position inside the clause-final prepositional phrase, and has left a gap after *with*. We understand the sentence as meaning that *double encore* is both the object of *videotaped* and of the preposition *with*. The fact that *that* refers to *the double encore* allows it to play a double role in the sentence.

There are other universal constraints on movement that we do not have space to properly explain here. For example, sentences like the following contain universally ungrammatical structures:

(22)   a.   *What did John eat ice cream and ___?
        b.   *Which ice cream do you believe the claim that John ate ___?

As we will see in Chapter 4, children never develop grammars that allow sentences that would violate universal constraints, such as these on movement.

Structure dependency is a feature of all syntactic operations in every human language; any possible human language – past, present, or future – must include structure dependent syntactic operations. Since Universal Grammar provides information about how the grammars of all human languages are organized and the general principles (like structure dependency) that all human languages possess, linguists can infer what properties would constitute an impossible human language. A grammar that had a syntactic rule that moved the third word to the front to form a question or reversed the words of an active sentence to make it passive would not be a possible grammar for a human language. It would be possible to formulate such a rule for a computer program or a language puzzle, but such a rule could never be part of a human language. This is true because the universal properties of human languages follow from the organizational features of the human brain. Human languages have the properties that they do because they are organized and stored in human brains, as we will examine in the next chapter.

▧   Pronominal reference

Pronouns – words like *I*, *me*, *myself*, and *mine* – are function words which replace noun phrases. Pronouns do not have absolute meanings (*I* refers to a different person, depending on the speaker), but rather get their reference from the context in which they appear. There are principles restricting the possible referents for pronouns, and these principles are also structure dependent, as the next examples illustrate:

(23)   a.   Peggy noticed that Mariah kicked herself.
       b.   Peggy noticed that Mariah kicked her.

Reflexive pronouns, like *herself* in (23a), must refer to a noun within their clause, whether the clause is a main or an embedded clause. So in (23a), *herself* may only refer to *Mariah*, and not to *Peggy*. In contrast, personal pronouns, like *her* in (23b), must refer to a noun outside of their clause. In (23b), it cannot be *Mariah* who is being kicked. Notice that these restrictions on the referents of pronouns are dependent on the notion of clauses.

The selection of referents for personal pronouns also provides more insights about how linguistic and psycholinguistic operations interact. The grammar tells us that *her* cannot be *Mariah* in (23b), but it does not tell us whether *her* refers to *Peggy* or to somebody else altogether (say, some female mentioned earlier). The grammar restricts the reference of pronouns by specifying what a pronoun cannot refer to. But the grammar never requires a pronoun to have a particular referent (except in the case of reflexives). How is the referent of a pronoun selected, then? Considerations beyond the sentence come into play, including the context in which the sentence was used, the plausibility of a given interpretation vis-à-vis another interpretation, and so on. Weighing these considerations to come up with an optimal interpretation of the sentence is a function of linguistic performance (psycholinguistic processing), not linguistic competence (grammar). We will return to this in Chapters 7 and 8.

▧   Summary: Syntax

The syntactic component of the grammar contains principles which govern the creation of simple and complex structures of hierarchically related constituents, and which move such constituents around. Syntactic principles are structure dependent and are restricted by structural factors, but not by non-structural considerations such as the number of embedded clauses in a sentence or the linear order of the words.

Metalinguistic Awareness and the Psychological Reality of Linguistic Structure

Throughout the preceding sketch of the operation of the syntactic component of the grammar, the examples (in the languages you know) have appealed to your **metalinguistic awareness**, the ability you have to think consciously about language and linguistic objects (sounds, words, sentences) apart from their use in ordinary communication. When people use language to communicate and interact with others, they are completely unaware of the linguistic system they are summoning to do that. But if asked to contemplate that system, they are able to do so – to a certain extent. Linguistic competence constitutes knowledge of language, but that knowledge is tacit, implicit. This means that people do not have conscious access to the principles and rules that govern the combination of sounds, words, and sentences; however, they do recognize when those rules and principles have been violated. The ability to judge such violations constitutes an important aspect of metalinguistic skill. It is also a powerful demonstration of the psychological reality of grammar. If you can judge when a principle or rule has been violated, you can be sure that it is mentally represented somehow. For example, when a person judges that the sentence *John said that Jane helped himself* is ungrammatical, it is because the person has tacit knowledge of the grammatical principle that reflexive pronouns must refer to an NP in the same clause. Another kind of metalinguistic skill is involved in perceiving the ambiguity of sentences. The perception of global structural ambiguity – that is, that a sentence can have two different meanings based on two alternative structures – illustrates the psycholinguistic information that can be obtained from metalinguistic judgments. Recall once again the ambiguous sentence from example (6):

(6)   The man saw the boy with the binoculars.

The fact that you can perceive this ambiguity demonstrates, first of all, that you have metalinguistic ability. Second, it demonstrates that your brain has used your grammar to create two distinct structural representations of the words in that sentence. Third, it demonstrates that linguistic knowledge is tacit: you are aware of the meanings associated with the two structures, but you are not aware of the structures themselves, nor can you describe the syntactic principles that created them. Fourth, it demonstrates that the meaning of a sentence is a function of the words of the sentence and their structural organization. Finally, it is a clear example of the distinction between linguistic and psycholinguistic processes: the grammar simply creates two possible structural representations of the sentence. It is completely indifferent with respect to which of the two representations is more appropriate. Selection of a preferred interpretation is purely a psycholinguistic activity. As with pronouns, the grammar presents the alternatives and the psycholinguistic system decides among them. The grammar is blind to plausibility considerations or facts about the world; it simply creates the representations. The psycholinguistic system, however, is able to weigh all the possibilities and make a decision. Since in the real world binoculars are instruments that aid vision, it might seem more plausible to select the meaning in which the man has the binoculars. Consider a slightly changed version of the sentence in (6):

(24)   The man hit the boy with the puppy.

When reading (24), you probably selected the meaning in which the boy is holding a puppy, since it is pretty far-fetched to imagine a man using a puppy to hit the boy. How you arrive at the meaning for globally ambiguous sentences is determined by psycholinguistic decisions that can rest on all sorts of information: linguistic (grammatical and lexical) and non-linguistic (plausibility).

Structural ambiguity is very common in language. Many of the sentences people process on a daily basis are either completely (globally) ambiguous or have local ambiguities in multiple places. An example of a local ambiguity is a sentence that begins *Mirabelle knows the boys*. You could think of many different ways to end this sentence; here are two possibilities:

(25)   a.   Mirabelle knows the boys next door.
       b.   Mirabelle knows the boys are rowdy.

The first sentence, (25a), has the simple subject–verb–object structure that was described in the previous section. In contrast, the second sentence,

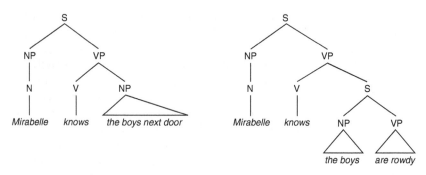

Figure 2.10   Diagrams for the sentences in (25).

(25b), has a complex structure: *the boys are rowdy* is a sentential complement that is an argument of the verb *knows*. Figure 2.10 illustrates the two possible structures for these two continuations of *Mirabelle knows the boys*.

Often, people can perceive structural ambiguity if asked to do so while studying psycholinguistics, but they rarely recognize such ambiguity in ordinary discourse. Even so, as we will discuss in Chapter 7, structural ambiguity (local as well as global) is an important variable that is linked to the ease with which sentences are processed.

▨ The Lexicon

Linguistic competence includes knowledge of a lexicon, as well as knowledge of a grammar. The lexicon is essentially an internalized dictionary consisting of all the words a person knows and the linguistic information connected with each. As we will see, a great deal of information is associated with each lexical entry: information about the word's meaning, information about the word's morphosyntax, and information about the word's morphophonology.

▨ Representing the meaning of words

A lexical entry includes information about the word's essential meaning. This is the word's **lexical semantics**. The meaning of a word will consist of those elements required to distinguish the word from other words, the semantic information all speakers of a language are assumed to share. Idiosyncratic information is assumed not to be among the semantic information listed in a speaker's lexicon. Suppose Bill's sister, Jane, is afraid of cats. Bill's lexical entry for *cat* will carry information that cats are small mammals with four legs, a tail, and whiskers, but not that Jane is afraid of them. Bill will have that information in his mind, but it will be stored in his general repository of knowledge about the world, rather than in his lexicon. (Notice that all speakers of English thus have very similar representations for the meanings of words like *cat*, but they will have different amounts of real-world knowledge about them.) The sentence *Jane saw the cat* does not have as part of its basic meaning that Jane was frightened. However, Bill will be able to infer that she was frightened because his knowledge of the world – highly personal and different from everyone else's – enables him to make that inference.

Lexical entries also contain information about a word's **selectional restrictions**. These are restrictions on what words can be combined with one another. Consider the following:

(26)   *The rock cried.

(27)   *Mary dispersed.

(28)   *John asserted the telephone.

(29)   ? We will grow the economy.

All these examples have an odd quality to them, because one of the arguments of their respective verbs violates the verb's selectional restrictions. For instance, the verb *cry* requires an animate subject, while the verb *disperse* requires a subject whose referent is a group. *The telephone* is an odd direct object for the verb *assert* in (28): telephones are not the kinds of things one can assert. Selectional restrictions can be subject to innovation, however, as the example in (29) illustrates. Generally, *grow* can be used transitively with direct objects like vegetables (*We will grow tomatoes*), but not people (*We will grow intelligent children*) or things concrete or abstract (*We will grow the house*, *We will grow the beauty*). Yet in certain circles (29) is a perfectly well-formed sentence. (The question mark preceding (29) indicates that the sentence is *marginally grammatical*, that is, its grammaticality is questionable.)

Like other aspects of lexical semantics, selectional restrictions are based on the basic meanings of words, rather than their idiosyncratic characteristics. Coming back to Bill, whose sister Jane is afraid of cats, a sentence like *Jane petted the cat* will be odd for Bill, because cats are not the sort of things that Bill knows Jane is likely to pet. All speakers of English will recognize the oddities in (26)–(28), but only Bill will recognize *Jane petted the cat* as odd.

All sorts of conceptual knowledge (including idiosyncratic things you know about the referents for words) is stored independently of lexical entries. Notice that you have concepts for which you lack words; it is likely that you don't have a word for the groove under your nose and above your upper lip, yet you know what it is, and use it regularly to recognize faces. (It is called the *philtrum*.) Notice also that different languages have different ways of naming the same concepts. For instance, English distinguishes between *fingers* and *toes*, while a language like Spanish calls both appendages *dedos*. Surely, Spanish speakers have different concepts for the *dedos* attached to their hands and the *dedos* attached to their feet, but they use the same word to talk about both.

Representing the grammatical properties of words

In addition to storing information about the meanings of words, the lexicon contains a great deal of information about the grammatical properties of words. Some of this information is morphosyntactic, some is morphophonological.

Each word must be identified in the lexicon according to its part of speech, and by extension as a *content word* or a *function word*. **Content words** are nouns, verbs, adjectives, and adverbs – all of which are also characterized as *open class words*, because an unlimited number of such words can be added to the lexicon. **Function words** are grammatical markers of various types – prepositions, conjunctions, determiners, and so on – and are known as *closed class words* because new function words cannot be added to the lexicon of a language. Content and function words are stored separately in the brain and accessed differently during sentence comprehension. Function words are particularly important for providing clues to sentence structure, because they introduce phrases and often signal boundaries between the clauses of complex sentences. Some function words have very little meaning of their own. What does *and* mean? What about *to* in *John wanted to go*? Other function words have some meaning, although such meaning merely relates other constituents of a sentence, like prepositions such as *in, on,* and *under*, or subordinating conjunctions such as *while, although,* and *since*.

Abstract morphosyntactic features are specified for nouns in the lexicon. For example, languages with grammatical gender, like Spanish or German, identify nouns as belonging to gender categories. Spanish has two categories: masculine (*libro*, 'book') and feminine (*mesa*, 'table'); German has three: masculine (*Mond*, 'moon'), feminine (*Sonne*, 'sun'), and neuter (*Auto*, 'car'). The lexicon also identifies nouns as either mass or count. Mass nouns, such as *sand* or *furniture*, do not take regular plurals (*sands*, *furnitures*), except when the expression means 'types of X' (e.g., *meats*). Mass nouns cannot be preceded by an indefinite article (*a sand*, *a furniture*), but they may be preceded by the quantifier *some* in their singular form (*some sand*, *some furniture*). Count nouns, like *cat* and *shoe*, behave in the opposite manner: *cats, shoes, a cat, a shoe* are all fine, but not *some cat* and *some shoe* (meaning a portion of a cat or a shoe).

An extremely important aspect of a verb's lexical representation, from a psycholinguistic point of view, is its **subcategorization information**. This is information about what kinds of arguments a verb must have and which arguments are optional. As discussed earlier, an intransitive verb is one that takes only a subject argument, and a transitive verb is one that must have a direct object. (See Figure 2.5 for other examples.) Every verb must have a subject, but for some verbs objects are optional, as illustrated in (30). Some verbs are transitive, but can be used intransitively only under special circumstances, as the example in (31) shows.

(30) a. John ate (the sandwich).
      b. Mary drove (the car).

(31) a. John broke the glass.
      b. *John broke.
      c. The glass broke.

Verbs are central in the creation of sentential complements and infinitive clauses, and this is information that is encoded in a verb's lexical representation. Some verbs, such as *know* and *believe*, subcategorize for sentential complements, as (32) illustrates. Other verbs, like *decide* and *like*, take infinitive clauses (33). Subcategorization information for verbs is used actively during sentence comprehension, as we will see in Chapter 7.

(32) a. John knew that Amanda was a brilliant pianist.
      b. Mary believed that Fred was a used car salesman.

(33) a. John decided to vote for Jane.
      b. Mary likes to play tennis.

In addition to storing a word's morphosyntactic properties (like its part of speech or its subcategorization information, if it is a verb), the lexicon stores morphophonological information. This part of a lexical representation contains information about a word's phonological representation: the features for pronouncing the word that are not predictable by the application of phonological rules. For instance, the lexical entry for *pin* does not indicate that the word begins with an aspirated /p/, since aspiration is derived by a phonological rule. It is necessary, however, for the entry to specify that *pin* is made up of the three phonemes /p/, /ɪ/, and /n/, since that information is not determined by any principle and is necessary to distinguish *pin* from words like *bin*, *pen*, *ping*, and so on.

Lexical entries generally consist of word stems, rather than forms derived by morphological principles. There will not, for example, be separate entries for *kiss* and *kissed*, since the latter is formed by a regular inflectional process that adds *–ed* to a verb. Irregular past tenses like *ate* must be represented separately, because their form is not predictable by any rule. Similarly, words that are formed by derivational morphological processes will not be listed separately. *Happy, sad, polite*, and other adjectives will be listed as separate entries, but not the nouns that are created by the addition of the derivational morpheme *–ness*, such as *happiness, sadness, politeness*, and so forth.

Lexical ambiguity

One final characteristic of the lexicon that has important psycholinguistic implications is that many words are multiply ambiguous. What this means is that words have a number of different meanings with a separate lexical entry for each one. Many ambiguous words are not only ambiguous in meaning, but in form class as well. The word *bat*, for instance, can be a noun that is a flying mammal or a noun that is a piece of baseball equipment. *Bat* can also be a verb indicating the movement that a cat makes when it plays with a piece of string, and *bat* is used for a specific movement made by eyelashes. When people produce and understand sentences, they will encounter not only structural ambiguity, but also **lexical ambiguity**, of the sort found in the following examples:

(34)   The two men approached the bank.

(35)   Eat everything he gives you with relish.

The word *bank* in (34) is multiply ambiguous: it could mean a place where money is deposited, the slope of land on the side of a river, and maybe even a large mountain of snow. The example in (35) is interesting because the lexical ambiguity of *relish* (which could be a feeling or a condiment) results in a different syntactic structure, so the sentence is both lexically and structurally ambiguous. Like structural ambiguity, lexical ambiguity is rarely perceived in ordinary discourse. The lexicon provides multiple meanings for the words people encounter in conversation, just as the grammar provides multiple structures for the sentences, yet both types of ambiguity are resolved unconsciously and rapidly by the hearer's language processing system.

Summing Up

This chapter has provided an overview of linguistic competence, describing the components that make up the grammar and the lexicon of natural languages. Grammatical competence, we have seen, includes knowledge of well-formedness principles for sounds (phonology), words (morphology), and sentences (syntax). The principles we have described have been illustrated with language-specific examples, but the way the principles work is universal, as we pointed out at the very beginning of the chapter. This knowledge of language is implicit, though indirect access is possible by means of metalinguistic ability – the ability to consciously examine language as a formal object. Finally, the chapter examined the meaning- and form-based components of lexical entries.

The grammar and the lexicon of a language constitute the linguistic competence of a person who knows that language. This is linguistic information, and as such it is not information about what is or is not plausible in the real world, nor is it idiosyncratic knowledge. Linguistic competence is thus an autonomous system, distinct from the store of general and idiosyncratic real-world knowledge that an individual develops over a lifetime. The ability to acquire and use a linguistic system is a fundamental aspect of being human, rooted in the biology of the human species.

Having laid out a basic understanding of linguistic competence, we can move forward to explore linguistic performance. Chapter 3 focuses on the biological foundations of language, Chapter 4 addresses language acquisition, and the remainder of the book deals with the psycholinguistic processes underlying sentence production and comprehension. In all of these chapters we will see how knowledge of language is acquired and put to use.

A Bibliographical Note

This chapter is unlike the rest of the book, in that it has no internal references. We have restricted the presentation to basic facts about the grammar and lexicon of natural languages. These same facts are available, in a less condensed form, in a variety of places. We recommend the following for more detailed introductions to the topics covered in this chapter: on phonetics, Ladefoged (2005); on phonology, Hayes (2009) and Roca and Johnson (1999); on morphology, Aronoff and Fudeman (2005); on syntax, Baker (2001) and Carnie (2006); on the lexicon, Aitchison (2003).

New Concepts

allophones
arguments
auxiliary (helping) verbs
bound morphemes
canonical word order
clause
   adverbial
   infinitive
   matrix (independent, main)
   relative
   subordinate (dependent, embedded)
complementary distribution
content (open class) words
contrastive (overlapping) distribution
derivational morphemes
direct object
do-support
free morphemes
function (closed class) words
grammatical category (part of speech)
head (phrasal head)
inflectional morphemes
intransitive verbs
lexical ambiguity
lexical semantics
manner of articulation
metalinguistic awareness
minimal pairs
mora
mora-timed languages

morphemes
morphophonological rules
noun phrase (NP)
null subject languages
parametric variation
phonemes
phonemic inventory
phones
phonetic inventory
phonotactic constraints
place of articulation
pronoun
prosody
recursive structure (recursion)
selectional restrictions
sentential complement
stress-timed languages
subcategorization frame
subcategorization information
subject
syllable
syllable-timed languages
tense, number, gender,
   and case
transitive verbs
Universal Grammar (UG)
verb phrase (VP)
voicing
vowel height
wh-movement

Study Questions

1. What is meant by the claim that human language is universal? Why is this claim a critical issue in psycholinguistics?

2. What is the difference between an allophone and a phoneme? Do all languages have the same sets of phonemes and allophones?

3. What are phonotactic constraints? How are they related to syllable structure?

4. How do phonological rules relate to the way words are pronounced?

5. What are some ways prosody is used to determine sentence meaning?

6. What is the distinction between bound and free morphemes? What are morphophonological rules?

7. Distinguish between derivational and inflectional morphemes. What are some examples of each?

8. What are the three major operations described by the syntactic component? Give an example of each.

9. What does it mean to say that the constituents of a sentence are hierarchically organized?

10. Use the substitution test to demonstrate that *running through the woods* is a constituent of the sentence *Daisy enjoys running through the woods.*

11. What does it mean to say that syntactic rules are structure dependent? What would a language be like if it didn't have structure dependent rules? Are there any such human languages?

12. What is meant by the statement that the rules of grammar are psychologically real? How do metalinguistic abilities suggest that this is true?

13. What information is included in the lexicon? What kind of information is not included?

3 The Biological Basis of Language

Psycholinguistics is a field primarily concerned with how language is represented and processed in the brain. The focus of this book is, therefore, on language as a system controlled by the brain that is different from but closely linked to general cognition. As such, language is an aspect of human biology. We will explore some of the evidence that psycholinguists – and scholars in related fields – have uncovered linking language to human biology. This chapter will also help you distinguish between language as a biological system and language as a sociocultural artifact.

The organization of this chapter is based on an important historical precedent. Over 40 years ago a neurologist named Eric Lenneberg adduced five general criteria that help determine whether a system is based in the biology of a species (Lenneberg 1964, 1967). These criteria, each described in the sections that follow, are as valid today as they were then, and we will use them to frame the arguments for the biological basis of language. According to Lenneberg (1967: 371–4), a system is biological if:

- its cognitive function is species specific;
- the specific properties of its cognitive function are replicated in every member of the species;
- the cognitive processes and capacities associated with this system are differentiated spontaneously with maturation;
- certain aspects of behavior and cognitive function for this system emerge only during infancy; and
- certain social phenomena come about by spontaneous adaptation of the behavior of the growing individual to the behavior of other individuals around him.

Later in the chapter, we will describe some of the anatomical and physiological correlates for language. We conclude with a summary of a system closely related to language but decidedly not biological: reading and writing.

As you read this chapter, you might stop to appreciate the great strides that have been made in research focusing on the biological foundations of language since Lenneberg wrote about them in the 1960s. Research in this area has moved at a strikingly rapid rate, even in the past decade or two, facilitated in part by technological advances.

▇ Language Is Species Specific

If we define *communication* loosely as a way to convey messages between individuals, we can generalize that every species has a communication system of some sort. If the system is **species specific** – that is, if it is unique to that species – the system is likely to be part of the genetic makeup of members of the species. Some communication behaviors arise in certain species even if the individual has never heard or seen adults perform the behaviors. Some kinds of crickets and other insects have such a system. Other communication systems, like language for humans and bird song for some species of birds, can be acquired only if the young animal has the opportunity to experience the system in use.

No other species has a communication system like the language used by humans. There are two ways to approach this claim, and thus meet Lenneberg's first criterion. One is rather obvious: no other animals talk, nor do any other animals have a gestural system with the organizational structure of human language. The other way to address this issue is to ask whether other animals can be taught a human communication system.

You have undoubtedly heard of experiments in which researchers have attempted to teach a form of human language to apes. That sort of experimentation is designed to test the claim that human language is species specific: if other species could learn human language, then human language would not be species specific. Primates do not have vocal tracts like those of humans, so the approach has been to teach them communication that involves gestures or manipulated objects. For example, the famous chimpanzee Washoe was taught to sign words taken from American Sign Language (Gardner and Gardner 1969; Brown 1970). Others, like the chimpanzee Lana (Rumbaugh and Gill 1976) or the bonobo Kanzi (Savage-Rumbaugh and Lewin 1994), have been trained on a variety of computer keyboard systems. Others, like the chimpanzee Sarah, have been taught to manipulate plastic symbols (Premack 1971, 1976). This type of research has been extended beyond primates. Parrots are excellent mimics of the sounds in their environment, and are particularly good at imitating human speech, even though their vocal tracts are very different from those of humans.

Research in interspecies communication has yielded a tremendous amount of information about the cognitive and social potential of non-human species. Some apes have been able to acquire remarkably large lexicons and use them to communicate about past events, to make simple requests, to demonstrate remarkable abilities of perception and classification, and even to lie. Apes have also demonstrated true symbol-using behavior (e.g., using a red plastic chip to stand for the color green) and the ability to recognize two-dimensional pictures of objects. The grey parrot Alex learned to label many objects, colors, and shapes, and also learned to combine sounds in ways that suggest some degree of awareness of the phonological units that make up speech (Pepperberg 2007).

Importantly, no animal has been able to learn a creative syntactic system. For example, Washoe, the chimpanzee, learned more than a hundred individual words and could combine them communicatively to request food or play. She did not, however, order them in consistent ways to convey meaning, nor was there any evidence that her utterances had any kind of structural organization (Fodor, Bever, and Garrett

1974: 443). Suppose Washoe wanted her trainer (call him Joe) to tickle her. She might sign, *Joe tickle Washoe, Washoe Joe tickle, Washoe tickle Joe, Tickle Joe Washoe,* or any other combination of those three gestures. The animals that use computers have been trained to press the keys in a particular order, otherwise they do not receive a reward. Lana, a chimpanzee trained this way, would ask for a drink of water by pressing three keys indicating *please, machine give, water.* Of course, no evidence exists that demonstrates Lana knows the meaning of any of the words associated with the computer keys. Lana has simply learned that this pattern of behavior will result in a reward of water, whereas other patterns will not. It is not news that smart animals can be trained to produce complex behavioral sequences for reward. However, their use of these sequences does not signify knowledge and use of syntax, particularly the recursive properties of syntax we discussed in Chapter 2. So Lenneberg's basic argument has not yet been falsified. None of these animals has acquired a system that incorporates anything approaching the formal complexity of human language (Hauser, Chomsky, and Fitch 2002).

Even if people had succeeded in teaching animals a communication system incorporating syntax, the claim that human language is biologically based would hardly have been damaged. Human language is certainly the only naturally occurring and naturally acquired system of its type in the animal kingdom. The fact that humans can fly under very special and artificial circumstances does not challenge the claim that flight is biologically based in birds but not in humans.

▉ Language Is Universal in Humans

Lenneberg's second criterion – that a biological system must be **universal** to all members of the species – is met by language in two ways. First, all human babies are born with a brain that is genetically prepared to organize linguistic information; thus, the psychological processes involved in both acquiring and using language are at play, no matter the person. Secondly, all human languages have universal properties.

There are close to 7,000 languages spoken in the world today and, on the surface, they differ greatly. However, there are profound similarities among the languages of the world – so many similarities, in fact, that *human language* can be thought of as a single entity. Language universals, some of which you read about in Chapter 2, embrace and unify all human languages. These universals do not derive from social, cultural, or general intellectual characteristics of humans. Instead, they result from the way the human brain organizes and processes linguistic information: language universals are a product of human neurology. Thus, a person's ability to acquire and use language is as natural as a person's ability to walk or a bird's ability to fly. Thinking of language in this way is similar to the way we think about having hair or walking bipedally, two aspects of being human that are rooted in our biology.

A fundamental goal of linguistics is to describe Universal Grammar, which consists of all the absolute universals of human languages plus a description of their parameters of variation. Universal Grammar represents the "blueprint" or "recipe" for human language that every person is born with. Chapter 2 dealt with language universals and with the type of information supplied by Universal Grammar. Every point made about the organization and functions of the grammar and lexicon is true of all human languages. All languages have a phonology, a morphology, a syntax, and a lexicon. All languages possess rules and principles that allow their speakers to combine meaningless phonetic or gestural segments to create meaningful words and sentences. All languages have an inventory of phonemes, phonotactic constraints on the way words can be formed, and phonological and morphological rules. Moreover, all languages have a recursive syntax that generates complex sentences, and because of this every human being has the capacity for unlimited linguistic creativity. Finally, all languages have a lexicon, which stores information about words by distinguishing form and meaning. Thus, the general organization of all human languages is the same. If languages were not biologically based, there would be no necessity for them all to have a similar organization – and we would expect great variation from language to language in terms of their internal organization.

The general organization of language is not the only aspect of linguistic universality. The general properties of grammatical rules are the same for all languages. For instance, in phonology the rules for syllable structure are shared by all languages, although some languages place limitations on syllable structures that other languages do not (as we discussed in Chapter 2, with examples from Spanish and Japanese). Similarly, in syntax there are restrictions on movement that are universal, and syntactic rules in all languages are structure dependent.

We can turn the concept of universality around and consider impossible languages and impossible rules. No human language could exist in which only simple sentences were used for communication, without the capacity to form complex ones. There are occasional attempts to categorize a language as being primitive. For example, the linguist

Daniel Everett has argued along these lines for Pirahã, a language spoken by hunter-gatherers in northwestern Brazil (Everett 2005). Everett's evidence includes a claim that Pirahã syntax lacks embedding, a charge that the language does not have complex syntax. More careful investigation of the facts about Pirahã syntax has strongly countered Everett's claims: the language does have recursive constructions (Nevins, Pesetsky, and Rodrigues 2009). It is possible, of course, that at some point our hominid ancestors had a language that consisted only of simple sentences, but that would be speculation, because researchers do not know what the language of protohumans was like (Evans 1998); the lack of fossil evidence about protohuman language is hard but not impossible to overcome, given advances in our understanding of the neural and genetic mechanisms for language (Fitch 2005). What is certain is that no language spoken by *Homo sapiens* – modern humans – could be so restricted as to not contain recursion. A corollary of this is that there is no such thing as a primitive human language. The languages spoken in communities of modern-day hunter-gatherers are as rich and complex as the languages of the most industrially and technologically advanced communities, and they all possess human linguistic universals. The same is true of vernacular (non-standard) languages, of languages without writing systems, and of languages that are signed: they are organized in the ways we have described in Chapter 2.

To examine directly whether humans can acquire rules that do not conform to Universal Grammar, a group of researchers attempted to teach a possible and an (impossible) made-up language to a polyglot savant – a person with an extraordinary talent for acquiring languages (Smith, Tsimpli, and Ouhalla 1993). For this investigation, the extraordinary language learner, Christopher, was exposed to Berber (a language spoken in North Africa, but which Christopher had never learned) and Epun (a language the experimenters invented for the study, containing rules that violated certain aspects of Universal Grammar). The researchers found that while Christopher learned Berber easily, he found it difficult to learn certain types of rules in Epun, particularly rules that violated structure dependency.

▪ Language Need Not Be Taught, Nor Can It Be Suppressed

Lenneberg's third criterion is about how biological systems consist of processes that are differentiated (develop) spontaneously as the individual matures. This has two correlates in language acquisition:

language does not need to be taught, and acquisition cannot be suppressed. Language acquisition in the child is a naturally unfolding process, much like other biologically based behaviors such as walking. Every normal human who experiences language in infancy acquires a linguistic system, and failure to do so is evidence for some sort of pathology. Contrary to the belief of many doting parents, language is not taught to children. The fact that children need to hear language in order to acquire it must not be confused with the claim that children need specific instruction to learn to speak. It is probably the case, however, that children need to experience social, interactive language in order to acquire language. A case study involving two brothers, Glen and Jim, who were the hearing children of deaf parents, illustrates both of these points (Sachs, Bard, and Johnson 1981). The boys were well cared for and did not suffer emotional deprivation, but they had little experience with spoken language other than from watching television. When discovered by the authorities, Jim (18 months old at the time) did not speak, and Glen (3 years, 9 months old) knew and used words, but his morphology and sentence structure were virtually non-existent. Glen would produce sentences such as the following:

(1) a. That enough two wing.
     b. Off my mittens.
     c. This not take off plane.

Speech-language pathologists from the University of Connecticut visited the home regularly and had conversations with the children. They did not attempt to teach them any particular language patterns, but they played with them and interacted linguistically with them. In 6 months, Glen's language was age-appropriate and Jim acquired normal language. When last tested, Glen was a very talkative school-age child who was in the top reading group of his class. The story of Glen and Jim illustrates the importance of interactive input for children during the years they are acquiring language. It also illustrates the fact that specific teaching is not necessary. In Chapter 4, we will explore further the role of caretakers in the acquisition process.

The fact that language learning cannot be suppressed is yet another manifestation of the biological nature of language. If language were more bound to the particular types of linguistic experiences a child has, there would be much greater variation in the speed and quality of language learning than is actually observed. In fact, people acquire language at about the same speed during about the same age span, no matter what kind of cultural and social situation they grow up in. Children from impoverished circumstances with indifferent parental care eventually acquire a fully rich human language, just as do pampered children of affluent, achievement-oriented parents. The biologically driven processes of language acquisition even drive the creation of new languages. Judy Kegl, Ann Senghas, and colleagues (Kegl 1994; Kegl, Senghas, and Coppola 1999; Senghas, Kita, and Özyürek 2004) describe how a signed language has developed in the deaf community of Nicaragua, as the natural product of language learning mechanisms. In the late 1970s, when schools for educating deaf children in Nicaragua were first opened, the deaf community had no systematic gestural system for communication, other than "home signs" that varied greatly from person to person. (A home sign is a sign or sign sequence made up by an individual.) Given the opportunity to interact more regularly with each other, deaf children began to develop a gestural system to communicate. As a result of continued use (both in and out of school), that system eventually expanded into a rudimentary sign language with systematic properties. The language now has over 800 users, and Senghas and colleagues report that the youngest signers are also the most fluent and produce the language in its most developed form.

The process of language birth witnessed in the case of Nicaraguan Sign Language resembles the process through which **pidgins** turn into **creole languages**. A pidgin is a communication system consisting of elements from more than one language. A pidgin emerges in situations of language contact, when people who speak different languages come up with ways to communicate with each other. Pidgins have simplified structure and a lexicon consisting of words from the various languages of their speakers. Importantly, a pidgin has no native speakers: its users have learned the communication code as adults, and their ability to use it will be uneven. When the pidgin becomes *nativized* – that is, when children begin to acquire it as their native language – the grammar stabilizes and becomes more complex, the lexicon grows, and the language is on its way to becoming a creole.

▪ Children Everywhere Acquire Language on a Similar Developmental Schedule

There is a remarkable commonality to the milestones of language acquisition, no matter where in the world children acquire language. Dan Slobin of the University of California at Berkeley has devoted his entire career to the cross-linguistic study of language acquisition and wrote a seminal essay entitled "Children and language: They learn the same all around the world" (Slobin 1972). Like the milestones of motor development (infants roll over, sit up, crawl, and walk at similar ages everywhere), the milestones of language acquisition are also very similar. Babies coo in the first half of their first year and begin to babble in the second half. The first word comes in the first half of the second year for just about everyone. In all societies, babies go through a one-word stage, followed by a period of early sentences of increasing length; finally, complex sentences begin. By the age of 5 the basic structures of the language are in place, although fine-tuning goes on until late childhood. Children all over the world are sensitive to the same kinds of language properties, such as word order and inflection. They make remarkably few errors, but their errors are of a similar type. While there is much individual variation in the age at which children acquire aspects of language, that variation is conditioned by individual characteristics of the child rather than by the language being acquired or the culture in which the language is used. One would never expect to hear, for instance, that Spanish-speaking children do not use their first word until they are 3, or that acquisition of Spanish syntax is not completed until adolescence. Nor would one expect to hear that infants in Zimbabwe typically begin speaking at the age of 6 months and are using complex sentences by their first birthday. There is clearly a developmental sequence to language acquisition that is independent of the language being acquired – although, as we will see in some detail in Chapter 4, some features of language are acquired more easily and earlier than others. In fact, those aspects of language that are easier and those that are more difficult are similar for all children. All children learn regular patterns better than irregular ones, and they actually impose regularities where they do not exist. For instance, children learning English will regularize irregular past tenses and plurals, producing things like *eated* and *sheeps*. All children make similar kinds of "errors" – no matter what language they are acquiring. Not only is the sequence of development similar for all children, the process of acquisition is similar as well. This is exactly what one would expect if the acquisition of a mental system is being developed according to a genetically organized, species specific and species-universal program.

Lenneberg's fourth criterion, claiming that certain aspects of behavior emerge only during infancy, points to an important property of language acquisition: for children everywhere there seems to be a **critical period** in the acquisition of their first language. Although the details of this concept are controversial, most researchers agree that the optimal period for first language acquisition is before the early teen years, after which a fully complex linguistic system will not develop. The evidence for this comes from reports of so-called "wild children," particularly from the case of Genie, a California girl who was locked in a closet by an abusive father for the first 13 years of her life (Curtiss et al. 1974; Curtiss 1977, 1988). During that time, Genie was deprived of any linguistic input of any kind. After she was rescued, in November 1970, researchers from the University of California at Los Angeles worked for years with her to help her acquire English, but to no avail. She acquired words and the ability to communicate verbally, but she never acquired the full morphological and syntactic system of English. Examples of her utterances in (2) illustrate the level of her language ability:

(2) a. Genie full stomach.
     b. Applesauce buy store.
     c. Want Curtiss play piano.
     d. Genie have mama have baby grow up.

Genie's hearing was normal, as was her articulation ability. There is some question as to whether her intelligence was completely normal, but even if it was not, this alone could not account for her inability to acquire language. Clearly, Genie had been terribly traumatized for many years, and her emotional development could not have been normal; however, the degree to which she was psychologically impaired could not account for her lack of language. Actually, Genie was quite friendly and used language well socially. Her problems were solely in morphology and syntax, the formal aspects of language structure that researchers suspect are subject to critical period effects.

Stories like Genie's or those of other "wild children" attempting to learn their first language beyond the early teen years illustrate the claim that after a certain critical period the brain can no longer incorporate the formal properties of language, but they are riddled with hard-to-answer questions related to the unusual life circumstances for these children. Less controversial evidence comes from studies of congenitally deaf adults who learned American Sign Language (ASL) at different ages. Elissa Newport and colleagues (Newport 1990) examined the linguistic competence of users of ASL who acquired the language from birth ("native"), around ages 4–6 ("early learners"), or after age 12 ("late learners"). The three groups of participants did not differ on tests tapping sensitivity to basic word order, but they differed greatly in tests tapping syntax and morphology. Native learners outscored early learners, who in turn outscored late learners.

While the existence of a critical period for first language learning is fairly well accepted, its relationship to second language learning is complicated. Lenneberg himself noted that people's ability to learn a second language in adulthood is puzzling: it is difficult to overcome an accent if you learn a language after early adolescence, yet "a person *can* learn to communicate in a foreign language at the age of forty" (Lenneberg 1967: 176). Research on age effects in second language acquisition confirms the intuition that older second language learners achieve lower levels of proficiency in their second language. Existing evidence taps different levels of linguistic competence, including: judgments of degree of foreign accent in speech (Flege, Munro, and MacKay 1995), performance on tests tapping competence in morphology and syntax (Birdsong and Molis 2001), and self-reported oral proficiency (Bialystok and Hakuta 1999). Studies like this have something important in common (Birdsong 2005): as the learner gets older, the achieved level of competence *gradually* gets lower. Importantly, studies like this suggest that aging makes some aspect or aspects of acquisition harder, but they do not demonstrate that there is a critical period for second language acquisition. Learning a new language later in life will be difficult, but it will not be impossible.

In Chapter 4 we will consider the extent to which an adult learner acquires a second language by processes similar to that of a child acquiring a first language. A related issue, which we will address a little later in this chapter, is whether a second language is represented in the brain in a similar way as the first language. Notice that the very act of posing questions such as these assumes a biological basis for both first and second language acquisition.

▨ Language Development Is Triggered by the Environment

Lenneberg's final criterion is about the necessity of stimulation from and interaction with the environment. Certain biological systems will not develop without environmental stimuli to trigger them. Children will not develop language if language is not accessible in their environment or nobody is there to interact with them. Earlier we described the example of how a sign language developed in the deaf community of Nicaragua, in the absence of language in the environment. Yet Nicaraguan signers had an important environmental stimulus: each other. For a biological system, the environmental input is a stimulus that triggers internal development. We will come back to this in more detail in Chapter 4, when we discuss what characteristics of the language in the environment are necessary for language development.

■ Anatomical and Physiological Correlates for Language

The most fundamental biological fact about language is that it is stored in the brain, and, more importantly, that language function is localized in particular areas of the brain. This is hardly a new idea, going back at least to Franz Joseph Gall, the eighteenth-century neuroanatomist who developed the field of phrenology. Gall believed that various abilities, such as wisdom, musical ability, morality, and language, were located in different areas of the brain and could be discovered by feeling bumps on a person's skull. Gall was, of course, wrong about the bumps, but it seems to be true that some neurally based abilities, such as language, have specific locations in the brain. The first conclusive demonstration that language was localized in the brain took place in 1861 when a French neurologist named Paul Broca presented to the Paris Anthropological Society the first case of **aphasia** (Dingwall 1993). Aphasia is a language impairment linked to a brain lesion. Broca had a patient who had received a blow to the head with the result that he could not speak beyond uttering *Tan, Tan*, and, thus, Broca called him Tan-Tan. Upon autopsy, he was found to have a lesion in the frontal lobe of the left hemisphere of his brain. Ten years later a German neurologist named Carl Wernicke reported a different kind of aphasia, one characterized by fluent but incomprehensible speech (Dingwall 1993). Wernicke's patient was found to also have a left hemisphere lesion, farther back in the temporal lobe. **Neurolinguistics** is the study of the representation of language in the brain, and the discovery of aphasias led to the birth of this interdisciplinary field.

The two predominant kinds of aphasia are still called by the names of the men who first described them, as are the areas of the brain associated with each. **Broca's aphasia**, also known as *non-fluent aphasia*, is characterized by halting, effortful speech; it is associated with damage involving Broca's area in the frontal lobe of the left hemisphere. **Wernicke's aphasia**, also called *fluent aphasia*, is characterized by fluent meaningless strings; it is caused by damage involving Wernicke's area in the temporal lobe of the left hemisphere. These two kinds of aphasias, among others, differ markedly in terms of the grammatical organization of the patient's speech. The speech associated with Broca's aphasia has been characterized as **agrammatic**; it consists of primarily content words, lacking syntactic and morphological structure. In contrast, the speech of people with Wernicke's aphasia has stretches of grammatically organized clauses and phrases, but it tends to be incoherent and meaningless. In conversation, it appears that people with Broca's aphasia comprehend what is said to them, while people with Wernicke's aphasia do not. Thus, a general clinical characterization has been that people with Broca's aphasia have more of a problem with speech production than with auditory comprehension, whereas people with Wernicke's aphasia produce fluent and well-articulated but meaningless speech, and have problems with auditory comprehension.

Psycholinguists studying the comprehension abilities of people with Broca's aphasia discovered something very interesting. People with Broca's aphasia had no difficulty in understanding sentences like (3a), but had difficulty with sentences like (3b) (Caramazza and Zurif 1976):

(3) a. The apple the boy is eating is red.
     b. The girl the boy is chasing is tall.

Both sentences are constructed of common words; both sentences also have identical structures, including a relative clause modifying the subject noun. There is, however, a profound difference between them: real-world knowledge allows a person to successfully guess the meaning of (3a), but not (3b). Comprehension of (3b) requires an intact syntactic processing system. Caramazza and Zurif's result suggests an explanation as to why people with Broca's aphasia seem to have little trouble with comprehension in conversational contexts. People with aphasia compensate for their impaired grammatical processing system by using real-world knowledge to figure out the meanings of sentences in discourse. In ordinary conversation with people one knows well and with whom one shares a great deal of real-world knowledge, one can understand much of what is said without having to do a full analysis of sentence structure. The question remains, of course, as to whether the grammatical problems of people with aphasia are a result of an impaired linguistic competence or are the result of difficulty in using that competence to produce and understand speech. It is very difficult to answer this question experimentally, but some researchers have found people with agrammatic aphasia whose metalinguistic skills with respect to syntax are better than their

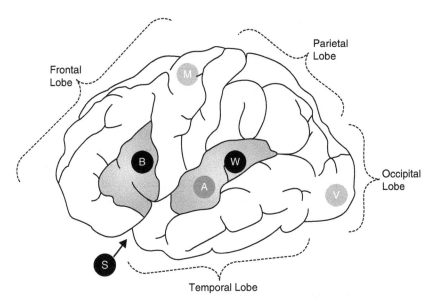

Figure 3.1 Diagram of the left hemisphere of the human cerebral cortex (side view). The diagram indicates the location of the primary language areas (Broca's and Wernicke's areas, 'B' and 'W', and the Sylvian fissure 'S'), as well as the approximate areas recruited for motor (M), auditory (A), and visual (V) processing.

ability to produce syntactically complex sentences (Linebarger, Schwartz, and Saffran 1983). This would suggest that the performance system is more impaired than the underlying grammar.

Figure 3.1 provides a sketch of the **left hemisphere** of the cortex of the brain, with Broca's and Wernicke's areas indicated. Broca's area is located near the motor area of the cortex, while Wernicke's is near the auditory area. Importantly, despite the proximity of these areas to motor and auditory areas, aphasias are purely linked to language, and not to motor abilities or audition. Users of signed languages can also become aphasic if they experience damage to the relevant areas in the left hemisphere. Their signs are non-fluent, halting, and agrammatic. This is true, despite the fact that they have no motor disability in their hands and can use them in everyday tasks with no difficulty (Poizner, Klima, and Bellugi 1987). The fact that signers become aphasic is dramatic confirmation of the fact that signed languages not only have all the formal properties of spoken language, but are similarly represented in the brain. It also demonstrates that the neurological damage that produces aphasia impairs language systems, rather than motor systems.

Aphasia is not a simple or clear-cut disorder. There are many different kinds of aphasia in addition to those classified as fluent and non-fluent, and many different behaviors that characterize the various clinical types of aphasia. Furthermore, much more of the left hemisphere is involved with language than just Broca's and Wernicke's areas; the area all along the Sylvian fissure, deep into the cortex, is associated with language function. Consequently, the localization of the damage for Broca's or Wernicke's patients does not always neatly correspond with the classical description (De Bleser 1988; Willmes and Poeck 1993). People with aphasia differ greatly in the severity of their symptoms, ranging from mild impairment to a global aphasia where all four language modalities – auditory and reading comprehension, and oral and written expression – are severely impaired.

Language lateralization

To say that language is lateralized means that the language function is located in one of the two hemispheres of the cerebral cortex. For the vast majority of people, language is lateralized in the left hemisphere. However, in some people language is lateralized in the right hemisphere, and in a small percentage of people language is not lateralized at all, but seems to be represented in both hemispheres. The hemisphere of localization is related to handedness, left-handed people being more likely than right-handed people to have language lateralized in the right hemisphere. Exactly why this should be the case is unclear, but, as illustrated in Figure 3.2, control of the body is **contralateral**: the right side of the body is controlled by the left motor and sensory areas, while the left side of the body is controlled by the right motor and sensory areas. Thus, left-handed people have right-dominant motor areas, while right-handed people have left-dominant motor areas.

Many investigations of hemispheric lateralization for language are based on studies of patients about to undergo brain surgery. In these cases, surgeons must be certain where their patients' language functions are localized so these areas can be avoided and an aphasic outcome prevented. Some procedures used to determine the localization of language in the brain are rather invasive. One common procedure for determining the hemispheric location of language functions in preoperative patients is the **Wada test**. In this procedure, sodium amytol is injected into one of the two hemispheres of a patient's brain. The patient is asked to count or name pictures presented on an overhead

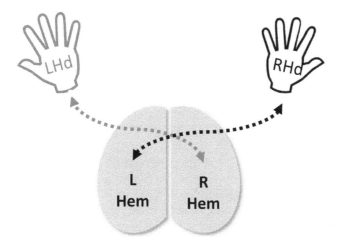

Figure 3.2 Schematic diagram of contralateral control. The shaded lobes represent the two hemispheres of the human brain, looked at from above. The dashed gray lines represent the direct paths from the right hemisphere to the left hand; the dotted black lines, paths from the left hemisphere to the right hand.

screen. Because each hemisphere controls the functioning of the opposite side of the body, the injection produces paralysis on the side of the body opposite from the affected hemisphere. The injection also disrupts verbal behavior, only briefly if the non-dominant hemisphere has been injected, but for several minutes if it has been the dominant hemisphere. A study of 262 people who were administered the Wada test (Rasmussen and Milner 1977) found that 96 percent of right-handers had language lateralized in the left hemisphere, and only 4 percent in the right. In contrast, only 70 percent of left-handers in the sample were left-lateralized, 15 percent were right lateralized, and 15 percent had language function located in both hemispheres. It is evident that the majority of left-handers are left lateralized, but there is a slightly higher probability that they will have language located in either the right hemisphere or in both.

Another procedure, called **brain mapping**, was originally developed by Penfield and Roberts in the 1950s (Penfield and Roberts 1959), and is still widely used to localize language function in preoperative patients; it is described extensively by Ojemann (1983). Patients are given a spinal anesthetic so they will be able to communicate with the clinician. The skull is opened and the brain is exposed, but because the brain itself has no nerve endings, this is not a painful procedure. Various areas are marked along the surface of the brain, and a brief electric current is administered at the same time the patient is performing a verbal task. For example, the patient is shown a picture of a ball and instructed to say, *This is a ball*. At the moment the word *ball* is about to be produced, a mild electric current is applied to a small area of the exposed brain. If that is a language area, the patient will experience a temporary aphasic-like episode, and will not be able to say *ball*. If the electric current is applied to a non-language area, there will be no interruption in speech. Surgeons do not cut within 2 centimeters of the areas identified in this manner.

Ojemann (1983) found that his patients had language areas located in Broca's area in the frontal lobe, in Wernicke's area in the temporal lobe, and all around the Sylvian fissure in the left hemisphere, but nowhere in the right hemisphere. Further, there seemed to be some areas that were specialized for word naming and others that were specialized for syntax (although most areas included both abilities). Ojemann's sample included seven Greek–English bilinguals, for whom there were a few areas in which Greek, but not English, was located, and other areas where English, but not Greek, was located. Importantly, in many areas, both languages overlapped. Ojemann's findings help explain some of the different recovery patterns reported for bilingual aphasics. A brain lesion could affect the two languages of a bilingual in parallel, or differentially (one language will be more affected than the other), or even selectively (one language will not be affected at all). These and other recovery patterns can be accounted for neuroanatomically (Green 2005): recovery will vary, depending on the area of the brain affected by a lesion.

A particularly fascinating demonstration of the lateralization of language function comes from patients who have had a surgical procedure called *commissurotomy*, in which the two hemispheres of the cortex are separated by cutting the *corpus callosum*, a thick sheaf of nerve fibers joining the two hemispheres. This procedure is performed in cases of severe epilepsy in order to prevent the electrical impulses that cause seizures from surging from one hemisphere to the other. Roger Sperry (1968) received the Nobel Prize for work with people who have had this surgery (Gazzaniga 1970). Bear in mind that the right side of the body is controlled by the left side of the brain, and vice versa. For a person who has had a commissurotomy, the neural pathways controlling the motor and sensory activities of the body are below the area severed by the commissurotomy, so the right motor areas still control the left hand and the right sensory areas receive information from the left side of the body. However, the right hemisphere of the brain cannot transfer information to the left hemisphere, nor can it receive information from the left hemisphere. Suppose that a commissurotomy patient has language lateralized in his left hemisphere. If his eyes are closed and a ball is placed in his left hand, he will not be able to say what it is. However, he would be able to select from an array of objects the object that he had held in his hand. The right hemisphere has knowledge of the identity of the ball, but it lacks the ability to name it. If the ball is placed in his right hand, he is able to name it, just as any person would be able to do with either hand. If a person with an intact corpus callosum were to close her eyes and have someone put a ball in her left hand, the information that it is a ball would register in her right hemisphere, then her right hemisphere would send the information to the left hemisphere, which would name it. If a person with a split brain is presented with a picture of a spoon in the left visual field (which we come back to below), he will not be able to name it, but he will be able to select a spoon from an array of objects with his left hand. This shows that the right hemisphere recognized the spoon, although it could not name it. The step that is missing for the person who has a split brain is the information transfer from the right to the left hemisphere.

Obviously, few people have split brains, so psycholinguists have developed a number of experimental techniques for studying the effects of lateralization in intact brains. These include visual field studies, dichotic listening studies, and studies involving neuroimaging. All demonstrate the language lateralization of the human brain.

Visual field studies rest on the fact that it is possible to present information to either the left visual field, which sends information to the right hemisphere, or to the right visual field, which sends information to the left hemisphere. The left visual field is not the same thing as the left eye; it is a bit more complicated than that. Information in the left visual field comes from both eyes (as does information in the right visual field), but what is of interest here is that the information from the left visual field goes only to the right hemisphere, and information from the right visual field goes only to the left hemisphere.

The fact that visual information can be presented to one or the other hemisphere has allowed psycholinguists to study in some detail the kinds of linguistic tasks each of the hemispheres can perform. While the right hemisphere is mute, it can recognize simple words, suggesting that there is some sort of lexical representation in the right hemisphere. However, there seems to be no representation of formal aspects of language. The right hemisphere cannot rhyme, suggesting that it does not have access to the internal phonological structure of lexical items. Neither does the right hemisphere have access to even simple syntax.

In an experiment that tested whether participants could match simple sentences presented to the right hemisphere with pictures they had been shown, participants could not distinguish between the (a) and (b) versions of sentences like the following (Gazzaniga and Hillyard 1971):

(4) a. The boy kisses the girl.
     b. The girl kisses the boy.

(5) a. The girl is drinking.
     b. The girl will drink.

(6) a. The dog jumps over the fence.
     b. The dogs jump over the fence.

Thus, while the right hemisphere may possess some rudimentary lexical information, it is mute and does not represent the phonological, morphological, and syntactic form of language.

Further evidence of the dominance of the left hemisphere for language comes from studies of **dichotic listening**. In this kind of experiment, participants are presented auditory stimuli over headphones, with different inputs to each ear. For instance, the syllable *ba* might be played into the right ear, while at the same exact time *da* is played to the left ear. The participant's task is to report what was heard. On average, stimuli presented to the right ear are reported with greater accuracy than the stimuli presented to the left ear. This is known as the **right-ear advantage for language**. It occurs because a linguistic signal presented to the right ear arrives in the left hemisphere for decoding by a more direct route than does a signal presented to the left ear. From the left ear, the signal must travel first to the right hemisphere, then across the corpus callosum to the left hemisphere (Kimura 1961, 1973). Thus, information presented to the right ear is decoded by the left hemisphere earlier than the information presented to the left ear. The right-ear advantage exists only for linguistic stimuli. Non-speech signals produce no ear advantage, and musical stimuli demonstrate a left-ear advantage (Kimura 1964).

Lateralization apparently begins quite early in life. Evidence suggests that the left hemisphere is larger than the right before birth, and infants are better able to distinguish speech from non-speech when the stimuli are presented to the left hemisphere (Molfese 1973; Entus 1975). Early language, however, appears not to be lateralized until the age of about 2. If the left hemisphere is damaged in infancy, the right hemisphere can take over its function. This ability of parts of the young brain to assume functions usually associated with other areas is called *plasticity.* An infant or young child who suffers left hemisphere damage is far more likely to recover without suffering aphasia than an adult, whose brain is far less plastic. Even children who have undergone surgery in which the left hemisphere is removed can develop quite good language functions. However, studies have shown that such children are deficient in the formal aspects of language morphology and syntax. Thus, the right hemisphere may be limited in its plasticity in that it cannot incorporate the structural analytical aspects of language associated with the left hemisphere (Dennis and Whitaker 1976).

Neuroanatomical correlates of language processing

Our understanding of how the brain represents and processes language has broadened dramatically with the development of neuroimaging techniques like event-related potentials and functional magnetic resonance imaging. Neuroimaging research focuses on identifying neuroanatomical correlates for the competence repositories and performance mechanisms for language.

While the brain is at work, active neurons emit electrical activity. This voltage can be measured by attaching electrodes to the scalp at different locations; the technical term for this is electroencephalography (EEG). **Event-related potentials** (or **ERPs**, for short) are changes in the electrical patterns of the brain that are associated with the processing of various kinds of linguistic stimuli. In ERP experiments, sentences are presented either visually (one word at a time) or auditorily, while measurements are collected that provide information about the timing, the direction (positive or negative), and the amplitude of the voltage.

The brain has different electrical responses to different types of linguistic anomalies. This is strong support for the proposition that different brain mechanisms are employed in processing semantic-pragmatic information on the one hand and morphosyntactic information on the other. One of the best-known ERP effects is the **N400 component**, so called because its signature is a negative (N) voltage peak at about 400 milliseconds following a particular stimulus. This component is sensitive to semantic anomalies, such as the ones in (7a) and (7b), compared to (7c) (Kutas and Van Petten 1988):

(7) a. *The pizza was too hot to cry.
     b. *The pizza was too hot to drink.
     c. The pizza was too hot to eat.

Studies investigating morphological and syntactic anomalies have discovered ERP components associated with structural processing (Friederici 2002). Morphosyntactic errors, like subject–verb agreement violations, elicit a **left anterior negativity (LAN)**, which occurs between 300 and 500 milliseconds. Another ERP component linked to syntactic structure building is a very **early left anterior negativity (ELAN)**. At around 150–200 milliseconds, the ELAN is even earlier than the LAN, and is characterized by electrical activity that is more negative when building syntactic structure is not possible, as in (8a), compared to (8b) (Neville et al. 1991):

(8)   a.   *Max's of proof
       b.   Max's proof

A late centro-parietal positivity, the **P600 component** (for positive voltage between 600 and 1000 milliseconds, also called the **Syntactic Positive Shift**, or **SPS**), is elicited with syntactic violations (Osterhout and Holcomb 1992), with sentences that require reanalysis (we will come back to these in Chapter 7), and with sentences that are syntactically complex (Friederici 2002).

Figure 3.3 summarizes some of the results from a study by Osterhout and Nicol (1999), which compared ERP responses to grammatical sentences and sentences with semantic anomalies (top panel), syntactic anomalies (middle panel), or both semantic and syntactic anomalies (bottom panel). The semantic anomalies elicited N400 effects, while the syntactic anomalies elicited P600 effects.

There are ERP components that have been associated with other aspects of language processing. For example, the **Closure Positive Shift (CPS)** is an ERP component linked to the processing of prosodic phrasing: intonational boundaries inside sentences elicit positivity (Steinhauer, Alter, and Friederici 1999). A different ERP component, the **P800**, is elicited when the intonation of a sentence does not match its form, for example, when a question has the intonation of a declarative, or vice versa (Artésano, Besson, and Alter 2004).

Studies using **functional magnetic resonance imaging (fMRI)** and **positron emission tomography (PET)** provide detailed information about the areas of the brain implicated in language processing. These technologies measure blood flow levels, capitalizing on the fact that increased neuronal activity in a particular area of the brain is supported by increased blood flow. fMRI data provide topographical information about what regions of the brain are specialized for different aspects of language representation and processing tasks. In addition to Broca's and Wernicke's areas,

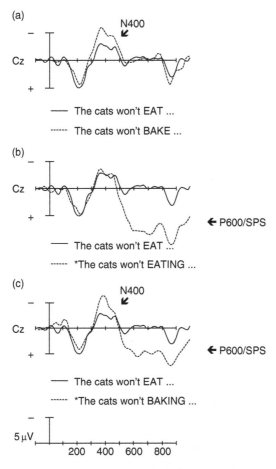

Figure 3.3 ERPs recorded at one electrode (labeled *Cz*), for contrasts between grammatical sentences (solid lines) and anomalous sentences (dotted lines). The anomaly was semantic (a), syntactic (b), or both semantic and syntactic (c). The graphs indicate voltage on the *y*-axis (negativity is up, positivity down), and time (in milliseconds) on the *x*-axis. Sentences with semantic anomalies elicited greater negativity at around 400 milliseconds (the signature of the N400 effect), while sentences with syntactic anomalies elicited greater positivity around 600 milliseconds (characteristic of the P600 effect). The figure is a composite of data reported by Osterhout and Nicol (1999). We thank Lee Osterhout for his permission to reproduce this figure.

other areas of the brain have been found to be involved in processing language, with specific neuroanatomical correlates for different types of processing (Bornkessel-Schlesewsky and Friederici 2007). ERPs are useful to study the time course of processing, while fMRI is better at detecting the areas of the brain that are involved in processing tasks.

The search for a genetic basis for language

The ultimate indicator of the biological nature of language would be the discovery of the genetic basis of language, as all aspects of human biology are directly encoded in our DNA. Researchers began genetic investigations by conducting pedigree studies. These are studies that examine the heritability of a particular trait (or disorder) in several generations of a family. Gopnik (1990, 1997) showed that members of over three generations of one family had suffered from specific language impairment (SLI), dyslexia, and other language disorders, indicating that genetic anomalies associated with language development can be inherited.

A major breakthrough came with the discovery by Lai and colleagues (Lai et al. 2001) of a specific gene, **FOXP2**, that was implicated in the language disorders of an extended family. Members of the family exhibited symptoms like those of agrammatic aphasics: effortful and non-fluent speech, lacking in syntactic organization. Their grammar appeared to be broadly impaired; they had difficulty manipulating phonemes and morphemes and understanding complex sentences (Watkins, Dronkers, and Vargha-Khadem 2002). The disorder was attributable to a mutation of the FOXP2 gene, which was transmitted by heredity. If a mutated version of a gene is responsible for language disorders, it is reasonable to infer that an intact version of that gene is implicated in normal language development and representation. It was suggested that a "gene for language" had been discovered.

The FOXP2 gene is associated with the development of other parts of human anatomy unrelated to language, including the lung, the gut, and the heart. It is also a gene that is not confined to *Homo sapiens*; it is also found in other mammals, including mice (Marcus and Fisher 2003). While the relationship of FOXP2 to heritable language disorders is an exciting breakthrough, it is important to remember that it cannot be *the* gene for language. All complex behaviors are attributable to the interaction of many genes and their schedules of expression. So FOXP2 is almost certainly only one gene in a network of multiple genes involved in the language abilities of humans.

■ Reading and Writing as Cultural Artifacts

We have discussed how human language meets all five of Lenneberg's criteria for biologically based systems. Language is specific to the human species, and universal for every member of the species (and every language used by the species). Language develops spontaneously, without explicit instruction, when children are exposed to it from infancy through early childhood. And language has a number of anatomical, physiological, and genetic correlates. But what about reading and writing, linked to human language as they are: are they also biological? The answer is that they are not.

Writing has existed for a mere 5,000 years (Sampson 1985) – a miniscule amount of time, compared to spoken language. The oldest known written language, *cuneiform*, was invented by the Sumerians around the end of the fourth millennium BCE, in the part of the world that is now southern Iraq. Cuneiform was developed as a means for keeping agricultural records. The earliest symbols were actually clay tokens that represented concepts (like bushels of wheat, for example), rather than speech.

Reading and writing are certainly species specific (as is driving a car or playing chess), but they are far from being universal in humans. Every known human culture has a spoken or gestural language, but, as we pointed out in Chapter 1, the speakers of many of those languages have not invented a written form of the language. In cultures where there is a written language, it is rarely acquired naturally without being taught – contrary to the way children acquire spoken languages. In addition, the success of reading and writing instruction is hardly uniform, as any elementary school teacher can attest: some learners make great progress with relatively little effort; others require a great deal of help. A person who has not learned to read and write will experience severe social disadvantages in many cultures, but is not considered to have a pathological condition – contrary to the way we perceive people who have been exposed to speech but who do not successfully acquire spoken language. There are pathological conditions, such as *dyslexia*, that will impair a person's ability to learn to read. We speak here of people who have had inadequate instruction and have therefore not learned to read. Reading is not a natural response to being exposed to written language. These facts all strongly indicate that written language is a cultural phenomenon, in stark contrast to the biologically based spoken language.

Unlike spoken languages, written languages vary greatly in the way they are organized and represented. One class of writing systems is called **phonographic**, meaning that their written symbols represent phonological properties of the language. For example, in the English alphabet, the symbols (letters) roughly correspond to phonemes. In the Sinhalese and the Japanese Katakana *syllabaries*, the symbols correspond to syllables. A second class of writing systems is **logographic**, like Chinese, in which each symbol represents an entire morpheme (or word), with no correspondence between the symbol and the sound. As it turns out, phonographic and logographic writing systems are learned and processed in different ways (Wolf 2007). For example, it takes much more effort to learn to write 1,000 words in Chinese than 1,000 words in English. This is because Chinese words all have unique symbols associated with them, whereas English words consist of combinations of a mere 26 letters. There is no correlate to this with spoken languages, which all appear to be variations on a single theme. The source of that single theme – the universality of the form of human language – is the organization and processing of information in the human brain.

Summing Up

The human ability to acquire and represent in the brain a linguistic system that conforms to Universal Grammar is, therefore, a property of our humanness just as is our upright posture and bipedal form of locomotion, along with all our other unique anatomical and physiological characteristics. The acquisition of language by children consists of the brain becoming organized in this genetically determined manner in response to the child's experience of language in the environment. Language is not the only system that works this way. The visual and auditory systems are genetically programmed to have a particular kind of organization and function, but if visual and auditory stimuli are not present at exactly the right time in development, they will not develop properly. Experience is absolutely critical to the unfolding of genetically specified systems of all sorts. The point is that the formal organization of the neurological response to that experience is precisely specified for each species.

There is a debate in psycholinguistic, linguistic, and neurolinguistic circles about whether language evolved as the human neurological system evolved. Some people are convinced that language must have evolved as the brain evolved. Others think that language was the result of the massive reorganization of the brain when it reached a particular size in human development. It is impossible to know which of these positions is correct because the fossils of our pre-human ancestors give few clues in this regard. However, fossil skulls of human ancestors have allowed anthropologists to conclude that they had larger left hemispheres than right. No matter how language arose in the human species, it is clear that this unique human ability is deeply rooted in human biology.

New Concepts

aphasia	logographic writing systems
brain mapping	N400 component
Broca's (agrammatic) aphasia	neurolinguistics
Closure Positive Shift (CPS)	P600 component (Syntactic
contralateral control	Positive Shift, SPS)
creole language	P800 component
critical period	phonographic writing systems
dichotic listening	pidgin
early left anterior	positron emission
negativity (ELAN)	tomography (PET)
event-related potentials (ERPs)	right-ear advantage
FOXP2	for language
functional magnetic resonance	species specificity
imaging (fMRI)	species universality
left hemisphere	Wada test
left anterior negativity (LAN)	Wernicke's aphasia

Study Questions

1. When psycholinguists say language is biologically based, do they mean that language has no social or cultural basis?

2. How does the universality of language support the view that language is biologically based?

3. Chimpanzees and gorillas have been taught rich communication systems using symbols of various kinds. Does this falsify the claim that language is species specific? Why or why not?

4. If a child has normal hearing but fails to acquire language, the child is judged to have a pathological condition. Explain the reasoning behind such a diagnosis, making reference to the biological basis of language.

5. What aspects of language did Genie fail to acquire? What did she acquire? What does this say about the critical period for acquisition of a first language?

6. What is meant by the lateralization of language? How does the study of aphasia support the view that language is lateralized?

7. How do studies of brain mapping demonstrate not only the lateralization of language but also the localization of language function in particular areas of the brain?

8. Why is a person with a "split brain" unable to name an object held in his left hand (assuming his eyes are closed)?

9. What is the right-ear advantage for speech? How do psycholinguists know that it is not simply a result of a general auditory superiority of the right ear?

10. What is the main difference between an N400 and a P600 ERP component? How does the existence of different ERP responses for different types of ungrammaticalities help demonstrate that language is biological?

11. How do studies of inherited language disorders contribute to the pursuit of the genetic underpinnings for language?

12. When language is compared to writing systems, it appears that the former flows from human biology, while the other is a product of human culture. What distinctions between language and writing lead to this conclusion?

4 The Acquisition of Language

Language acquisition is one of the most fascinating facets of human development. Children acquire knowledge of the language or languages around them in a relatively brief time, and with little apparent effort. This could not be possible without two crucial ingredients, which we discuss in the first two sections of this chapter: a biologically based predisposition to acquire language, and experience with language in the environment. All children pass through similar stages of linguistic development, which we will describe later in the chapter, as they go from infancy through middle childhood. We will close the chapter with a section on how older children and adults acquire second languages.

■ A Biological Predisposition for Language

In Chapter 3, we pointed out that language acquisition is central to the demonstration of the biological nature of language. Language acquisition is a natural developmental process; all children progress through similar milestones on a similar schedule. This could not be so were it not for the fact that language is rooted in human biology. If human language is a genetically based characteristic of humans, represented and processed in the human brain, then it follows that a human infant will acquire that system as its brain develops. This is called the **nativist model of language acquisition**.

It is important to be very clear about how we frame the nativist conception of language acquisition. The claim is not that humans acquire language without experience – on the contrary. In fact, biologically based systems, for humans and other animals, require **environmental input** to trigger or stimulate development. For example, the biologically based system for human vision is already well developed at birth, but newborns cannot differentiate the input they receive from their left versus their right eye, so they have no depth perception. During an infant's first month of life, visual input triggers important changes in how the brain organizes stimuli that enter from the left versus the right eye, and eventually the baby is able to perceive perspective, distances, and depth. If something interferes with the processing of visual stimuli during a critical period of development (the first few months of life), the child will not develop normal vision.

Just as external input is crucial in the development of vision, external input is important – indispensable, actually – in language acquisition. Infants who are born deaf, and therefore cannot experience speech, cannot acquire spoken language: they lack the appropriate environmental stimulation. Deaf infants can, however, acquire a signed language with the same facility that hearing infants acquire spoken language, if sign language is present in their environment. The nativist claim is that the developing brain provides the infant with a **predisposition to acquire language**; but language acquisition will not happen in a vacuum. The child must be exposed to external input to construct a grammar and a lexicon with all the properties associated with human language.

Precisely what human biology endows the child with and what is derived from the environment is perhaps the central question in language acquisition research. Most psycholinguists endorse some version of the nativist view of language acquisition, though differences exist among them concerning exactly what aspects of language and cognition are biologically based and what role experience plays in the acquisition process. Many psycholinguists agree that language is acquired under the guidance of Universal Grammar: innate knowledge of language, which serves to restrict the type of grammar the child will develop. In addition, acquisition strategies help the child impose structure on the input. Universal Grammar accounts for the similarities observed among the world's languages, as we argued in Chapter 2. Universal Grammar and acquisition strategies are both derived from the structure and operational characteristics of the human brain, as we discussed in Chapter 3.

The child has been whimsically called – originally by Chomsky (1965) – a **LAD**, or **Language Acquisition Device**. The LAD is, of course, not the child but rather a property of the child's brain that endows it with a predisposition for acquiring language. The child, exposed to language through the environment, processes the input using biologically endowed systems for language acquisition (Universal Grammar and acquisition strategies), and the eventual outcome is a grammar and a lexicon. The medium for the input is not important: the same internal processes will take place if the signal consists of speech or gestures. The specific language of the input is also not important, as long as it is a human language: English, Spanish, Chinese, or any other language can be acquired by any human child. And if the environment provides sustained exposure to more than one language, more than one grammar and more than one lexicon will develop. This model of language acquisition is diagramed in Figure 4.1.

Of course, a full adult-like grammar and lexicon do not develop instantly. The Language Acquisition Device generates a series of increasingly more adult-like child grammars and lexicons, each of which conforms to the general pattern of human language. Most of the basic aspects of grammar and vocabulary are in place by the time a child starts school (around age 5 or 6); the size of the lexicon, as well as processing abilities and metalinguistic skills, will continue to expand beyond childhood.

The speed and ease with which a child acquires language is largely attributable to Universal Grammar (UG), which is the general form of human language and is part of the child's genetic makeup. Recall that all languages have a similar organization of their respective grammars into phonological, morphological, and syntactic components. For each of those components, UG provides a set of principles that are part of the grammars of all human languages and a set of parameters that reflect

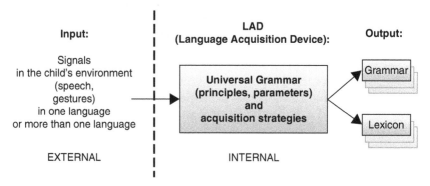

Figure 4.1 Schematic diagram of the relationship between external stimuli and internal knowledge in language acquisition. Input from the environment activates internal processes that lead to the acquisition of a grammar and a lexicon, which are the output of the process of acquisition. If the input provides experience in more than one language, a grammar and lexicon will develop for each language.

the ways languages can differ. UG, then, guides language development in three ways. First, the child will develop a grammar consisting of phonological, morphological, and syntactic components. Second, those components will include the principles basic to all languages. Third, the parameters specified in UG will guide the child's discovery of the particular characteristics of the target language. The child will not have to discover these organizational properties of language through experience; they are provided by the child's developing brain. Likewise, universal principles for lexical organization will guide the mental vocabulary as it develops, sorting new words into content or function categories, and associating with each phonological, morphosyntactic, and semantic information.

Research has demonstrated the involvement of UG in language acquisition. The development of the phonological, morphological, and syntactic components has been studied extensively. Child grammars never violate universal principles of language. For instance, they will never contain rules that are not structure dependent (Crain 1991). Nor will they allow the construction of sentences that violate universal constraints on movement, such as *What did John eat ice cream and?* We can also observe that children set the parameters of their language very early. For example, languages vary in the order of their grammatical elements (referred to informally as *word order*). All languages have subjects, objects, and verbs, but different languages have different preferred ways to order these constituents. Recall from Chapter 2 that the canonical word order for English is SVO (subject–verb–object), while for Japanese it is SOV (subject–object–verb); these are the two most common basic word orders, but other languages have other canonical word orders (VSO for Gaelic languages, VOS for some Austronesian languages). The word order parameter is among the earliest set by children acquiring all languages. In fact, it is almost certainly the case that children have acquired the word order of their language before they have begun to speak in two-word sentences; we will return to this issue later in the chapter.

Another part of the child's biological endowment is a set of **acquisition strategies** that enable the child to take the input from the environment and construct a grammar that conforms to the organizational principles of UG. These strategies, or *operating principles* (Slobin 1973, 1985), determine what will be the most salient and easily acquired aspects of language. For instance, children are highly sensitive to the regularities of language. In fact, as we will see below, a characteristic of early child language is that it overextends regularities of the language. Children expect linguistic devices to be meaningful and will look for linguistic ways to convey new ideas of their developing cognitive systems. Children anticipate morphological variations that systematically alter the form of words, so suffixes, prefixes, and infixes are easily acquired. The ends of words are salient, as is order of all kinds, and children expect their new words to fit systematically into their existing morphological and phonological categories.

Some psycholinguistic theories of language acquisition rely primarily on learning strategies of various kinds, which exploit the child's ability to detect patterns in the target language and respond to elements that are of high frequency of occurrence. For instance, the **constrained statistical learning framework** model (Saffran 2003) places an emphasis on learning strategies based on statistical learning. The claim is that infants extract statistical regularities from the input and use those to identify the properties of the language they are learning (Saffran, Aslin, and Newport 1996). Such approaches to studying language acquisition reject the claim that UG guides acquisition, and propose that the similarities among languages are a result of the biologically based way that humans learn languages and, more generally, the biologically based way that humans are sensitive to patterns. The nativist model of acquisition presented in this chapter relies on acquisition strategies based on pattern discovery and attention to frequency. However, the nativist model proposes that it is not possible for the child to acquire underlying features of language – such as the components of grammar, universal principles, and features of variation – without the biologically based UG. As we explained in Chapter 2, the surface representation of language is not adequate to provide information about the abstract, structural features of language. The model we advocate here, then, is one in which learning strategies operate on the child's linguistic input and allow it to be organized according to universal principles to create a grammar of the target language.

We can summarize this section by pointing out that children approach the task of language acquisition with a sophisticated toolkit that makes them extremely biased learners; as Ray Jackendoff puts it, children possess "preconceptions" about language acquisition which ultimately "give them the right solutions" (Jackendoff 2002: 84). Human biology supplies knowledge of universal principles for organizing language and knowledge of the handful of ways languages can vary, and limits the way the input is processed by means of general principles of acquisition. Thus equipped, children can take input from the environment to rapidly and efficiently acquire the language or languages around them.

Characteristics of the Language in the Environment

The primary purpose of a child's linguistic environment is to provide information about the language the child is acquiring. Psycholinguists call this type of information **positive evidence**. It supplies the data that the child needs in order to set parameters and develop a grammar that is adult-like. Obviously, the main providers of input are the people who interact with the child: parents, caretakers, siblings, and any other children or adults engaging in routine linguistic interactions with the child. In this section we consider the general characteristics of caretaker speech. We stress that children need to be talked to: experiencing input provides children with positive evidence about how the language works. But to what extent do children need to be talked to in specific ways?

There are some important facts about language acquisition that limit significantly how we view the role of the language in the environment: every child in every known culture acquires language with similar ease, by going through similar stages at about the same rate. This implies that any characteristics of the input in the environment that are identified as essential for language development must exist in every language community in the world. Parents in the United States, for example, consider interacting verbally with children to be very important, assuming that they "teach language" to their children and that this sort of interaction is necessary for language acquisition to take place. There are cultures, however, in which adults rarely talk with children. Children in such cultures get most of their information about the language from older children. In some communities in northwestern Brazil, certain cultural practices lead to a complex multilingualism and to very non-Western-like values regarding verbal interactions with children (Chernela 2004). Women must marry outside of their linguistic background, a practice known as *linguistic exogamy*. When they marry, they relocate to their husband's village, because the community is *patrilocal*. Children grow up hearing both the maternal and paternal languages, alongside any additional languages spoken by others in their village. However, children are actively discouraged from openly using the language of their mother, whereas a great deal of guidance is offered with their paternal language because the latter is more highly valued – since it is the primary language of the village. Crucially, even though they are discouraged from speaking their mother's language, children are constantly exposed to it and so they grow up competent in it, though they will be reluctant to demonstrate their ability.

It is clearly not the case that parents or other caretakers need to "teach" language to their children. Children around the world acquire language in vastly different cultural and social settings, so it should not come as a surprise that many caregiver behaviors (even those particularly favored by one culture) are not necessary features of the linguistic environment. Research over the years has revealed what kind of language experience caregivers need to provide for children and what kind they do not. Caregivers *do* need to provide linguistic input to their children, and opportunities for interaction with the input enhance acquisition (recall the story of Jim and Glen, described in Chapter 3). In cultures where information about the language comes from people other than caretakers (for instance, other children, as mentioned above), the information must be conveyed in an interactive setting. But children do not need to be rewarded, or encouraged to imitate the language around them, or corrected when they produce an error, and caregivers do not need to alter the way they speak (or sign) to guarantee successful language acquisition.

A very old view of language acquisition was that children had to be *rewarded* when they said something correctly and not rewarded when they said something grammatically incorrect. (The concept of reward and non-reward being necessary for language learning was a major component of the behaviorist view of language, discussed in Chapter 1.) Studies have demonstrated that parents do not interact with their children in the way this theory would predict. Brown and Hanlon showed that parents show approval when children make accurate statements, whether or not they are grammatical. Parents generally enjoy talking to their children and reward everything their children say (Brown and Hanlon 1970; Hirsh-Pasek, Treiman, and Schneiderman 1984).

Another theory about the role of the environment in language acquisition is the notion that children acquire language by imitating their caregivers' language. It is important to be very specific about precisely what the term *imitation* means. Imitation occurs when a child repeats what an adult has said, or at least produces a child version of it, immediately after the adult has said it. As an example, consider a scenario where the adult says, *This is a big blue ball*, and the child immediately replies, *Blue ball*. There seems to be a great deal of individual variation when it comes to imitation during language acquisition. It turns out that not all children imitate, and those who do imitate do not do it most of the time. Moreover, there is no evidence that imitators acquire language any faster than non-imitators, nor is there evidence that the children of adults who regularly encourage imitation acquire language any faster than other children.

Parents and other primary caregivers generally feel that they have some obligation to help their children acquire language, and might have the intuition that *correcting errors* is important. Caregivers do correct when their children say something that is factually inaccurate (Hirsh-Pasek, Treiman, and Schneiderman 1984) or socially stigmatized (parents typically do not tolerate cursing or certain types of slang). But more frequently, rather than correcting an error, adults will think it is cute. In fact, children's errors find their way into children's literature; the children's books character Junie B. Jones (Park 1992) produces a range of errors that sound familiar to anyone who has been around English-speaking children: *stoled*, *stucked*, *bestest*, *splode* (from *explode*), and *mergency* (from *emergency*). More importantly, errors produced by children usually go unnoticed; when they are noticed, they are frequently not corrected; and when they are corrected, the correction does absolutely no good (McNeill 1966). A child who says *eated* instead of *ate* will continue saying *eated* no matter how many times she is corrected. The following exchange between a child and a parent is typical (Braine 1971: 160–1):

(1) Child: Want other one spoon, Daddy.
    Adult: You mean, you want the other spoon.
    Child: Yes, I want other one spoon, please, Daddy.
    Adult: Can you say "the other spoon"?
    Child: Other ... one ... spoon
    Adult: Say "other."
    Child: Other.
    Adult: Say "spoon."
    Child: Spoon.
    Adult: Other ... spoon.
    Child: Other ... spoon. Now can I have other one spoon?

Parents only sporadically correct their children and children fail to respond as their parents might desire. While the language in the environment supplies plenty of positive evidence in the form of well-formed words and sentences, it provides very little, if any, **negative evidence**, that is, evidence about what is *not* grammatical in the language. Yet children make very few mistakes, although they rely only on positive evidence about their language. Take word order, for instance. Infants as young as 14 months have acquired information about the word order of their language (Hirsh-Pasek et al. 1978) and have set the word order parameter. They have accomplished this based exclusively on the positive evidence they receive about word order in the language in their environment. This is well before they can produce two-word sentences, and therefore well before they might have ever been corrected for word-order errors.

If rewarding correct behavior, encouraging imitation, and correcting errors are not important, are there any aspects of the way caregivers speak to children that might make a difference? Some characteristics of the language in the child's environment have been observed in a great many different cultures. The conjunct of these characteristics is referred to as **infant-directed speech** or **motherese**. One important characteristic is prosodic: when people talk to very small children, they tend to use an overall higher and more variable pitch than when speaking to adults. Cross-linguistic studies have shown that the prosody of infant-directed speech is similar in many different cultures (Fernald 1994). This prosodic adjustment has been linked to maternal nurturing behaviors, and has been claimed to be without linguistic significance. Later, exaggerated prosody might assist infants in acquiring the phonemes of their language, segment words, and discovering phrasal boundaries. However, children will acquire phonemes, words, and phrases without the assistance of exaggerated prosody; so this is not a necessary characteristic of the language learner's input.

Another characteristic of speech directed to children is that it consists of short, highly grammatical, and semantically simple sentences. These characteristics have not been studied cross-linguistically as thoroughly as has the prosody of speech to infants. However, they do seem typical of the way many caretakers in the English-speaking world address young children. Studies attempting to relate specific features of child language to specific characteristics of caretaker speech have been unsuccessful (Gleitman, Newport, and Gleitman 1984), and there is no evidence that children spoken to in typical child-directed speech acquire language with any greater facility than children who receive more adult-like input. However, speech with the characteristics of child-directed speech is probably easier to understand, and is thus a better vehicle for positive evidence. Importantly, speech addressed to children, while it might be semantically simple, is not syntactically or morphologically simple. Children must receive positive evidence about the full variety of syntactic and morphological forms in their language, and caretaker speech provides much of that evidence. Since child-directed speech is semantically simple, it is a good vehicle for communicative interaction between caretaker and child, which is critical for language acquisition.

To summarize this section, we emphasize two important points about the role of input in language acquisition. First, interactive input is necessary: Jim and Glen were not able to acquire spoken English simply by experiencing language via television, although Glen did learn a few words (Sachs, Bard, and Johnson 1981). This observation has been confirmed experimentally, in a study of American 9-month-old children exposed to a foreign language, Mandarin Chinese (Kuhl, Tsao, and Liu 2003). In the study, children exposed to a live speaker performed much better, when tested on their perception of sounds specific to Mandarin, than children whose exposure to the same speaker was pre-recorded (presented via a television set or only as audio). Clearly, interactive experience with language enhances acquisition. Second, interactive experience is all that is needed: Jim and Glen did not receive any special instruction, reward, or correction, and neither did the children exposed to Mandarin in the study by Kuhl and colleagues.

Developmental Stages

We have mentioned several times in the preceding pages that children everywhere develop linguistically at similar rates and experience similar developmental milestones. In this section we describe the major developmental stages that children go through over the course of language acquisition.

From before birth to 12 months

A growing body of evidence indicates that infants are attuned to human language from the moment they are born. In fact, sensitivity to language seems to be present even before birth, since the earliest exposure to linguistic input is *in utero*. Hearing begins to develop during the second trimester, at around 18 weeks of gestation, and by the beginning of the third trimester, the fetus responds to auditory stimulation. A study by Barbara Kisilevsky and colleagues (Kisilevsky et al. 2003) demonstrated that full-term fetuses (38 weeks of gestation) have a preference for their own mother's voice over that of a stranger, as indicated by increased fetal heart rate and body movements.

By the time they are born, then, babies have had considerable access to the general prosody (the rhythm and intonation) of the language of the environment; this is reflected in their bias for their mother's voice over the voices of others, and in their recognition of their mother's language as distinct from other languages (Mehler et al. 1988). Much of the research with newborns uses non-nutritive devices to measure newborns' sucking rates while they are exposed to different pre-recorded stimuli. The non-nutritive devices are, simply, nipples hooked up to a device that measures sucking rates: in infants, sucking rates increase proportional to increases in attention. Newborns are very attentive to the language around them: infants as young as 10 weeks prefer to look at a face whose movements are synchronous with speech they are hearing than a face with non-synchronous speech movements (Spelke and Cortelyou 1981; McKain et al. 1983). In fact, very young infants can discriminate languages by visual cues alone, as demonstrated by a study of monolingual and bilingual 4-month-old infants, who could distinguish between French and English just by watching talking faces with the accompanying sound turned off (Weikum et al. 2007).

Prosody plays a central role in the baby's discovery of many aspects of the grammar being learned. Babies use regularities in the rhythm and intonation of the input to assist in the identification of the phonemic inventory and phonotactic constraints of the language or languages in their environment, and will eventually use rhythmic and intonational signals to help identify the boundaries of syntactic constituents. Note that we are referring to the natural prosody of the speech of the environment, not the exaggerated prosody associated with some infant-directed speech.

An important accomplishment that takes place over the baby's first year is the identification of the phonemic inventory for the language being learned. The target set of phonemes will be a subset of all the possible sounds that exist in the world's languages. Logically, the infant must approach this task by being able to **discriminate** all sorts of different phonemic contrasts, whether or not they are present in the environment. Studies measuring brain activity by using event-related brain potentials (ERPs) have demonstrated that infants as young as 2 months are able to discriminate many phonemic contrasts, including vowel and consonant duration, and vowel and consonant articulation (Männel and Friederici 2008).

Janet Werker and her colleagues (Werker and Lalonde 1988; Polka and Werker 1994; Werker and Tees 2002) have produced seminal findings regarding the phonemic discrimination abilities of babies in their first year. This research uses procedures that measure discrimination in infants by conditioning them to turn their head toward a visual display when they hear a change in an auditory stimulus presented to them. Werker's research has demonstrated that infants aged 6 to 8 months can discriminate speech sounds that are not phonemic in their language, even though older children and adult speakers of their language cannot. For instance, Japanese infants can discriminate /r/ versus /l/ as well as English-speaking adults can, although Japanese adults find this distinction very difficult. Infants who experience English in their environment can discriminate two types of stop consonants – alveolar /t/ versus retroflex /ʈ/ (produced by curling the tongue backwards) – a contrast that is phonemic in Hindi but does not exist in English. English-speaking adults cannot discriminate those sounds, but their babies can. This perceptual ability vanishes gradually over the second half of the first year of life, and by about 12 months of age infants perform like adults, reliably discriminating only those speech sounds that are phonemic in the language of their environment. Their phonemic inventory has been set. Of course, if children are exposed to another language, they will be able to recover the phonemic distinctions in the new language. Werker's research serves as a metaphor for all language acquisition. Infants are born with the ability to acquire any language; then experience with the language of the environment allows them to acquire their target language.

Many babies grow up with two or more languages in their environment. Bilingual language acquirers must, therefore, set two or more phonemic inventories. There is a growing body of research demonstrating that, in order to distinguish between the languages in the environment, bilingual infants rely on phonetic information that they extract from the input (Werker and Byers-Heinlein 2008). Recall the broad rhythmic distinctions between languages described in Chapter 2. Languages like English and Dutch are stress-timed, whereas languages like Spanish and Catalan are syllable-timed. It turns out that newborns can discriminate languages from different rhythmic classes (e.g., English and Spanish), but not from the same rhythmic class (e.g., Spanish and Catalan); however, by 4 or 5 months infants can distinguish even between languages of the same rhythmic class. All infants are able to discriminate languages in their environment from unfamiliar languages, but an interesting difference has been documented between monolingual and bilingual infants: bilinguals will take longer to attend to a stimulus in one of their native languages than to a stimulus in an unfamiliar language, while monolinguals will take longer to orient to an unfamiliar language than to their native language (Bosch and Sebastián-Gallés 1997). Presumably, the delay has to do with the time it takes the bilingual baby to identify which of the two native (and familiar) languages is being presented.

Bilingual babies, then, might need to attend to the speech of their environment differently than monolingual babies do, because it necessarily contains information about two languages, rather than just one. The study cited earlier about 4-month-olds' attentiveness to muted talking faces, by Weikum et al. (2007), also demonstrated that in older babies, 8-month-olds, only the bilinguals still successfully discriminated between English and French. By the end of their first year of life – particularly when exposure to the two languages is regular and sustained – bilingual babies have developed a system that distinguishes between all of the phonemic contrasts in each of their languages, although the details of how they get there are still not well understood (Werker and Byers-Heinlein 2008).

In the first half of the first year of life infants interact in a variety of ways with their caretakers, but their vocalizations are primarily soft coos and gurgles that are not at all like actual language. In the second half of the first year, true **babbling** begins. Babbling consists of single syllables at first, always consisting of a consonant and a vowel. Usually the consonant is a stop consonant and the vowel is /a/. At first the babbles will be strings of similar syllables, like *baba baba*. Later, the babbles will become more varied, e.g., *baga bada*. This type of babbling is called *segmental babbling* because the vocalizations sound like phonemic segments. The vocalizations also have sentence-like intonation, so the strings of babbles might sound like declarative or interrogative sentences made up of nonsense words. This is a very interesting stage of language development because as far as one can tell the babbles have no content. Hearing such a child, one sometimes has the sense that the child is trying to convey something meaningful, but in fact it is more likely that the child is playing with the sound structures of the language. During this period, children babble as much when they are alone as when they are with other people. Even though babbling is not used for communication, it may play a role in interactive "pretend" conversations.

Laura Ann Petitto and her colleagues have demonstrated that babbling reflects a stage of linguistic development, rather than merely being a side effect of the development of the vocal tract (Petitto et al. 2004). This discovery offers insights into the biological nature of language acquisition. Their work compares hand gesture activity in babies acquiring sign language and babies acquiring spoken language. Babies exposed to sign language produce hand gestures that are not only far more regular and frequent than their spoken-language acquiring counterparts, but also crucially different from the gestures of hearing children, because they are based on the signs used in the sign language around them, just as hearing babies make sounds that are similar to syllables in the spoken language they are hearing. Babies acquiring sign language babble with their hands.

From 12 to 24 months

Infants as young as 9 months can segment individual words from a string of speech and recognize them later (Aslin et al. 1996). However, it is not until between 12 and 18 months that children produce their first word. The first word is often indistinguishable phonologically from babble, but it is identifiable as a word because it has a consistent referent. The child will spend a few months in the **one-word stage** of language, also called the **holophrastic** period, because each word conveys as much meaning as an entire phrase. The word *milk*, for instance, will not only be used to refer to milk, but it will also be used to request milk, to observe that the cat is drinking milk, that milk has been spilled, and so forth. Early vocabulary items tend to be those things that are very salient for the child, like toys and articles of clothing. Rarely would an early word be a large, stationary object like a refrigerator. Nor would the words be function words, except for perhaps *up* and *down*. The vast majority of early words are nouns.

During this early one-word period, the twin phenomena of **underextension** and **overextension** are features of word use. Underextension is a case in which the child will acquire a word for a particular thing and fail to extend it to other objects in the same category. For example, if a child learned the word *flower* in connection with a rose and did not extend its meaning to other kinds of flowers, this would be an example of underextension. Overextension is more common, or perhaps it's just more noticeable. Overextension is when the child will extend a word incorrectly to other similar things. For example, a child might call all four-legged animals *doggie*, or everything that is bright *light*. This behavior is almost certainly not because children are unable to discriminate cats from dogs or light bulbs from lightning. It is because children just do not have a big enough vocabulary to use words very precisely. A study by Fremgen and Fay (1980) demonstrated that children's overextensions in production do not carry over into a receptive task. Children who called all four-legged animals *doggie* were perfectly able to discriminate between dogs and cats in a picture-selection task. This suggests that such children have both *cat* and *dog* in their lexicons but have difficulty retrieving *cat* in speech production.

When the child's vocabulary approaches about 50 words, two interesting things happen. The child starts putting words together to form rudimentary sentences. Words are learned more rapidly than before, so much so that most children are said to go through a **vocabulary spurt**, and the rate of acquisition of vocabulary increases dramatically. It has been estimated that a 6-year-old child has a vocabulary of about 8,000 to 14,000 words. Beginning with one word at 12 months, this means that the child must acquire an average of four to eight new words every day during the preschool years (Carey 1978). This rapid acquisition of lexical items begins with the vocabulary spurt. A very interesting characteristic of spurting is **fast mapping** (Carey 1978), which occurs when a child hears a word once or twice, learns its grammatical class, but has only a vague sense of what it means. The child will then use the word in sentences, while gradually acquiring the full meaning of the word. For example, one of us has a stone cat in her living room, and a visiting child who was spurting said that the cat was *shy*. She had no doubt heard the word *shy*, probably applied to quiet children at her nursery school. The immobile cat, therefore, fit her fast-mapped meaning of *shy*. The result was a grammatical but amusing sentence.

Eventually, of course, children acquire the full meaning of words that have been fast mapped initially. It is not at all clear how they manage to do this. Referential words are often taught explicitly, but not complete meanings. One of us had the following experience, where her son aged 2-and-a-half came home from nursery school and asked his mother to be his friend. After several exchanges, it became clear that he wanted his mother to sit on the floor with him and work a jigsaw puzzle. It turned out that an older child in his school had said *Will you be my friend?* then worked on a puzzle with him. He had evidently fast mapped the word *friend*. By the time the child started first grade, several years later, he had acquired the meaning of the word *friend* in all its detail and subtlety. Yet no one had taught him. Children acquire the meanings of words by experiencing them in communicative contexts, not by explicit instruction.

Dapretto and Byork (2000) suggest that much of what appears to be expanding vocabulary is actually improvement in lexical retrieval skills for production. They studied 2-year-olds who differed in vocabulary size. Small toys, which all the children could name, were placed in boxes. When asked to retrieve each toy, all the children were able to do it, if the boxes were open and the toys in full view of the children. However, when the boxes were closed, so that the toys were no longer in full view, only the children with larger vocabularies were able to name the toys. Dapretto and Byork argue that the task reflects inferior lexical retrieval skills of the children with small vocabularies, which explained their inability to use their full vocabularies in production.

Tests measuring vocabulary development have been normed on children who are learning only one language. Such tests include parent checklists (in which parents are asked to check off which words in a list their child produces spontaneously) and word lists (which measure what words in a list a child understands). More and more, these measures are being used to detect language delays, as early as when the child is 8–15 months (Fernson et al. 1994). How to adapt such measures to bilingual children is challenging (Pearson 1998). Recall from Chapter 2 that knowing a word requires knowing both its form and its meaning. If a bilingual knows two translation-equivalent words (*duck* and *pato*, for example), there is no guarantee that there are two separate representations for the meaning of these two forms. There are also plenty of words that exist in one language but not the other; food-related words are frequently like this. Furthermore, some words have language-specific semantic details. For example, *bread* and *pain* could mean dramatically different things for a child raised in a community where

Wonderbread and baguettes do not mix; *dragon* and 龍 – which means 'dragon' in Chinese – could elicit very different mental images for a Chinese–English bilingual child. An additional category of words, called *blends*, have elements from the two languages, like *socketines*, a combination of *socks* and *calcetines*. There is also a complication added by idiosyncratic differences in the phonological complexity of translation-equivalent words. A child might prefer *agua* over *water* but *shoe* over *zapato*, maybe because the preferred forms have simpler syllable structures.

When researchers take care to create testing instruments that are sensitive to the complexities of bilingual vocabulary development, the findings are very interesting. In a longitudinal study of 25 Spanish–English bilingual children between ages 8 and 30 months, Barbara Pearson and colleagues (Pearson, Fernández, and Oller 1993) demonstrated that bilingual children followed lexical development patterns that closely matched those of monolingual children. Interestingly, growth spurts occurred mostly in one language at a time, and these spurts followed estimates of shifts in how much the child was being exposed to one language or the other (Pearson et al. 1997).

A number of **lexical learning principles** guide the child's rapid acquisition of vocabulary. One of these is the **whole object assumption**, which works for adults as well as for children (Markman 1992). Suppose a mother points to an animal her child has never seen before and announces *skleet*. Her child will likely assume that *skleet* refers to the entire animal, not to just some part of it, like its tail, or to just some property of it, like its coloration or texture. The whole object assumption is very helpful for children, for whom things are constantly being named. If every new word were as likely to refer to parts of things as to whole objects, it would be very difficult for a child to sort out exactly what was being named. It helps to assume that new words refer to whole objects.

Another principle allows children to acquire labels for parts of things: according to the **mutual exclusivity assumption**, everything has only one name (Markman and Wachtel 1988; Golinkoff, Mervis, and Hirsch-Pasek 1994). If a parent points to a horse – a word the child already knows – and says, *That's a skleet*, the child will not assume that *skleet* is another word for *horse*. The child will assume that it is a word for a part of the horse he does not yet have a word for, or that the word refers to the type of horse it is. Bilingual children face an interesting dilemma: a horse is a *horse* or a *caballo*. An experiment examining the use of mutual exclusivity by monolingual and bilingual 3- and 6-year-old children confirmed that monolingual and bilingual children alike use mutual exclusivity to name whole objects, but that older bilingual children are more likely to suspend the mutual exclusivity assumption than are all monolingual children and younger bilingual children (Davidson and Tell 2005). This is obviously a wise move on the part of the bilingual children, as mutual exclusivity does not hold across languages: there are two words for every object, one in each language.

Many experiments with children explore how the whole object and the mutual exclusivity assumptions interact in lexical acquisition. If a novel object is given a novel name, the child assumes the name refers to the whole object. If a novel name is applied to an object the child already has a name for, the child assumes that the novel name applies to a part of that object (Markman 1994). Both of these principles reflect universals of lexical semantics in the world's languages. Object parts will not have words associated with them unless the entire object has a name, and thus the naming of whole objects occurs prior to the naming of object parts. It is also true that few true synonyms exist in languages, and those that do are usually dialect variations. The relationship between principles of lexical learning and universal characteristics of lexicons is not nearly as clear as the relationship between UG and the child's acquisition of the structural features of languages. This is because far less is known about the universal properties of lexicons than is known about the universal properties of grammars. Moreover, psycholinguists who study acquisition of the lexicon have not attempted to account for lexical acquisition in light of universal principles to the same extent as researchers who study acquisition of grammar have. There is, however, a growing debate about whether the principles of lexical learning are biologically based or are learned. Considerations of universality must play a role in this debate.

A final principle of lexical learning that assists the child's rapid acquisition of a vocabulary is the **principle of extendability** (also called the **taxonomic assumption**). This principle gets the child in trouble during the one-word stage, leading to overextension, but it can be helpful later on. Extendability creates the expectancy that individual words will refer to categories of similar things. For example, when a mother points to a dog and says, *That's a dog*, the child will expect that other similar things will also be dogs, and the child will attempt to discover that category of animal. Studies have shown that even though young children prefer to sort things into groups of things that are functionally related – dolls with bottles and diapers, children with balls and bats – they will shift to categories of things if given a label (Markman and Hutchinson 1984). This is a particularly important result because it demonstrates that the principle of extendability is not a property of the child's general cognitive orientation, but of the child's expectations about lexical items. Thus, a child's acquisition of the linguistic system is distinct from a child's general cognitive system.

Even very young children are sensitive to the non-verbal behavior of their caretakers when they learn words for things. It is often the case that the child will be attending to one thing while the adult is attending to – and labeling – something entirely different. Children would be in real trouble if they took the adult's label to refer to whatever the child was attending to, ignoring the adult's different focus. In fact, children do not make this kind of mistake. Baldwin (1991) showed that children pay attention to the direction of the adult's gaze and acquire labels only for those objects that both the child and the adult are looking at.

The lexical learning principles we have discussed so far apply primarily to the acquisition of nouns. Verbs, however, present a different sort of problem for the learner, because they label an ongoing activity, rather than a stationary object. As Gleitman (2000) has pointed out, a novel verb, such as *moak*, can mean *chase* if a sentence like *The cat is moaking the mouse* is predicated of a cat in the visual context of the cat chasing a mouse. However, in the same context, if the sentence is *The mouse is moaking the cat*, then *moak* can be taken to mean *flee*. Gleitman argues that to learn a new verb, a child must pay attention to the syntactic context in which the verb occurs. Naigles (1990) demonstrated elegantly how the structure of a sentence affects a child's interpretation of a novel verb. Her experiment used a technique called preferential looking with 2-year-old children. While sitting on their mothers' laps, all the children saw a video of a rabbit repeatedly pushing a duck down into a squatting position; each time the duck pops back up. Throughout the video, both the rabbit and the duck are waving their arms around in circles. Half the children heard the transitive sentence (2a), which describes a transitive action, the pushing. The other half of the children heard the intransitive sentence in (2b), which describes the intransitive action of arm waving:

(2) a.   The rabbit is gorping the duck.
     b.   The rabbit and duck are gorping.

After this training period, the children were shown two videos, one depicting the rabbit pushing the duck, the other depicting both animals arm waving. They were instructed by the experimenter: *Show me gorping*. The children who had heard the transitive version of the sentence looked toward the video showing pushing, while those who had heard the intransitive version looked toward the video depicting arm waving. Clearly, the children had identified the action referred to as *gorping* based solely on the structure of the descriptive sentence.

The preschool years

As the child leaves the one-word stage, vocabulary development speeds up and children begin to combine words to form small sentences. Even at the earliest stages of combinatorial speech, it is obvious that syntactic principles govern the creation of the child's sentences.

When children begin combining words, the resulting rudimentary sentences reflect the structure of the child's target language. English-speaking children obey word order very strictly, with subjects preceding verbs and verbs preceding objects (e.g., *Mommy push, Pull car*). Sentences can also consist of just a subject and an object (e.g., *Baby cookie*), but they always get the order right. Adjectives precede nouns (e.g., *Big doggie*), and the rare function word is correctly placed (e.g., *That kitty*).

Children acquiring languages with other word orders will reflect that order in their earliest sentences. Both German and French are canonically SVO languages, but they differ in a few ways: in French, constituents can sometimes be moved from their canonical position, so sentences can sometimes begin with a verb; in German, a so-called V2 language, the verb must appear in second position in a matrix clause and in final position in a subordinate clause. Children learning German or French follow these basic word order patterns. Meisel (1989) studied the word order of sentences produced by German–French bilingual children, and found that the word orders the bilingual children produced in each language were different: clause-final verbs occurred in German, not French; clause-initial verbs occurred in French, but not German; word orders characteristic of V2 languages only appeared in German, but not French.

Bilingual children respect canonical word order, depending on the language they are speaking, and even in utterances with components from both languages. Bilinguals – both children and adults – sometimes switch from one to another language within the same conversation, and sometimes also within the same sentence. This is called *code-switching*, a topic we will address in more detail in Chapter 5. In bilingual children's speech, a sentence containing a code-switch will follow the word-order constraints of the language of the sentence, so a French–English bilingual child might say *rouge bird* ('red bird') in an English sentence, but – because French adjectives follow the noun – the child will say *bird rouge* ('bird red') when the sentence is in French (Paradis, Nicoladis, and Genesee 2000).

Monolingual children learning English will not use bound morphemes at this stage, but monolinguals acquiring highly inflected languages, like French, will begin to acquire inflections as soon as they begin to use words. In a study of three French–English bilingual children, tested at three different intervals in early childhood, Paradis and Genesee (1996) found that the children's utterances in French consistently had more inflections than in English, at all three intervals. Deuchar and Quay (2000) examined the emergence of morphology in a Spanish–English bilingual child, and reported that inflectional morphemes appeared in each language, in their language-specific forms: no Spanish morphemes ever appeared bound to English verbs, or English morphemes bound to Spanish verbs.

As sentences gradually lengthen, a useful index of language development is **mean length of utterance (MLU)**. The MLU for a child is computed by adding the bound and free morphemes in a language sample (e.g., 100 intelligible utterances) and dividing by the number of utterances. There is a high correlation between MLU and age. MLU increases with age for two reasons. First, sentences become longer presumably because the child's working memory capacity allows the child to plan and execute longer sentences. (Working memory is temporary memory storage, for storing information briefly, while processing a sentence or completing a computational task; in Chapter 8 we will discuss it in more detail, including how it differs from long-term memory.) Second, the child is acquiring more bound morphemes and function words. Figure 4.2 provides an estimate of the MLU ranges observed in children of different ages. MLU is an average computed over sentences of varying lengths. A child with an MLU of 2 will have many one-word sentences, many two-word sentences, and many sentences that are longer. Another interesting indicator of development is the child's longest sentence.

Researchers working on the acquisition of languages that are typologically different from English have adapted the MLU measures used to study children acquiring English, or have developed alternative ways to index language development (Thordardottir and Ellis Weismer 1998). For example, for highly inflected languages, words rather than morphemes are counted to calculate MLU. This is because child

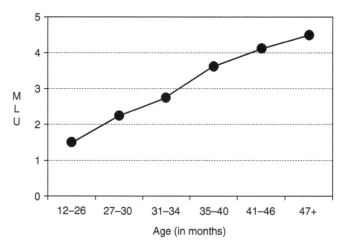

Figure 4.2   Mean length of utterance (MLU) as a function of age in months, for children learning English. Data from Owens (2001: 308), based on Brown (1973).

utterances in languages rich with inflections inflate the morpheme-based MLU measure disproportionately.

The morphological and syntactic characteristics of speech at this time are of more interest than simple length (although, as noted above, the two are related). Early speech of children acquiring English has been called "telegraphic" because it is missing many function words and bound morphemes. (When people used to send telegrams, they tried to omit as much as they could, since they were charged by the number of words in the message.) It is important to point out that during this stage the child's production may be telegraphic, but the child is nonetheless sensitive to the presence of those elements in the speech of others (Gerken and McIntosh 1993). Early speech sounds like a telegram written by an adult. The following utterances collected from a 23-month-old girl, Hannah, are typical of early telegraphic speech:

(3)   No Hannah mess.
      No Daddy mess.
      Where go, Mom?
      Mom, talk phone.
      Mommy like it.
      Want juice.
      More cracker.
      Daddy push in swing.
      Go subby [subway].

In Hannah's speech there are no bound morphemes, no tense markers on verbs, no plural markers, and so on. *No, it, in,* and *where* are the only function words in this 25-word sample; articles and prepositions are essentially absent. The single *wh*-word (*where*) is not syntactically organized. Similarly, the negative sentences simply begin with no. Hannah's utterances contain no modals (e.g., *can, would,* or *do*), no auxiliaries (e.g., *is* as in *is talking*), and no complex structures or structures that result from movement. However, the utterances do pay strict attention to word order. The MLU for this tiny sample is 2.8 (25 morphemes in 9 utterances). A larger sample would probably contain many one-word utterances and would produce a smaller MLU.

Another thing Hannah does that is very common – no matter what language a child is acquiring – is omit subjects. She says *Want juice* instead of *I want juice,* and *Go subby* when she means to say *Mommy go subby.* Typically, children omit subjects much more than they omit objects, and this asymmetry in subject omission has been a topic of great interest to psycholinguists for some time. There are languages (e.g., Spanish and Italian) in which one can omit the subject under certain circumstances, so a grammar that allows sentences without subjects (a null subject language) is possible in a human language; we discussed languages like this briefly in Chapter 2. In fact, this is a parameter of variation specified in UG, known as the **null subject parameter**. It has been suggested that at this stage English-speaking children have not yet obtained sufficient information to know that subjects are always required in their sentences and set their parameter accordingly (Hyams 1986). Others think that the subject omission in English speakers is the result of children having limited working memory space within which to plan sentences (Bloom 1990; Valian 1990). This debate illustrates a common problem that psycholinguists face in understanding language acquisition. Psycholinguists must try to determine which features of child language reflect the child's growing linguistic competence, and which features reflect properties of the child's developing performance system, both expressive and receptive.

By the age of 3 (or earlier) children have set the parameters for their target languages. The null subject parameter is an example, as is the word order parameter. V2 languages, such as German, mentioned above, result from the correct setting of the V2 parameter, which is set early enough for the first rudimentary sentences to reflect it. The correct placement of the negative marker *pas* in French results from the setting of a parameter that determines where the verb appears in basic sentences. It accounts for the difference of the placement of adverbs in languages such as French versus those such as English, and is acquired by the age of 2 (Pierce 1992). Such early acquisition of complex features of language is a remarkable accomplishment. It almost certainly could not happen were it not for the fact that UG narrows the possibilities of language variation and, therefore, the language-specific information that children must seek in their target languages (Wexler 2002).

There is an interesting continuity between features of children's early and later language skills. Marchman and Fernald (2008) measured picture-naming speed in 25-month-old children, then correlated those measures with vocabulary growth during the subsequent years. Children who were faster at naming pictures showed faster vocabulary growth. Furthermore, naming speed at 25 months was a strong predictor of scores on standardized language tests when the children were 8 years old. A similar continuity has been demonstrated between communicative gestures in infancy and vocabulary development. Recent work by Rowe and Goldin-Meadow (2009) shows that children who had more communicative gestures (such as pointing, head nodding and shaking, etc.) at the age of 14 months had larger vocabularies at age 4-and-a-half than did children who had fewer gestures at 14 months.

With respect to vocabulary size, bilingual children have been found by some studies to have smaller vocabularies in each of their languages than do their monolingual peers. This may appear to be a deficit, but these studies also show that the number of words in both lexicons of a bilingual is greater than in the single lexicon of a monolingual; thus, there is no deficit in lexical capacity. The difference is probably due to the fact that bilingual children do not have as much exposure to individual words as do monolinguals, since they are experiencing input from two languages. Since bilinguals hear each of their languages less often than monolinguals, it takes them longer to acquire individual words.

Bilingualism appears to have positive consequences for cognitive control. Bilingualism requires greater attention and control of language functions than does monolingualism. We have already cited studies demonstrating that bilingual babies attend more carefully to the environmental input than monolingual babies, because they are developing two phonemic inventories. As he or she matures, the bilingual child must also learn to inhibit the language not active in the current conversation. Indeed, there is evidence that bilingual children outperform their monolingual peers in tasks that require controlled attention and inhibition (Bialystok 2009).

Throughout the third year of life, sentences gradually lengthen, bound morphemes and function words emerge, and some movement operations begin. Psycholinguists have found that the order in which some of the bound morphemes and function words are acquired is similar for all children acquiring English (Brown 1973). Earliest of all is the *-ing* marker on verbs signaling the present progressive form of the verb. Sentences such as *Kitty sleeping* are very common, but the auxiliary form, such as *Kitty is sleeping*, comes much later. Other early bound morphemes are the plural /s/ and the possessive /s/. These are to be expected from the point of view of Slobin's operating principles, because they are suffixes that carry meaning. The function words *in* and *on* are also acquired very early; children acquire *the, a,* and *an* slightly later. Auxiliaries and the copula (a form of the verb *to be*, as in *That is a doggie*) are acquired late, as is the /s/ that is a third person singular marker on verbs (e.g., *he works*); in both cases these are virtually meaningless grammatical elements.

Past tense marking on verbs is interesting because it illustrates a common feature of child language. The most common verbs have irregular past tenses and children tend to acquire these first (e.g., *ate* and *went*). They then acquire some regular past tenses (e.g., *hugged, kissed*), and at some point they seem to recognize that the past tense is governed by rules. At that point, children begin to **overgeneralize** the past tense marker and mispronounce many irregular verbs, producing utterances with forms such as *eated* and *goed* or even *ated*. Plurals also get overgeneralized, and it is common to hear utterances such as *foots* and *feets*.

These examples in English illustrate the tendency of all children to over-regularize irregular processes in their language. Overgeneralization in other languages will look different on the surface from overgeneralization in English – because the rules being over-regularized are different – but the underlying mechanisms are the same. Children learning Spanish are faced with many irregular past first person singular verbs: *supe* for *saber* ('to know'), *puse* for *poner* ('to put'), *tuve* for *tener* ('to have'). The regular past tense is created by adding *-é* or *-í* to the stem of the verb: *canté* for *cantar* ('to sing'), *bebí* for *beber* ('to drink'). Spanish children will routinely produce over-regularized irregulars: *sabí, poní,* and *tení*. Regular processes, in any language, are more easily acquired than irregular ones, and regularity is forced by the child where it does not exist.

As auxiliaries and copulas enter the child's speech, so do modals and negative modals, such as *can't* and *don't*. The negative modals and words such as *wanna* and *hafta*, which, for adults, are contractions of *want to* and *have to*, are examples of *fixed forms*. A fixed form is a word that is derived in the adult language, but is a single lexical item for the child. When a child begins saying *can't*, the child does not create it as a contraction of *can* and *not*. The child just uses it as a negative word. Also associated with the use of auxiliaries and modals is the consistent use of subjects in sentences. As the grammar is restructured to include auxiliaries and modals, it no longer allows subjects to be omitted (Hyams 1986).

Children at this age rarely produce passive sentences, but one can observe the beginning of movement in question formation. Recall that both yes/no and *wh*-questions involve the fronting of the auxiliary element of the verb phrase. About the time auxiliaries enter the child's speech, the child will begin inverting them in yes/no questions, progressing from questions like (4a) to questions like (4b). Around the same time inversion of auxiliaries and modals in *wh*-questions also begins (Weinberg 1990). The child first produces questions like (5a), and later questions like (5b):

(4) a. Doggie sleeping?
     b. Is doggie sleeping?

(5) a. Why I can't go outside?
     b. Why can't I go outside?

Around the age of 3 (with much individual variation), the child will begin to produce complex sentences. This is a very important linguistic development, because it means the child has developed the last capacity of the syntax – to create complex sentences out of simple ones. A complex sentence is one with two verbs. The sentences *I wanna go potty* or *I hafta get the ball* do not count as complex because when they are first used, *wanna* and *hafta* are being used like modals (as in *I can go potty* or *I will get the ball*). These are, however, precursors of complex sentences. Early complex sentences consist of a clause being substituted for a constituent of the sentence that was earlier filled by a single phrase. Examples of this are when a child says sentences like the following (Limber 1973):

(6) I want Mommy do it.
     I see you sit down.
     Watch me draw circles.
     I don't know who is it.

A precursor of relative clauses are sentences such as *Looka what my made*, to be followed by true relatives, *I want the one what you got*. These sentences illustrate an invariant feature of early English sentences. The more complex material, whether it is a complex noun phrase or an entire clause, is always placed at the right end of the sentence. In early sentences, noun phrases involving coordination (e.g., *Mommy and Daddy*) or modification (e.g., *pretty blue flower*) are much more likely to appear in the object position than in the subject position. This probably reflects a tendency of the production processing system to plan for the least complex part of the utterance to be produced first (Bloom 1990).

Children begin producing relative clauses spontaneously around the age of 3 or 4, and elicited production studies have shown that children even younger can produce them (McKee, McDaniel, and Snedeker 1998). However, some types of sentences contain relative clauses that are much easier to understand than others. The most difficult kind is one in which the subject of the sentence is modified by a relative clause and serves as the object of the verb (known as a *subject–object relative clause*). An example of such a sentence is in (7a), below. *The cow* is the main-clause subject of this sentence. It is modified by the relative clause *that the horse kissed*, making the cow the object of the verb kissed. Notice how much easier sentence (7b) is:

(7)   a.   The cow that the horse kissed nuzzled the sheep.
      b.   The horse kissed the cow that nuzzled the sheep.

In (7b) (an *object–subject relative clause*) the relative clause *that nuzzled the sheep* is attached to the object noun phrase *the cow*, which is, in turn, the subject of the verb *nuzzled*. Both sentences are formed by the same grammatical operations, but they differ in ease of processing. In the more difficult sentence, the relative clause intervenes between the main-clause subject and verb, putting a strain on short-term memory. The relative clause *that nuzzled the sheep* is also out of standard subject–verb–object word order, a feature that always increases processing difficulty. The easier sentence has neither of these troublesome features. Still, even children of early school age have difficulty with sentences of the first type, not because they lack the underlying grammar of relative clauses, but because they are more vulnerable to those features of sentences that make them difficult to process for performance reasons.

All the characteristics of development that have been described here appear gradually in the child's speech, and in different "stages" they may overlap. For instance, there is a considerable period between the time a child first uses a past tense marker and consistent use of past tense. When a child begins to invert the auxiliary in *wh*-questions, the child will not do it consistently for a considerable period of time. The best way to get a sense of how child language really sounds is to take a language sample from a fairly verbal child between the ages of 2 and 3. In that sample it will be possible to observe many of the features that have been described here, including the overlapping of more and less mature features of language.

When you think about it, it is quite remarkable that child language between the ages of 2 and 3 is so similar. Children learning English are speaking a language we can call Child English. It is different from adult English, but the same for all children acquiring English. They all speak a language they have never heard; in fact each child lives in a very different language environment. Some are spoken to often, others are not; some attend preschool or day care, others stay at home. Yet the form of Child English and the period of childhood during which children speak it are virtually identical for all English-learning children. The only similarity is that they have all experienced the English language in their environment. The fact that they all construct a common language (Child English) must be because they have similar learning strategies with which they approach the target language and similar biologically based grammatical forms with which to organize it. We make this point with respect to English, but the same thing can be said of children speaking every language that has ever been studied: Child Spanish, Child Italian, Child Russian, etc. Furthermore, all the child versions of human languages have their own similarities because all children construct their languages on a similar developmental timetable with similarly developing brains.

Later Language Development

As children grow older, they develop much more proficiency with language. Their processing capacity increases and their ability to produce and interpret longer and more syntactically complex sentences improves. In fact, the ability to process difficult sentences, such as those with relative clauses described in the previous section, is related to reading ability in the early school years. Lexical learning continues at a rapid rate, and around school age, children begin using derivational morphemes and the word combinations provided by derivational morphemes. A production study by Jarmulowicz (2006) showed that children of 7, 8, and 9 years of age could correctly produce words with derivational morphemes that do not alter the pronunciation of the stem to which they are attached (such as *–ness*, *–ful*, and *–ment*). The younger children, however, were not proficient with derivational morphemes that alter the pronunciation of the stem (such as *–ity*, *–tion*, and *–ic*). This ability improved with age; 9-year-olds were successful 80 percent of the time, but still did not perform as well as adults.

A child's interpretation of sentences also changes in later childhood, making it appear that there are changes in the child's syntactic knowledge. It is probably the case, however, that much of this change is due to increased knowledge about the grammatical characteristics of lexical items and an enhanced ability to create grammatical structures. Both these factors probably account for the observation that it is not until later childhood that children develop adult interpretations for sentences that contain clauses that appear to be missing subjects, like the following examples:

(8)   a.   John met Mary before seeing the show.
      b.   John invited Mary to see the show.

In both sentences, the subject of *see* is not stated and must be inferred from the sentence structure. In (8a), *John* will see the show; in (8b), *Mary* will see the show. Young children, however, interpret both sentences as meaning that Mary will see the show. The adult interpretation of such sentences depends on detailed knowledge of the properties of verbs and subordinating conjunctions, and of the structures those properties require. It is such knowledge that probably develops in later childhood (McDaniel, Cairns, and Hsu, 1990; Cairns et al. 1994).

Another example of a change in processing ability in late childhood relates to the comprehension of sentences like the following:

(9)   Put the frog on the napkin into the box.

Experimental studies are set up so that the child listens to instructions like the sentence in (9) while sitting in front of a display in which there is a toy frog on a napkin, another toy frog not on a napkin, an empty napkin and an empty box. Upon hearing the instruction, young children will simply put the frog that is not on a napkin onto the empty napkin, ignoring the issue of the box (Trueswell et al. 1999). Adults and children over the age of 8 will initially consider *the napkin* as a goal for the frog, but when they hear *into the box* they are able to revise their understanding, realize that *on the napkin* modified the frog and that *into the box* is the correct goal. So they take the frog from the napkin and put it directly into the box. The point here is that it is not until the age of 8 that children can revise initial incorrect hypotheses about the meaning of this sentence (Trueswell 2008). A similar phenomenon is that young children will interpret sentences like the one in (10) as meaning that leaves should be used to chop the tree, rather than interpreting *with the leaves* as a phrase to identify which tree should be chopped (Kidd, Stewart, and Serratrice 2006):

(10)   Chop the tree with the leaves.

Only in later childhood will children be able to alter their interpretation of this instruction. Trueswell suggests that before approximately the age of 8, children cannot overcome what he calls "cognitive impulsivity," which renders them unable to revise initial hypotheses about meaning. After the age of 8 the development of cognitive control allows them to be more flexible in abandoning initial interpretations and reprocessing sentences (Trueswell 2008).

Discourse ability

Very young babies exhibit incipient conversational abilities by making eye contact and exchanging coos or babbles with caretakers. In early childhood children can take turns in conversations and maintain a topic over a limited number of conversational turns. It is in late childhood, however, that people acquire a mature ability to converse for the exchange of information. Brown and Yule (1983) distinguish between *interactional discourse*, which serves primarily a social function, and *transactional discourse*, in which communicating information is the main purpose. (We will discuss these two types of discourse again in Chapter 8.) It is the latter type of discourse that develops in late childhood. Crucial to successful transactional discourse is the ability of the person who is speaking to evaluate the communication needs of the person being spoken to, an ability that develops only gradually during late childhood.

The ability to take to take another person's informational needs into account was studied by Anderson, Clark, and Mullin (1994) in an investigation of the ability of children aged 7 to 13 to give successful instructions to a partner. The children were divided into pairs, each of which had similar maps, but one map of the pair was slightly different. One child was the giver of information, the other the receiver. Their goal was to communicate the path between a starting and ending point. Of course, the children could not see one another's maps, so the information giver had to be alert to the information needs of the receiver, and the receiver had to be able to communicate information needs to the giver. While communication success improved with age, even the 13-year-olds were not completely skilled at perceiving the information needs of others and communicating their own information needs. We will revisit this experiment in Chapter 8.

An excellent example of the development of the ability to take into consideration the information needs of another is the child's use of pronouns. In order to communicate successfully, the referent of each pronoun must be recoverable by the person being spoken to. Young children are notorious for producing pronouns whose referents are ambiguous. Consider the following narrative of a young child reported by Shin (2006: 50; translation from Spanish by Shin):

(11)   Once upon a time there was a little pig that was called José and another, Carlos. One day he invited him to his house. After they sat on the rug to chat … after he invited him to his room, and they drew. He also showed him many toys that he had.

Clearly, it is impossible to identify any of the pronouns as referring uniquely to either José or Carlos. Beliavsky (1994) studied the ability of children from Kindergarten to fourth grade to use pronouns unambiguously in storytelling. While there was improvement with age, even the fourth graders used many ambiguous pronouns. The use of pronouns is what is called an *interface phenomenon*, which means that syntactic devices (in this case, pronouns) serve a non-linguistic goal (in this case, communication). The development of interface usage lags far behind basic acquisition of grammar.

Another aspect of language use that develops in late childhood is the ability to create a narrative, tell a story. Young children's narratives tend to be very simple, consisting of a few loosely connected sentences. Older children can construct narratives that have a simple plot: main characters, a problem, and a resolution. The ability to create narratives is closely related to the ability to conduct discourse. Both must have the characteristics of being coherent, in that each piece of the narrative, like each conversational turn, must relate clearly to a central theme or topic.

There is a great deal of individual variation in the ability to engage in transactional discourse and create cohesive narratives, not only among children, but among adults, as well. We all know adults who use ambiguous pronouns and are very bad at giving directions. Unlike grammatical development, whereby all individuals in a language community have acquired a complete grammar by the age of 4 or 5, mature communication skills are mastered at different ages by different children, and vary in adult speakers of a language.

Metalinguistic awareness

Probably the most important skill that develops in later childhood is metalinguistic awareness. The reason these skills are so important is that they are highly correlated with early reading ability. Metalinguistic skill is the awareness of language as an object, rather than simply as a vehicle for communication. Metalinguistic skills include the ability to appreciate and explain metaphors, puns, and figurative language. The person who is metalinguistically aware is able to think consciously about linguistic objects.

The metalinguistic skill most obviously related to early reading is *phonological awareness*, which is the ability to perceive speech as a string of phonological units. Phonemes are literally hiding inside the speech signal, which is continuous and highly variable because of the way speech is produced. When the child realizes that *cat* is composed of three separate phonological units, it is because the phonological units are represented as separate segments in the child's mind, not in the speech signal itself. When children learn to read, they must acquire letter–sound (grapheme–phoneme) correspondence so that they can decode written words. Phonological awareness allows children access to the phoneme part of that relationship. There are many tests of phonological awareness, all of which correlate with early reading skill (Adams 1990). One such test involves asking a child what word is created if a sound is removed from a word, such as taking the /s/ or the /p/ out of *spit*. Another test involves presenting an array of pictures, say of a pig, a pool, and a beak, pronouncing the words for the child, and then asking which begin with the same sound. The most difficult test of phonological awareness is teaching the child to tap once for each phoneme in a word. In such a test, one taps twice for *boo*, and three times for *boot* (Liberman et al. 1977). It is very important to provide children with large amounts of experience involving language, reading, rhyming, and word play, in order to enhance their metalinguistic skills and increase the probability that they will be successful early readers. Phonological awareness skills predict reading success in pre-readers, and instruction in phonological awareness assists children who are having difficulty learning to read.

The ability to *detect ambiguity* is also a metalinguistic skill that develops in the late preschool and early school years and is highly correlated with reading skill. Children of this age discover lexical ambiguity and become mad punsters. One study relates the ability to appreciate jokes that depend upon ambiguity with reading ability. For example, only children with strong reading abilities can appreciate jokes such as *How can hunters in the woods best find their lost dogs? By putting their ears to a tree and listening to the bark* (Hirsch-Pasek, Gleitman, and Gleitman 1978). Children below the age of 4 do not recognize that the word for a flying *bat* and the word for a baseball *bat* sound the same (Peters and Zaidel 1980), and many 4-year-olds cannot recognize the ambiguity of *The boys saw a bat in the park*. Structural ambiguities, like the one in (12), are more difficult for children to detect:

(12)   The girl tickled the baby with the stuffed animal.

Cairns, Waltzman, and Schlisselberg (2004) did a longitudinal study of ambiguity detection and early reading ability. They found that the children's ability to judge the ambiguity of lexically ambiguous sentences when they were pre-readers was a strong predictor of their reading ability at the end of second grade (ages 6–7). Furthermore, their ability to detect the ambiguity of structural ambiguities in second grade predicted their reading ability in third grade. The researchers suggested that ambiguity detection predicts reading skill because the same psycholinguistic processing operations are used in both. A subsequent study by Wankoff and Cairns (2009) demonstrated that ambiguity detection involves both sentence processing skill and metalinguistic ability. Chapters 6 and 7 will describe the psycholinguistic processing operations that are involved in sentence comprehension, which Cairns and colleagues (2004) argue are also employed in reading text. Zipke, Ehri, and Cairns (2009) demonstrated that teaching third graders to detect the dual meanings of homophones and ambiguous sentences improved their reading comprehension, and Shakibai (2007) demonstrated that Kindergarteners can also be taught to recognize homophones and lexically ambiguous sentences. It is entirely possible that ambiguity detection, like phonological awareness, will be employed in future reading readiness programs. Similarly, it could be used to identify children at risk for reading difficulty and as part of intervention programs for struggling readers.

A final metalinguistic skill is *awareness of ungrammaticality*: the ability to judge that a sentence is not well-formed, that it is ungrammatical. Some kinds of judgments are easier than others. Word order errors, like in (13a) are the easiest to detect. Errors of reflexive pronoun agreement, like in (13b), are also easy to detect. Errors in subject–verb agreement, like in (13c), are more difficult to recognize (Schlisselberg 1988).

(13)   a.   *Grover slid the slide down.
       b.   *Bert hurt herself.
       c.   *The horses is drinking water.

The ability to detect and correct grammatical errors is also highly correlated with early reading skill (Menyuk et al. 1991; Tunmer and Hoover 1992). Cairns et al. (2006) argue that the ability to detect the ungrammaticality of sentences and correct them is related to psycholinguistic processing skills.

Second Language Acquisition

In the sections above, **bilingual language acquisition** came up in various places. Children who are exposed to two languages simultaneously from birth are **bilingual (simultaneous) acquirers**. Other bilinguals acquire their two languages one after the other (**sequentially**). The study of how people learn languages after their first is called **second language acquisition** – even when the language being learned is the third, or fourth, or fifth.

A great deal of research on second language acquisition is concerned with identifying the similarities and differences between how people acquire their first and second languages. Developmental sequences are very similar in first and second language acquisition. Many early studies of second language acquisition focused on the morphosyntactic development of learners, and the general finding was that bound morphemes appear in the same order in the first and second language (Bardovi-Harlig 1999). Second language learners are also able to produce and process simple sentences before complex sentences (Pienemann et al. 2005), just like first language learners.

Some crucial differences exist between learning a first and a second language. The *pace of acquisition* (how quickly the learner makes progress) and the *level of ultimate attainment* (how proficient the learner eventually becomes) are both much more variable with the second compared to the first language. The development of a second language grammar can be influenced by forms in the first language, a phenomenon known as *transfer* (which we describe in Chapter 5), and certain deviations from the target language grammar will persist indefinitely in second language learners, a phenomenon known as *fossilization* (Han 2009). And as we discussed in Chapter 3, the level of ultimate attainment in second language acquisition is subject to age effects: older learners are not as good as younger learners, even though acquiring a second language as an adult is not impossible (Birdsong 2005).

There are proposals about these differences between first and second language acquisition that appeal to internal changes caused by maturation: as the learner gets older, the neurological mechanisms that support language acquisition change or atrophy, or both (Birdsong 2005). Other explanations have proposed that psycho-social or affective variables are the cause: older learners are psycho-socially distant from the culture of the target language (Schumann 1975), are afraid or embarrassed to make mistakes, or are not sufficiently motivated to learn the language (Gardner 1985). Another class of research has focused on differences in the input: older learners experience much less exposure to the target language than young children acquiring their first language, and the input older learners experience places greater communicative demands on them (VanPatten 1987). It is likely that combinations of these factors contribute to the overall observed differences between first and second language acquisition.

▮ Summing Up

The process of language acquisition is a natural unfolding of genetically based neurological organization in response to the linguistic experience of the environment. The lexicon and grammar develop according to principles and sequences that are common to all children and highly similar for all children acquiring the same language. Despite some complications, similar principles and sequences are also observed in second language learners. As language knowledge develops, so does the ability to put that knowledge to use in the production and comprehension of sentences and in the social use of language. Finally, the child develops awareness of the linguistic system as distinct from a vehicle for social interaction and communication. This awareness enables the child to grasp and use the written form of the language.

New Concepts

acquisition strategies
babbling
bilingual (simultaneous) language
   acquisition
constrained statistical learning
   framework
discriminate
environmental input
extendability principle (taxonomic
   assumption)
fast mapping
infant-directed speech
   (motherese)
Language Acquisition Device (LAD)
lexical learning principles
mean length of utterance (MLU)

mutual exclusivity assumption
nativist model of language
   acquisition
negative evidence
null subject parameter
one-word (holophrastic) stage
overextension
overgeneralize
positive evidence
predisposition to acquire
   language
second (sequential) language
   acquisition
underextension
vocabulary spurt
whole object assumption

Study Questions

1. What is the nativist claim about the nature of biologically based components in language acquisition?

2. How does Universal Grammar assist the child in acquiring language? How about acquisition principles?

3. What characteristics of the child's linguistic environment are important for language acquisition? What aspects are not important? What evidence exists to support this?

4. Describe how children approach the task of acquiring the phonemic inventory for their language. How is this process a metaphor for all of language acquisition?

5. Do bilingual language acquirers differentiate the phonemic inventories for each of their languages? Do they show syntactic differentiation, when the syntax differs between their two languages?

6. What are some of the principles of lexical learning that assist the child in acquiring a large lexicon very rapidly? Explain both what they are and how they are useful to the word-learning child.

7. There are individual differences in language acquisition among children learning the same language, as well as among children acquiring different languages. What kinds of variation would one expect to observe? What kinds of variation would one not expect to observe?

8. In general, what kinds of morphemes are acquired at an early age? What kinds are acquired at a later age?

9. How do metalinguistic abilities develop in the child? Why are they considered to be particularly important?

5 The Speaker: Producing Speech

The processes that underlie the production and comprehension of speech are information processing activities. The speaker's job is to encode an idea into an utterance. The utterance carries information the hearer will use to decode the speech signal, by building the linguistic representations that will lead to recovering the intended message. Encoding and decoding are essentially mirror images of one another. The speaker, on the one hand, knows what she intends to say; her task is to formulate the message into a set of words with a structural organization appropriate to convey that meaning, then to transform the structured message into intelligible speech. The hearer, on the other hand, must reconstruct the intended meaning from the speech produced by the speaker, starting with the information available in the signal.

In this and the next three chapters, we will describe the information processing operations performed rapidly and unconsciously by the speaker and the hearer, as well as the mental representations constructed by those operations. It is worth emphasizing that a hearer's successful recovery of a speaker's intention when uttering a sentence involves shared knowledge that goes well beyond knowledge of language and well beyond the basic meaning of a sentence – a topic we will explore in Chapter 8. But before we can examine contextualized language use, we describe the operations that use knowledge of language in encoding and decoding linguistic signals. This chapter focuses on production.

Since the mid-1970s, production has gradually become a central concern in the study of language performance (Bock 1991), alongside the study of perception. The sections that follow provide an introduction to some of that research. We will first discuss the components of a general model for language production. We will then describe the mental mechanisms that constrain how speakers encode ideas into mental representations of sentences, which are eventually uttered, written, or signed. The chapter concludes with details on how those mental representations are transformed into an acoustic speech signal.

■ A Model for Language Production

The production of a sentence begins with the speaker's intention to communicate an idea or some item of information. This has been referred to by Levelt (1989) as a **preverbal message**, because at this point the idea has not yet been cast into a linguistic form. Turning an idea into a linguistic representation involves mental operations that require consulting both the lexicon and the grammar shared by the speaker and hearer. Eventually, the mental representation must be transformed into a speech signal that will be produced fluently, at an appropriate rate, with a suitable prosody. There are a number of steps to this process, each associated with a distinct type of linguistic analysis and each carrying its own particular type of information. Figure 5.1 summarizes, from left to right, the processing operations performed by the speaker.

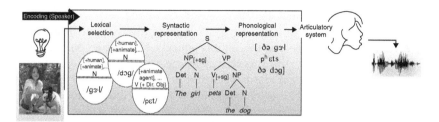

Figure 5.1 Diagram of some processing operations, ordered left to right, performed by the speaker when producing the sentence *The girl pets the dog*. (This figure expands on parts of Figure 1.3, Chapter 1.) Production begins with an idea for a message (the light bulb on the far left) triggering a process of lexical selection. The capsule-like figures represent lexical items for the words *girl*, *dog*, and *pet*, activated based on the intended meaning for the message; these include basic lexical semantic and morphosyntactic information (top half) and phonological form information (bottom half). The tree diagram in the center represents the sentence's syntactic form. The phonetic transcription to the right represents the sentence's eventual phonological form, sent on to the articulatory system, which produces the corresponding speech signal. The different representations are accessed and built very rapidly and with some degree of overlap.

The first step is to create a representation of a sentence meaning that will convey the speaker's intended message. This semantic representation triggers a lexical search for the words that can convey this meaning. (In Figure 5.1, the words *girl*, *dog*, and *pet* are activated.) The meaning of a sentence is a function of both its words and their structural organization (*The girl pets the dog* does not mean the same thing as *The dog pets the girl*), so another encoding stage involves assigning syntactic structure to the words retrieved from the lexicon. This process places the words into hierarchically organized constituents. Morphosyntactic rules add morphemes to satisfy grammatical requirements – for example, the requirement that a verb and its subject must agree in number. A phonological representation can then be created, "spelling out" the words as phonemes. Phonological and morphophonological rules then apply to produce a final string of phonological elements. This phonological representation will specify the way the sentence is to be uttered, including its prosodic characteristics. The final representation incorporates all the phonetic detail necessary for the actual production of the sentence. In this representation phonological segments are arranged in a linear sequence, one after the other, as if they were waiting in the wings of a theater preparing to enter the stage.

This representation is translated into instructions to the vocal apparatus from the motor control areas of the brain, and then neural signals are sent out to the muscles of the lips, tongue, larynx, mandible, and respiratory system to produce the actual speech signal.

Recall that Chapter 1 drew a number of important distinctions between language and speech, between language and other aspects of cognition (like general intelligence), and between language and communication. Language is a distinct, autonomous system that can be described without reference to other systems (as we did in Chapter 2). Yet the interaction of linguistic and non-linguistic systems, a recurring theme in this book, is key to understanding psycholinguistic processes. Psycholinguists disagree on some details regarding the nature and the degree of interaction between linguistic and non-linguistic systems, but that they do interact is uncontroversial. Sentence planning offers an excellent example of this phenomenon: the processes inside the gray box of Figure 5.1 use the speaker's knowledge of language to link ideas to signals, two non-linguistic and quite distinct representations. An idea is a product of the speaker's general cognition and intellect. Speech is a complex motor activity engaging the vocal tract and respiratory physiology. The elements outside the gray box – ideas, articulatory processes, and acoustic signals – are not part of language and do not have abstract linguistic representations (though they certainly have abstract non-linguistic properties). All of the representations inside the gray box of Figure 5.1 are abstract linguistic representations. Linguistic theory provides a vocabulary and a framework to represent syntactic structure, morphemes, and phonological segments.

The general model presented in Figure 5.1 can account for two aspects of language production not covered in this chapter: writing and signing. If a sentence is to be written rather than uttered, its phonological representation will be sent to the motor system responsible for engaging the hands either in handwriting or typing. Very little is known from a psycholinguistic perspective about the writing process, though occasionally psycholinguists employ writing as the medium for eliciting production. For signed languages, the phonological representation of a sentence will be very different than for spoken languages, and the articulation of that representation will be handled by a motor system that engages the hands and face to create gestures. Other than those differences, writing and signing involve the same stages of sentence planning as we will describe in detail below about speaking.

The model in Figure 5.1 – a much simplified version of models like Levelt's (1989) or Garrett's (1988), among others – has been refined empirically over the years. A great deal of what is known about the levels of production planning comes from analyses of **speech errors** (also called **slips of the tongue**) by Garrett (1980a, 1980b, 1988), Fromkin (1971, 1980, 1988), and others. This research draws on speech error corpora, collected by the investigators, by noting the occasions when they or their interlocutor produced a speech error. An **interlocutor** is a participant in a conversation. Other evidence comes from studies using a range of techniques to elicit speech production under controlled laboratory conditions; the objective of such work is to examine how fluent speech is produced, and what conditions cause fluent speech to break down.

Production in bilinguals and second language learners

Few adjustments need to be made to the working model in Figure 5.1 to account for production by people who speak two or more languages. We need to assume that a bilingual has two language-specific grammars, and a lexicon with language-specific entries, and we need to specify how these language-specific knowledge repositories are activated (or deactivated) – but that is all. When a bilingual is speaking in a **unilingual mode** (only one language), only one of the grammars is consulted to build structural representations, and the active language's lexical entries are activated. When in a **bilingual mode** (when the bilingual's two languages are being used in the same conversation), access to both grammars and lexical items from both languages must be possible (Grosjean 2001). Models of bilingual language production, like de Bot's (2004) or Green's (1986), incorporate mechanisms to control activation of the language or languages of the conversation (or inhibition of the language or languages not being used). Choosing what language (or languages) to activate during a conversation is guided by the speaker's communicative intent and other non-linguistic variables like conversation participants, topic, and context. (For more discussion of language choice, see Chapter 8.) The process resembles how a monolingual chooses between speaking formally or informally.

Importantly, the steps for production continue to be the same in both the unilingual and the bilingual mode of production, and for monolingual and bilingual speakers: lexical items are selected; a syntactic structure is built; a phonological representation is generated. However, knowledge of two languages has at least two important consequences for language production: it permits intentional switching from one language to the other, and it triggers occasional unintentional slips into a language not active in the conversation.

One type of alternation between languages in bilingual speech is **code-switching**. Code-switching is switching between two *codes* (two languages, or two distinct dialects of the same language) within the same discourse. A switch can take place between sentences (*intersentential code-switching*). A switch can also occur within the same sentence (*intrasentential code-switching*), at clause boundaries, or at smaller phrasal boundaries. A third category, *tag-switching*, involves the insertion of frequently used discourse markers, like *so, you know, I mean*, etc. (Lipski 2005). The example in (1), produced by a Spanish–English bilingual (cited by Romaine (1995: 164)), illustrates all three types of code-switching; the underlined phrases are translated below the example:

(1)   … they tell me 'How'd you quit, Mary?' I don't quit I … I just stopped. I mean it wasn't an effort that I made [a] <u>que voy a dejar de fumar por que me hace daño o</u> this or that uh-uh. It's just that I used to pull butts out of the waste paper basket yeah. I used to go look in the … [b] <u>se me acaban los cigarros en la noche</u>. I'd get desperate [c] <u>y ahí voy al basurero a buscar, a sacar,</u> you know.

      [a] 'that I'm going to quit smoking because it's harmful to me or'
      [b] 'I run out of cigarettes at night'
      [c] 'and so I go to the trash to look for, to get some out'

Code-switching is a discourse style that is most typical in bilinguals who are highly proficient speakers of both languages (Poplack 1980), which is not surprising: producing utterances that alternate between two languages requires sustained activation of the grammars and lexicons of each language, and of the rules that govern grammatical switching.

Code-switching generally serves a communicative function (Myers-Scotton 1988). A bilingual may switch to the other language to emphasize something just said, to quote something or someone, or to modify a statement further; code-switching can also be used to include or exclude an interlocutor, or to signal power relations between interlocutors. In the example in (1), the speaker switches into Spanish for the more personal parts of her message. In some bilingual speech communities, the default communication style when in a bilingual mode involves frequent alternation between two languages (Myers-Scotton 1988).

Code-switching is guided by the same production mechanisms involved in unilingual production. Research examining large code-switching corpora has demonstrated that naturally occurring code-switching is highly principled behavior (Myers-Scotton 1993). As such, code-switching offers insights about the cognitive architecture that supports bilingualism.

In Chapter 2 we used the phenomenon of **borrowing**, in which a word from one language is incorporated into the lexicon of another, to illustrate how a borrowed word might be transformed to conform with the phonotactic constraints of the incorporating language. Borrowing is also a feature of bilingual language use, and it is sometimes difficult to distinguish from code-switching. One difference between the two is the degree of integration of the guest word in the host language. A borrowed word (also called a *loan*) typically undergoes both orthographic and phonological adaptation into the host language; the example in (2a) illustrates orthographic adaptation (the loan in English is not capitalized and loses the umlaut over the third vowel). Loans are sometimes translated into an equivalent word in the host language, and are then called *loan translations* or *calques*; an example is in (2b). Bilinguals often borrow to fill lexical gaps in one of their languages. Loanwords sometimes become established in the language, and even monolinguals will begin to use them.

(2) a. doppelganger
         'ghostly counterpart of a person'
         (from German *Doppelgänger*)
     b. thought experiment
         (from German *Gedankenexperiment*)

It is important to distinguish between deliberate alternations, like code-switching or borrowing, and unintentional non-native-like elements in the speech of a second language learner. A second language grammar may differ – slightly or dramatically – from the grammar of a native monolingual speaker. No doubt, you have heard second language learners speak with an accent, use words in ways that do not match native speakers' intuitions, and even produce sentences with unusual syntax. Non-native-like production by second language learners can be the result of rules from the first language being incorporated into the second language, a phenomenon called **transfer**. Non-native-like production can also be linked to the use of acquisition strategies like overgeneralization (see Chapter 4).

▨ Planning Speech Before It Is Produced

Producing a sentence involves a series of distinct operations and representations: lexical, syntactic, morphological, and phonological. The following sections discuss some of the evidence that has led researchers to posit these different levels of production planning.

Accessing the lexicon

As mentioned above, the process of language production begins with an idea that is encoded into a semantic representation. This sets in motion a process called **lexical retrieval**. Remember that the lexicon is a dictionary of all the words a speaker knows. A lexical entry carries information about the meaning of the word, its grammatical class, the syntactic structures into which it can enter, and the sounds it contains (its phonemic representation). A word can be retrieved using two different kinds of information: meaning or sound. The speaker retrieves words based on the meaning to be communicated and has the task of selecting a word that will be appropriate for the desired message. The word must also be of the appropriate grammatical class (noun, verb, etc.) and must be compatible with the structure that is being constructed. It is most certainly not the case that the structure is constructed before the words are selected, nor are all the words selected before the structure is constructed. In fact, the words and the structure are so closely related that the two processes take place practically simultaneously. Ultimately, the speaker must retrieve a lexical item that will convey the correct meaning and fit the intended structure. This means that a speaker must enter the lexicon via information about meaning, grammatical class, and structure, only later to retrieve the phonological form of the required word. The hearer's task, which will be discussed in detail in the next chapter, is the mirror image of the speaker's. The hearer must process information about the sound of the word and enter his lexicon to discover its form class, structural requirements, and meaning.

Important psycholinguistic questions concern the organization of the lexicon and how it is accessed for both production and comprehension. The speed of conversational speech varies by many factors, including age (younger people speak faster than older people), sex (men speak faster than women), nativeness (native speakers are faster than second language speakers), topic (familiar topics are talked about faster than unfamiliar ones), and utterance length (longer utterances have shorter segment durations than shorter ones); on average, though, people produce 100 to 300 words per minute (Yuan, Liberman, and Cieri 2006), which, at the slower end, is between 1 and 5 words (or 10 to 15 phonetic elements) per second. (Notice that this includes the time it takes to build syntactic and phonological representations and to move the articulators, not just time actually spent in lexical retrieval.) Clearly, the process of accessing words is extremely rapid.

According to Miller and Gildea (1987), adults with a high school education know around 40,000 words. All the different versions of a single word count as one word. For example, *write, writer, writes, written,* and *writing* together count as one word. If one adds to that total another 40,000 proper names of people and places, the adult lexicon is estimated to contain around 80,000 words. If each word a person uses must be retrieved from a bank of 80,000 in less than half a second, it is obvious that the processes employed in lexical retrieval must be extremely efficient, and these processes are affected by the way the lexicon is organized.

One way the lexicon is organized is by frequency of use, a topic we will explore in more detail in Chapter 6. During production, more common words are retrieved more rapidly: for example, it is easier and faster to retrieve the word *knife* than the word *dagger*. Studies of pauses and hesitations in speech have shown that hesitations often occur before low-frequency words (Levelt 1983).

Words are also organized by their meaning, so close associates are stored near one another. Speech errors can give some insight into this meaning-based organization. It is extremely common for a word retrieval error to result in the selection of a semantically and structurally similar word. Consider the following examples:

(3)   a.   I just feel like whipped cream and mushrooms.
          {I just feel like whipped cream and strawberries.}
      b.   All I want is something for my elbows.
          {All I want is something for my shoulders.}
      c.   Put the oven on at a very low speed.
          {Put the oven on at a very low temperature.}
      d.   I hate … I mean, I *love* dancing with you!

(In all examples of speech errors in this chapter, the intended utterance is in curly brackets, beneath the actual utterance containing the slip.) In each of the examples in (3), the speaker has erroneously selected a word that is of the same grammatical class (nouns) and that shares many aspects of meaning with the intended word. This kind of error is very common and is probably responsible for many of the so-called *Freudian slips* that people make, such as the one in (3d). However, rather than representing a repressed desire for mushrooms or a secret loathing of one's dance partner, the errors in (3) are more likely driven by the fact that words sharing semantic features are stored together. Antonyms – words that are the opposite of one another, like *love* and *hate* – actually share a great many aspects of meaning. *Love* and *hate* are both verbs that refer to internalized feelings one person can have about another; the only difference between them is that they refer to distinct (and opposite) feelings. Speech errors often involve the production of *forget* instead of *remember*, *give* instead of *take*, and so on.

Sometimes words that sound alike are implicated in speech errors, like the following:

(4) a. If you can find a gargle around the house ...
         {If you can find a garlic around the house ...}
     b. We need a few laughs to break up the mahogany.
         {We need a few laughs to break up the monotony.}
     c. Passengers needing special assistance, please remain comfortably seated until all passengers have complained ... uh, deplaned.

In these errors, the grammatical class of the intended and the intruding word is the same, even though the meaning is completely different. Errors like these suggest that words are organized by phonological structure, forming "neighborhoods" of words that sound similar.

Semantically based and phonologically based errors, like those in (3) and (4), respectively, provide evidence for the distinction between two components of lexical representations discussed in Chapter 2: meaning-based and form-based.

A phenomenon in lexical retrieval that has fascinated psycholinguists for decades is the **tip-of-the-tongue phenomenon** (Brown and McNeill 1966; Aitchison 2003). A tip-of-the-tongue state occurs when the speaker knows the word needed but cannot quite retrieve it. It is a very uncomfortable mental state, and when people experience it, they might say "I've got that word right on the tip of my tongue!" What people experience during a tip-of-the-tongue state offers a glimpse into the steps involved in lexical retrieval. Typically, people have access to the meaning-based part of the lexical representation, but experience a tip-of-the-tongue state when they fail to find a fully specified form-based representation (Bock and Levelt 1994). However, people typically know something about the word they are unsuccessfully searching for. They can often think of the initial or final sounds or letters, how many syllables it has, where primary stress is located, and even words that sound similar. People experiencing a tip-of-the-tongue state will often also perform gestures that are suggestive of the meaning of the word, though it is not necessarily the case that gesturing helps retrieval (Beattie and Coughlan 1999).

While no one really understands tip-of-the-tongue states, it is a phenomenon that demonstrates that when people enter the lexicon through meaning, in order to produce a word, a great deal of information may be available even if the entire representation of the word is not retrieved. Tip-of-the-tongue states, of course, are a rare occurrence, as are lexical retrieval errors like the ones in (3) and (4). Usually lexical retrieval produces an appropriate set of words required for the speaker's sentence.

Building simple sentence structure

Levelt (1989) refers to the creation of sentence structure during sentence planning as **grammatical encoding**. For this the speaker must consult the internalized grammar to construct structures that will convey the intended meaning. Again, speech errors provide information about some of the characteristics of the representations that are constructed.

We know, for instance, that words are represented as separate units. Speech errors like the ones in (5) provide evidence for this:

(5)   a.   I left the briefcase in my cigar.
          {I left the cigar in my briefcase.}
      b.   ... rubber pipe and lead hose ...
          {... rubber hose and lead pipe ...}

These examples illustrate a common type of error, **exchange errors**; the exchange units here are two words. **Word exchange errors** never occur between content words and function words and are usually limited to words of the same grammatical class, nouns in the case of the examples above.

An exchange error can involve units larger than individual words. Such errors provide evidence that sentences are organized structurally during language production. Constituents that are larger than words, but which are units in the hierarchical organization of the sentence, can exchange with one another. Consider the following error:

(6)   The Grand Canyon went to my sister.
      {My sister went to the Grand Canyon.}

A noun phrase, *the Grand Canyon*, has changed places with another noun phrase, *my sister*. Thus, a constituent larger than an individual word has moved. Movement of two words that are not part of the same constituent is never observed. An error such as *The grand my sister to canyon went* would never be produced. In speech errors, syntactically defined constituents are moved, and the resulting sentences are always structurally well-formed sentences of English.

Exchange errors also demonstrate the existence of a level of representation where bound morphemes are represented separately from their stems, as the following examples illustrate:

(7) a. He had a lot of guns in that bullet.
         {He had a lot of bullets in that gun.}
     b. You ordered up ending.
         {You ended up ordering.}
     c. We roasted a cook.
         {We cooked a roast.}
     d. ... gownless evening straps ...
         {... strapless evening gowns ...}

In (7a), *gun* and *bullet* have been exchanged, but the plural morpheme *–s* appears in the intended structural position. In (7b), the words *end* and *order* have been exchanged, but the morphemes *–ed* and *–ing* appear in their intended structural positions. The same type of analysis applies to (7c), in which *roast* and *cook* have been exchanged, but the morpheme *–ed* has not moved. These examples suggest that while speech errors may produce sentences with odd meanings, they rarely produce structurally bizarre sentences. The error in (7b), for instance, was not *You ordering up ended*, as it would have been if the bound morphemes and the stem had formed a unit at the time of exchange.

How are errors like those in (7) possible? Free morphemes, and the bound morphemes that attach to them, are separate units in the mental representations built during sentence production. Inflectional morphemes, like *–s*, *–ed*, and *–ing*, are added to specific structural positions, based on the syntax of the sentence, rather than based on the words they eventually attach to. The error in (7d) suggests that much the same applies to derivational morphemes, like *–less*. There is a level of representation at which free and bound morphemes are represented separately.

Errors like those in (7) also suggest that morphemes are added to the mental representation before morphophonological rules operate to specify the phonetic form by which the morpheme will be realized. The example in (7c) is particularly relevant. (Notice that (7c) might initially appear to contradict the observation that only words of the same grammatical class are exchangeable, since *cook* is a verb and *roast* is a

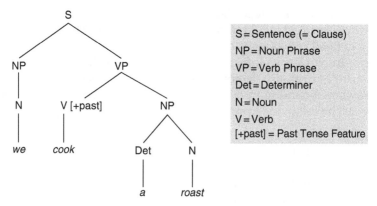

Figure 5.2   Representation of a past tense morpheme before the application of morphophonological rules.

noun. However, both words can be either a noun or a verb, so the example is not a contradiction.) The past tense morpheme –*ed* differs in the way it is pronounced depending upon the final segment of the verb to which it is attached. The past tense morpheme on *cook* surfaces as [t], while on *roast* it surfaces as [ɪd]. In the speech error in (7c), the past tense feature is "spelled out" according to morphophonological rules attaching it to *roast*. Clearly, *roast* and *cook* were exchanged before morphophonological rules applied. The exchange error resulting in (7c) thus provides evidence for a level of representation as shown in Figure 5.2, where past tense is an abstract feature in the syntactic structure, but the morpheme that marks past has not yet been added to the word *cook*. The words were exchanged at a processing level before morphophonological rules had applied. If the exchange error had occurred at a later processing stage, the sentence would have been uttered as *We roast a cooked*. Such a speech error would never occur.

The following speech error illustrates a similar interplay of morphology and phonology:

(8)   If you give the nipple an infant ...
       {If you give the infant a nipple ...}

In this example, *nipple* and *infant* have been exchanged before the morphophonological rule specifying the pronunciation of the indefinite determiner has applied. The determiner would have been pronounced *a* before *nipple*, but instead became *an*, given the initial segment of *infant*. Had the exchange error occurred after the application of the morphophonological rule, the resulting sentence would have been **If you give the nipple a infant*.

Creating agreement relations

The errors we have described so far illustrate aspects of sentence planning related to placing lexical material in structural positions in a syntactic representation. There is another class of errors, which has been studied extensively in English and several other languages, involving subject–verb agreement. These errors are informative about the role of agreement features in production planning and execution.

Agreement is a requirement of the grammar, with some very language-specific properties. English requires that verbs and their subjects agree in number (and person). Since English has limited morphology, number agreement is only marked (by a bound morpheme) on verbs with third person singular subjects, like (9a), or on subjects when they are plural, like (9b):

(9) a. The bridge closes at seven.
     b. The bridges close at seven.

Other languages have richer morphology for agreement, and require not only agreement of number and person features, but also of gender features. (Examples of some of these are in Chapter 2.) Many languages require agreement between verbs and their subjects, and some languages also require agreement between verbs and their objects.

For an English speaker, producing sentences with grammatical number agreement is relatively straightforward, with one important exception. When a plural feature intervenes between a singular subject and its verb, the phenomenon of **plural attraction** can trigger an error, like the following:

(10) a. The time for fun and games are over.
      b. The illiteracy level of our children are appalling.

In a landmark series of experiments, Bock and Miller (1991) presented English speakers with pre-recorded audio sentence preambles like the ones in (11); the participants' task was to complete the sentences as quickly as possible.

(11) a. The bridge to the islands ...
      b. The bridges to the island ...
      c. The bridge to the island ...
      d. The bridges to the islands ...

Bock and Miller found that in the sentence completions produced by participants, agreement errors were about ten times more likely with preambles like (11a) than any of the other three. (Bear in mind that the overall proportion of errors in the experiments was always extremely low, typically below 2 percent.) Errors like *The bridge to the islands close at seven* are frequent, not only in speech but also in all sorts of writing – from unedited student essays to heavily edited periodicals and books. The effect has also been replicated in dozens of studies, not only in English but also in a number of other languages, including French, Dutch, Italian, and Spanish (Vigliocco et al. 1996).

Evidently, there is something special about plural morphemes. When the structural path between a singular verb and its subject is interrupted by a plural feature, an error is more likely than when a singular feature interrupts the path between a plural verb and its subject. Applying grammatical constraints in real time is something we are able to do automatically and without conscious effort, but certain configurations, structures like those in (10) and (11a), are more likely to trigger errors.

Plural attraction errors are yet another instance of the interplay between linguistic and non-linguistic information; the *marking and morphing* model developed by Kay Bock and colleagues (Bock et al. 2001) makes some explicit links between intended meanings and the linguistic representations created during sentence production. Plurality is assigned to nouns based on the intended meaning, a process called *number marking*. A separate process, called *number morphing*, adds number features to verbs, based on the subject they must agree with. Attraction errors emerge during number morphing.

Building complex structure

A major goal of grammatical encoding is to create a syntactic structure that will convey the meaning the speaker intends. This requires accessing the speaker's grammar. In Chapter 2 we noted that one of the tasks of the grammar is to combine simple sentences into complex, multi-clausal sentences. It turns out that this function of the grammar has a number of important psycholinguistic ramifications. Ferreira (1991) compared speech initiation times associated with sentences with a simple subject NP, such as (12a), to sentences with complex subjects, such as (12b) (which contains a relative clause), and found that speech initiation times for sentences with complex subjects were significantly longer than for sentences with simple subjects.

(12)   a.   The large and raging river ...
       b.   The river that stopped flooding ...

This finding, replicated by Tsiamtsiouris and Cairns (2009), indicates that planning complex sentence structure recruits more computational resources than does planning simple structures.

In the production of complex sentences, the clause appears to be the primary planning unit. Most speech errors that involve two elements – like the exchanges discussed above, and some other error types discussed below – take place within a single clause. This suggests that sentences are organized in clause-sized bundles before they are produced. Not surprisingly, clause boundaries have been identified as loci for sentence planning. Numerous studies report more pauses at the beginnings of clauses than within them (Boomer 1965; Ford 1978; Beattie 1980; Butterworth 1980), indicating the presence of planning processes. McDaniel, McKee, and Garrett (2010) elicited sentences containing relative clauses from children and adults, and found that pauses clustered at the clause boundaries.

Evidence for increased production planning cost associated with subject–object relative clauses (described in Chapter 4, sentence (7a)) comes from a study by Tsiamtsiouris, Cairns, and Frank (2007), who report longer speech initiation times for sentences with subject–object relatives than for sentences with object–subject relative clauses (like (7b) in Chapter 4). Tsiamtsiouris and colleagues (2007) also observed longer speech initiation times for passive sentences than active sentences, suggesting that producing sentences that are out of canonical word order increases planning cost.

The phenomenon of **syntactic priming** provides further insight into the mechanisms of production planning. Bock (1986) and Bock and Griffin (2000) described an effect they referred to as *syntactic persistence*, by which a particular sentence form has a higher probability of occurrence if the speaker has recently heard a sentence of that form. For example, if you call your local supermarket and ask *What time do you close?*, the answer is likely to be something like *Seven*, but if you ask *At what time do you close?*, the response is likely to be *At seven* (Levelt and Kelter 1982). Speakers (and hearers) automatically adapt themselves to the language around them, and as a consequence align their utterances interactively to those produced by their interlocutors; this process of *interactive alignment* has the useful consequence of simplifying both production and comprehension (Pickering and Garrod 2004). Syntactic priming studies are designed to explore to what extent a structure just heard can affect the structure for an utterance being planned. They exploit the fact that certain messages can be structured more than one way, as illustrated by the following examples (from Chapter 2):

(13)   a.   Robert gave a cashmere sweater to his girlfriend.
     b.   Robert gave his girlfriend a cashmere sweater.

(14)   a.   John hit the ball.
     b.   The ball was hit by John.

The example in (13) illustrates alternation between prepositional and double-object datives; the example in (14) illustrates the alternation between actives and passives. In syntactic priming experiments, participants are asked to describe images depicting scenes such as those described by (13) or (14). Prior to their descriptions, participants have just heard (either from a recording, or from an investigator or another participant in the experiment) a different sentence containing one of the structures of interest. For example, a person asked to describe a picture of John hitting a ball might have just heard a completely different sentence structured as active (e.g., *Mary is eating the cherries*) or passive (e.g., *The cherries are being eaten by Mary*). The sentence just heard will prime the structure of the sentence being produced; that is, the participant's description of the target picture will be more likely to match the structure of the prime sentence just heard.

Syntactic priming has been used to study a number of aspects of production. One such aspect is production complexity. Smith and Wheeldon (2001) demonstrated that production is facilitated for a structure that has just been heard; speech initiation times were shorter for sentences with primed structures than for those with unprimed structures. Tsiamtsiouris and Cairns (2009) replicated those findings. Another question pursued by this line of research is what psychological mechanisms underlie syntactic priming. A common view is that once a particular structure has been constructed, it remains for some time as a memory trace and facilitates the construction of a similar structure.

Syntactic priming is a robust effect, which has even been documented across languages, when the two languages involved have comparable alternative structures. Studies that have examined priming between languages, with bilinguals or second language learners, have confirmed that the structure of an utterance heard in one language can affect the structure of an utterance produced in another language (Loebell and Bock 2003; Hartsuiker, Pickering, and Veltkamp 2004). The study of syntactic priming between languages contributes to current models of the type of cognitive architecture that supports some of the linguistic behaviors bilinguals can engage in: code-switching, borrowing, and transfer (Loebell and Bock 2003). If structures in one language can prime structures in another language, the two languages of a bilingual are not impermeable and fully separate; instead, the same language production mechanism (susceptible to what the system has previously perceived) is recruited for language production, regardless of the language of the utterance.

Preparing a phonological representation

The mental representation of a sentence that serves as input to the systems responsible for articulation (speech, writing, or gestures) is phonological. Some examples of slips of the tongue discussed earlier reflect the application of morphophonological rules, as a phonological representation for a sentence is prepared during production. There is an entire class of speech errors involving units of analysis that are smaller than phrases or words or morphemes, and these errors shed further light on the nature of the phonological representations built during language production. Consider the following:

(15) a. hass or grash
          {hash or grass}
      b. I can't cook worth a cam.
          {I can't cook worth a damn.}
      c. taddle tennis
          {paddle tennis}

The example in (15a) is an example of a **segment exchange error**, in which the exchange is between two phonological elements: the final consonants in the two words. In (15b), we have an example of a **perseveration error**, in which a segment (in this case the /k/ of *can't*) perseveres and intrudes in a later word (so the speaker utters *cam* rather than *damn*). In (15c), the example is of an **anticipation error**, in which a speech sound that has not yet been produced (the /t/ of *tennis*) intrudes in an earlier word.

Speech errors involving phonological segments never create phonemes that are not part of the phonemic inventory of the speaker's language, nor do they create words that violate the phonotactic or phonological rules of the speaker's language. A speaker might slip and say *tips of the slung*, but never **tlips of the sung*, because in the latter a sequence has been created that violates phonotactic constraints for English (Fromkin 1973). There are many other phonologically based regularities connected with speech errors. Consonants and vowels never substitute for one another, and substitutions and exchanges take place only between elements that are phonologically similar.

Errors like those in (15) demonstrate that there is a level of representation in which phonological elements are represented segmentally. Such errors are revealing about the psychological reality of linguistic representations before sound is produced. Errors like these – anticipation errors in particular – demonstrate that there is a mental representation containing the phonological form of a sentence, some time before a sentence is actually produced. This representation is quite abstract, as illustrated by the following exchanges, where what is exchanged is not a full phonological segment but only some of its phonological features:

(16) a. pig and vat
          {big and fat}
      b. spattergrain
          {scatterbrain}

In (16a), what is exchanged is voicing: voiced /b/ is produced as voiceless [p], and voiceless /f/ is produced as voiced [v]. In (16b), place of articulation is exchanged: velar /k/ becomes bilabial [p], and bilabial /b/ becomes velar [g].

A final type of word exchange errors, in (17), illustrates that prosodic information is also supplied by the mental representation of a sentence, independently of the lexical items involved, but based on the syntactic structure of the sentence. This includes information about which words in the sentence will receive prosodic prominence (words with a focus accent are in capital letters):

(17) a. When the PAPER hits the story ...
          {When the STORY hits the paper ...}
      b. Stop beating your BRICK against a head wall.
          {Stop beating your HEAD against a brick wall.}

In (17a), a focus accent occurred on *paper*, which landed in the same position in the sentence as *story* should have been: prosodic prominence applied based on the structure of the clause, rather than based on being associated with a particular lexical item. Put a different way, the focus accent – being associated with the structure of the sentence, rather than a particular word – did not move with the lexical item. If that had happened, the result would have been *When the paper hits the STORY*. The same phenomenon is illustrated in (17b), where again the prosodic prominence is associated not with a particular word but with a particular structural position in the sentence.

Summary: Sentence planning

Sentence planning is the link between the idea the speaker wishes to convey and the linguistic representation that expresses that idea. It must include words organized into an appropriate syntactic structure, as sentence meaning depends upon lexical items and their structural organization. From speech errors we have evidence for the psycholinguistic representation of words and their phonological forms, the representation of morphemes, and levels of sentence planning. Experiments that elicit various types of sentences offer evidence that clauses are planning units, and that multiple factors influence the resources recruited in sentence production.

The sentence planning process ends with a sentence represented phonologically (at both the segmental and suprasegmental level), to which phonological and morphophonological rules have applied to create a detailed phonetic representation of the sentence, which now needs to be transformed into an actual signal, an utterance. This is the topic of the next section.

Producing Speech After It Is Planned

The abstract phonetic representation of the speaker's sentence is sent to the central motor areas of the brain, where it is converted into instructions to the vocal tract to produce the required sounds. Speaking is an incredibly complex motor activity, involving over 100 muscles moving in precise synchrony to produce speech at a rate of 10 to 15 phonetic units per second (Liberman et al. 1967). During silence, the amount of time needed for inhaling is about the same as for exhaling. Respiration during speech is very different: the time for inhaling is drastically reduced, sometimes to less than half a second, and much more time is spent exhaling, sometimes up to several seconds. During speech, air from the lungs must be released with exactly the correct pressure. The respiratory system works with the muscles of the larynx to control the rate of vibration of the vocal folds, providing the necessary variations in pitch, loudness, and duration for the segmental (consonants and vowels) and suprasegmental (prosody) content of the utterance. Muscles of the lips, the tongue, and other articulators must be carefully coordinated. Much precision of planning is required. For example, to make the vowel sound [u], different sets of nerves lower the larynx and round the lips. Impulses travel at different rates down those two sets of nerves, so timing must be carefully orchestrated: one impulse must be sent a fraction of a millisecond sooner than the other. This is an example of the level of planning carried out by the central planning system in the brain.

In this section, we examine how vowels and consonants are produced, with a focus on how the articulation of speech converts a sequence of discrete mental units (a phonological representation) into a continuous acoustic signal. The signal, as the end product for the speaker and the starting point for the hearer, must contain sufficient information for successful decoding. Our objective, then, is to identify some of the characteristics of the signal which carry information that will be used by the hearer.

The source-filter model of vowel production

Speech consists of sounds generated at the vocal folds being filtered as they travel through the vocal tract. (Figure 5.3 repeats a diagram used in Chapter 2, identifying the organs involved in producing speech, for your reference while reading this section.) The **source–filter model** of vowel production breaks down the process of producing vowels into two component parts: a source and a filter.

We will illustrate how the source–filter model works by considering the vowels [i], [a], and [u]. To articulate these vowels, you open your mouth and force air from your lungs through your larynx, where the vocal folds reside. This causes the vocal folds to vibrate – that is, to open and close in rapid sequence. The frequency of this vibration is called the **fundamental frequency** (or F_0), and this is, in essence, the **source** in the source–filter model of speech production. Sounds with higher frequency are higher in **pitch**, pitch being the perceptual

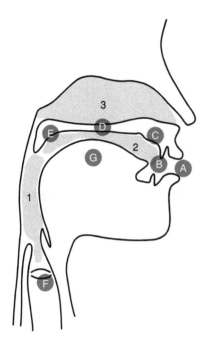

Articulators:

A. Lips (bilabial sounds)

B. Teeth (labiodental and dental sounds)

C. Alveolar ridge (alveolar sounds)

D. Hard palate (palatal sounds)

E. Velum, soft palate (velar sounds,
   and nasal/oral distinction)

F. Larynx, vocal folds, glottis (glottal sounds)

G. Tongue

Cavities:

1. Pharyngeal

2. Oral

3. Nasal

Figure 5.3   Diagram of the vocal tract, identifying the organs involved in producing speech (articulators) and the spaces in which speech sounds resonate (cavities). This figure repeats Figure 2.1 from Chapter 2.

correlate of fundamental frequency. Overall, men have lower pitch than women, who in turn have lower pitch than children (Katz and Assmann 2001). These differences are directly related to sex- and age-based differences in size of physique. In general, smaller vocal folds vibrate at a higher frequency, so people with small larynxes speak with higher overall pitch. Different vowels also vary in pitch: high vowels like [i] and [u] tend to have higher fundamental frequency than low vowels like [a] (Whalen and Levitt 1995). However, it is not F_0 that serves to distinguish vowels from one another – after all, hearers distinguish between vowels uttered with high pitch just as well as between vowels uttered with low pitch. Vowels are distinct from each other based on their acoustic form, or spectral properties, which we describe below.

A tuning fork creates a *simple* sound, with energy at a single frequency. The left panel of Figure 5.4 shows some of the acoustic characteristics of a simple sound, a computer-generated pure tone: its waveform is evenly sinusoid (a sine wave) and its spectrogram has

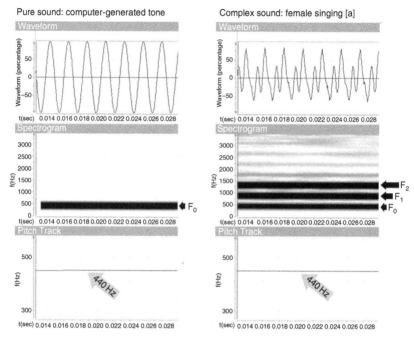

Figure 5.4 Waveform, spectrogram, and pitch track for a computer-generated pure tone (left panel) and a human-articulated complex tone (right panel). The two bottom graphs indicate that both tones have the same pitch, 440 Hz – which happens to be the pitch for the note called Concert A (the A above middle C). Notice how the waveform of the computer-generated pure tone is perfectly sinusoid, unlike the waveform of the human-generated complex tone. Notice also, by comparing the spectrograms, that the pure tone has only one band of energy (the fundamental frequency, F_0), while the complex sound has multiple bands of energy, the strongest being the fundamental frequency (F_0), and the first two formants (F_1 and F_2).

only one band of energy, the one corresponding to the tone's F_0. Yet most sounds people hear on a daily basis – speech, music, and so on – are *complex*. A **complex acoustic signal** is one that has energy at many frequencies in addition to the fundamental frequency. The graphs in the right panel of Figure 5.4 correspond to another tone, with the same fundamental frequency as the pure tone, only this one was produced by a female singing the vowel [a]. The complex sound wave generated by the vibrations of the human vocal folds is a complex sound, with acoustic energy at many frequencies. The frequencies carrying acoustic energy are multiples of the fundamental frequency of the voice. So a person who is speaking with a fundamental frequency of 150 cycles per second (cps) – also referred to as 150 Hertz (Hz) – will produce a complex sound wave with energy at 300 cps, 450 cps, 600 cps, and so forth. These bands of energy are called **harmonics**. For a given speech sound, the F_0 and its **formants** – which we will define in a moment – are the sound's **spectral properties**.

How to read waveform graphs, spectrograms, and pitch track graphs

Some of the figures in this chapter (and elsewhere in the book) incorporate images generated by acoustic analysis software. The software we used is *Speech Analyzer* (SIL International 2007); other similar tools include *Computerized Speech Lab* (KayPENTAX 2008) and *Praat* (Boersma and Weenink 2009).

The figures contain waveforms, spectrograms, and pitch tracks for audio recordings illustrating various types of sounds. **Waveform** graphs, also called *oscillograms*, display time horizontally and air pressure variations vertically. **Spectrograms** display the spectral properties of the recorded sounds. A spectrogram plots information along three dimensions: time is displayed horizontally, frequency (in Hz) is displayed vertically, and energy intensity is indicated by shades of gray (the darker the gray, the more intense the energy). Finally, **pitch track** graphs give an estimate of pitch movements by plotting time on the horizontal axis and fundamental frequency (in Hz) on the vertical axis.

Key to understanding how the vocal tract acts as a **filter** is the concept of **resonance**. The vocal tract changes shape when different sounds are articulated. For example, when the vowels [i] and [u] are articulated, the tongue body is relatively high, compared to when [a] is articulated; the tongue body is farthest in the front of the mouth when articulating [i], slightly farther back for [a], and farthest in the back for [u]. For these three vowels, then, the oral and pharyngeal cavities are shaped slightly differently, relative to each other. Consequently, for a sound generated at the vocal folds traveling through these differently shaped cavities, some harmonics will be reinforced, and other harmonics will be cancelled. In other words, energy at some frequencies will increase, and energy at other frequencies be eliminated. This is resonance.

Figure 5.5 shows plots of the average fundamental frequency and two bands of reinforced harmonics (**formants**) associated with the vowels [i], [a], and [u], as produced by four different speakers. The formant with the lowest frequency is called the **first formant (F_1)**,

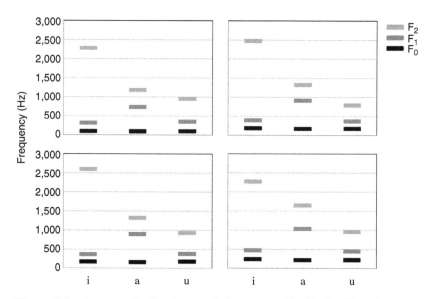

Figure 5.5   Average F_0 (fundamental frequency, black), F_1 (first formant, medium gray), and F_2 (second formant, light gray), for the vowels [i], [a], and [u], as uttered by four speakers of American English: an adult male (top left), an adult female (top right), a young male (12 years old, bottom left), and a young female (11 years old, bottom right).

the second lowest is the **second formant (F_2)**. While all four speakers have different F_0 averages (the adult male has the lowest, 180 Hz on average, the young female the highest, 221 Hz on average), the pattern for F_1 and F_2 with respect to each other and with respect to F_0 is remarkably similar. Figure 5.5 sketches only F_1 and F_2 because those two formants are sufficient to illustrate the distinctions between our example vowels. In Figure 5.5, it is clear that [a] has a much higher F_1 than [i] or [u]; [i] is distinct from [u] because it has a very high F_2.

The vowels [i], [u], and [a] are often called *point vowels* because they represent the maximal extent of F_1 and F_2 variation. A graph plotting these two dimensions relative to each other, also called a *vowel triangle*, is presented in Figure 5.6. All of the world's languages have, at minimum, these three vowels, but many languages have several others, representing other combinations of F_1 and F_2 within the vowel space. Resonance depends on the size and shape of the filter – the cavities a sound travels through. F_1 and F_2 thus vary based on the size and shape of the pharyngeal and oral cavities, the size of which is determined by the position of the tongue. F_1 correlates with the width of the pharyngeal

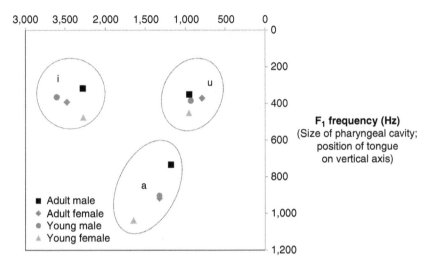

Figure 5.6 F_1 and F_2 data from Figure 5.5, plotted together to represent the vowel triangle. If you connect the dots from [i] to [u] to [a] and back to [i], for the data points corresponding to each of the speakers, you will come up with an upside-down triangle for each. The horizontal and vertical axes in the graph are plotted in reverse, so that the high front vowel is plotted on the top left, as in conventional vowel charts.

cavity and with the position of the tongue on a vertical axis: F_1 frequency is higher when the pharynx is narrow and the tongue is low, as with the low vowel [a]. F_2, in contrast, correlates with the length of the front of the oral cavity and the position of the tongue on a horizontal axis: F_2 frequency is higher when the oral cavity is short and the tongue is forward in the mouth, as in the production of [i]. The vowel [u] has a low F_2 because the oral cavity is elongated, as the lips are rounded and the larynx is lowered.

The exact frequencies of the formants will differ from speaker to speaker, generally being higher for women than for men. For instance, Kent (1997) reports – based on data from Hillenbrand et al. (1995) – an average F_1 and F_2 for the vowel [i] for male speakers of 342 Hz and 2,322 Hz, respectively. For female speakers, the formants average 437 Hz and 2,761 Hz. Exact frequencies will also differ in rapid speech, because the articulators might not have time to reach their target position. However, the relationship between F_1 and F_2 will be the same for vowels in every speech situation.

Acoustic characteristics of consonants

A complete description of the **acoustic characteristics** of speech sounds is beyond the scope of this book, but there are some general properties of certain classes of consonants that are worth pointing out. Table 5.1 has additional details and examples. In Chapter 2 we distinguished between obstruent and sonorant consonants. We use this distinction here again. Obstruents are characterized by an obstruction in the vocal tract during articulation. Full closure followed by release is the characteristic feature of **stops**, like [p] and [t]. The acoustic indicator of closure is silence.

A feature distinguishing between many consonants is voicing. For voiced sounds, like [z], the vocal folds are engaged during the articulation of the consonant. For voiceless sounds, like [s], voicing will not begin until the vowel that follows is articulated. The acoustic indicator of voicing is fundamental frequency. For stops, like [b] and [p], the key acoustic indicator of voicing is *voice onset time* (frequently abbreviated as *VOT*). VOT is the time between the release of closure of a stop and the onset of voicing. Voiced stops have very short VOTs, while voiceless stops have relatively longer VOTs. In Chapter 6, we will discuss how the continuous variation in VOT is perceived categorically by speakers of different languages.

Fricatives, like [s] and [ʃ] are produced by creating turbulence as air is forced through two articulators, a sound much like the hiss of white noise; the acoustic indicator of such turbulence is high-frequency noise. Articulating the third class of obstruent consonants, **affricates**, like [tʃ] and [dʒ], involves combining a stop and a fricative. Affricates, therefore, have acoustic properties of both stops and fricatives: silence followed by sustained high-frequency noise.

Sonorants, being close to vowels in their articulation, are close to vowels in their acoustic form, and therefore have the characteristic formant configurations of vowels. In articulating **nasals**, like [n], [m], and [ŋ], the velum – the flap that opens and closes the opening between the nasal cavity and the oral cavity – is lowered; as a result, the resonance of the air in the nasal cavity combines with the resonance of the oral cavity. The nasal cavity causes resonances to decrease in energy, resulting in an overall attenuation of the signal. (You might have noticed that humming is never as loud as regular singing. Humming involves resonance in the nasal cavity.) **Approximants** – which include **liquids** (e.g., [l] and [r]) and **glides** (e.g., [w] and [y]) – are very vowel-like and have clear formant structure. The two liquids in English, [l] and [r], have similar articulation, but differ in terms of tongue placement, as described in Table 5.1. The acoustic consequence of this articulation difference is reflected acoustically in the shape of the third formant (F_3), as shown in the spectrograms for these sounds in Table 5.1.

Coarticulation

Probably the most important psycholinguistic aspect of speech production is the phenomenon of **coarticulation**. Coarticulation simply means that the articulators are always performing motions for more than one speech sound at a time. The articulators do not perform all the work for one speech sound, then another, then another. The genius of speech production is that phonological segments overlap, so the articulators work at maximum efficiency, in order to be able to produce 10 to 15 phonetic segments per second – more in rapid speech. This transmission speed would be close to impossible to achieve if each phonological unit were produced individually. As it is, speech is produced more slowly than necessary for the speech perception system. People can actually understand speech that has been sped up (compressed) at several times the normal rate (Foulke and Sticht 1969). But coarticulation is not just a matter of convenience for the speaker: if speech were not coarticulated – that is, if phonological units did not overlap – speech would actually be too slow and disconnected for the hearer to process it efficiently.

A simple example of coarticulation is the articulation of [k] in *key* and *coo*. When uttering *key*, while the back of the tongue is making closure with the top of the mouth for the [k], the lips – not ordinarily involved in articulating [k] – begin to spread in anticipation of the following vowel [i]. Similarly, when uttering *coo*, the lips round during the articulation of [k], in anticipation of the upcoming [u]. One aspect of coarticulation, then, is that the actual articulation of a phonological segment can be influenced by upcoming sounds. This is sometimes referred to as *regressive assimilation*.

Coarticulation can also be influenced by a phonological segment that has just been produced, a phenomenon sometimes called *progressive assimilation*. The [t] in *seat* is pronounced slightly more forward in the mouth than the [t] in *suit*. This is because the tongue position for the [t] is influenced by the preceding vowel ([i] is a front vowel and [u] is a back vowel).

Table 5.1 Articulatory and acoustic features for some obstruent consonants (this page) and sonorant consonants (following page). For each example: The first row (A) describes the articulatory characteristics of the class of sounds. The second row (B) describes the acoustic characteristics. The third row (C) provides an example (in a context between two vowels), and a waveform and spectrogram of a recording of that example.

	Obstruents		
	Oral stops	Fricatives	Affricates
A.	Full closure followed by release	Approximation of articulators and air forced between	Full closure followed by approximation of articulators and air forced between
B.	Silence followed by burst of noise	Sustained turbulent high-frequency noise	Silence followed by turbulent high-frequency noise
C.	a pin	a shin	a chin

Table 5.1 (cont'd)

	Sonorants		
	Nasal stops	**Lateral approximants**	**Central approximants**
A.	Full closure in oral cavity; lowered velum permits release of air through nasal cavity	Tip of tongue touching alveolar ridge, air flows around it	Tongue tip near alveolar ridge, sides of tongue touch upper molars, air flows through center
B.	Formant structure, but resonance in nasal cavity decreases energy, and signal is attenuated (less intense formants)	Clear formant structure, very high third formant (F_3)	Clear formant structure, very low third formant (F_3)
C.	*a mit*	*a limb*	*a rim*

Coarticulatory effects can span several segments. For example, the [b] in *bag* will be articulated slightly differently than the [b] in *bat*, as a consequence of the differences in the syllable-final phonemes [g] and [t]. What is most important for the present discussion, however, is that sounds produced by speakers are not discrete (separate) units, but rather form part of a continuous speech signal. The mental representation of the phonological form of an utterance is definitely segmental, phonemes lined up one after the other; however, in the process of speaking, phonemes overlap and blur together. The linguist Charles Hockett offered an apt metaphor for coarticulation (1955: 210):

> Imagine a row of Easter eggs carried along a moving belt; the eggs are of various sizes, and variously colored, but not boiled. At a certain point, the belt carries the row of eggs between the two rollers of a wringer, which quite effectively smash them and rub them more or less into each other. The flow of eggs before the wringer represents the series of impulses from the phoneme source; the mess that emerges from the wringer represents the output of the speech transmitter. At a subsequent point, we have an inspector whose task it is to examine the passing mess and decide, on the basis of the broken and unbroken yolks, the variously spread-out albumen, and the variously colored bits of shell, the nature of the flow of eggs which previously arrived at the wringer.

Hockett's words foreshadow discussion, in Chapter 6, of the effect of coarticulation on the perception of speech.

One final aspect of coarticulation is central to understanding the production (and perception) of stop consonants. Stops involve producing a complete closure somewhere in the vocal tract: [p] and [b] involve closure at the lips, [t] and [d] closure at the alveolar ridge, and [k] and [g] closure at the velum. The effects of coarticulation can be seen in Figure 5.7, which provides the waveform and spectrogram for the same vowel preceded by three stop consonants with different place of articulation: bilabial [ba], alveolar [da], and velar [ga]. F_1 is very similar in all three syllables, curving upwards from the onset of voicing to the steady formant of the vowel. F_2, in contrast, is slightly different for each syllable: it starts low and curves upwards for [ba], but it starts high and curves downwards for [da] and [ga].

The spectrogram reflects the changing shape of the oral cavity from the moment the stop is released (when voicing begins) and the tongue moves into position for the vowel. The movement of the tongue is tracked as **formant transitions**, visible in Figure 5.7 as lines of frequency

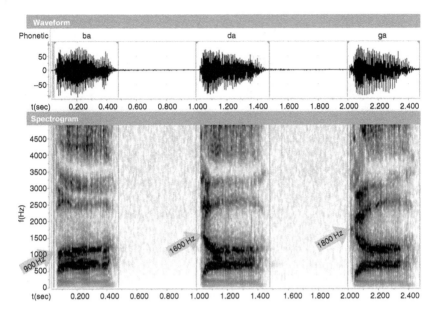

Figure 5.7 Waveform and spectrogram for three syllables produced by a male speaker of American English: [ba], [da], and [ga]. F$_1$ is similar for all three syllables, but F$_2$ differs. The F$_2$ for the vowel is about 1,100 Hz in all three cases, but F$_2$ begins at 900 Hz and rises to 1,100 Hz for [ba] on the left; F$_2$ begins at 1,600 Hz and falls for [da], in the middle; and F$_2$ begins at 1800 Hz and falls for [ga], on the right.

that change rapidly, as the shape of the oral cavity rapidly changes before assuming the final position for the vowel. The segmental nature of the representation before production has been transformed into a continuous signal, with information about the two segments combined and spread over less than 100 milliseconds of sound. Most remarkable about this is the fact that place of articulation information for stop consonants is actually carried by the vowel rather than the consonant itself.

Words in Speech

The speech rate of 10 to 15 phonetic units every second works out to about 125 to 180 words per minute; conversational speech can be much faster, reaching up to 300 words per minute. When people talk, they do

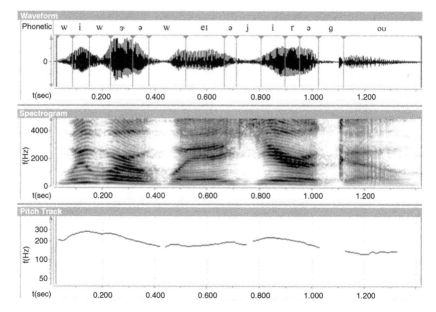

Figure 5.8 Waveform (top panel), spectrogram (middle panel), and pitch track (bottom panel) for the sentence *We were away a year ago*, spoken by a female speaker of American English. The vertical lines in the waveform indicate the approximate boundaries between segments. As can be appreciated by inspecting all three graphs, the signal is continuous.

not pause between words; words are run together just as the phonetic units are. In a continuous speech signal, neither the phones nor the words are segmented. Figure 5.8 provides an acoustic snapshot of the sentence *We were away a year ago*, produced by a female speaker.

The figure shows how words flow continuously, without spaces or discontinuities, from one to the next. In fact, the only period of silence is associated with the stop consonant [g] in the word *ago*. The word boundaries are completely obliterated by the continuous movement of the articulators as the sentence is produced.

■ Summing Up

The production of even a fairly simple sentence requires a complex coordination of preproduction planning of structure, lexicon, and phonology, followed by a series of movements that are highly organized and precisely coordinated. Underlying the actual production of a continuous, coarticulated speech signal is an abstract representation of individual words made up of segmented phones. Psycholinguists know that this representation precedes the production of speech because speech errors demonstrate that individual phones and words move as units. Like all psycholinguistic processes, the planning and execution of sentence production is effortless and unconscious, even though it is extremely complex. The complexity is related to the fact that language production recruits vast amounts of information (lexical and grammatical, as well as real-world knowledge), and it is sensitive to both the context of the conversation and the speaker's and hearer's communicative intents. The speaker transmits the speech signal, which is the outcome of this process, to the hearer, whose job it is to recover the speaker's idea by making sense of those sound waves, by recreating an abstract representation of discrete linguistic units, using the information carried by the continuous speech signal. Chapter 6 focuses on the hearer's task.

New Concepts

acoustic characteristics of:
  affricates
  approximants
  fricatives
  glides
  liquids
  nasals
  stops
anticipation errors
bilingual mode
borrowing
coarticulation
code-switching
complex acoustic signal
exchange errors
F_0, fundamental frequency
F_1, first formant
F_2, second formant
filter
formant transitions
formants
grammatical encoding

harmonics
interlocutor
lexical retrieval
perseveration errors
pitch
pitch track
plural attraction
preverbal message
resonance
segment exchange errors
source
source–filter model
spectral properties
spectrogram
speech errors (slips of the tongue)
syntactic priming
tip-of-the-tongue phenomenon
transfer
unilingual mode
waveform
word exchange errors

Study Questions

1. How can the study of speech errors demonstrate that speech consists of segmented words and phonemes before it is produced? Why is this interesting?

2. What are some of the similarities and differences between monolingual and bilingual models of production?

3. How does the study of speech errors demonstrate that speech is represented at various processing levels before it is actually produced?

4. What characteristics of speech errors demonstrate that they are not random, but honor linguistic classifications and constraints?

5. At some point before an utterance is produced it is represented in a form to which phonological and morphophonological rules have not yet applied. What characteristics of speech errors support this claim?

6. Freud suggested that word retrieval errors were a result of repressed feelings. Consider the following spoonerism: *Work is the curse of the drinking classes.* What is the psycholinguistic view of this error?

7. How do studies of syntactic priming demonstrate that speakers and hearers align their utterances interactively in conversations?

8. In the source–filter model of vowel production, what is the source? What is the filter? How do the source and filter operate together?

9. What are the primary acoustic characteristics of different classes of consonants? How is the acoustic signal related to articulation?

10. What is coarticulation? Why is it such an important feature of speech production?

11. Why do psycholinguists say that the speech signal is continuous? Are mental representations of sentences, before they are produced, also continuous? What is the evidence for this?

6 The Hearer: Speech Perception and Lexical Access

Chapter 5 dealt with the operations the speaker performs, using knowledge of language, when encoding a mental message into a physical signal accessible to the hearer. The hearer's task is almost the mirror image of the speaker's task. First, using information from the acoustic signal, the hearer reconstructs a phonological representation. The hearer enters the lexicon using that phonological representation to retrieve the lexical items that match. This permits the hearer to recover the semantic and structural details of the words in the message. The next

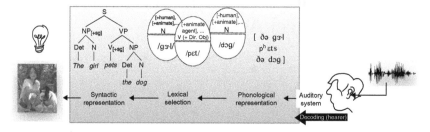

Figure 6.1 Diagram of some processing operations, ordered right to left, performed by the hearer when decoding the sentence *The girl pets the dog*. (This figure expands on parts of Figure 1.3, Chapter 1, and is parallel to Figure 5.1, Chapter 5.) The speech signal on the far right, perceived by the auditory system, serves to recover the phonological form for the sentence, indicated by the phonetic transcription. The capsule-like figures in the middle represent lexical items, activated by their phonological form (bottom half), but whose morphosyntactic features (included in the top half) help the processor recover the intended syntactic structure. The tree diagram on the left represents the sentence's syntactic form, used to decode the meaning of the sentence. The light bulb indicates that the hearer has successfully recovered the idea the speaker intended to convey.

step is to reconstruct the structural organization of the words, to create a syntactic representation – necessary for recovering the meaning of the sentence. This chapter and Chapter 7 describe these operations, represented graphically (from right to left) in Figure 6.1.

Chapter 7 focuses on syntactic processing (parsing). In this chapter, we examine the two steps in perception that precede parsing: **speech perception** and **lexical access**. We address these two aspects of perception together because they interact in interesting ways. Both phonetic elements and words must be extracted from a continuous, unsegmented, highly coarticulated signal. There are no spaces between phonetic units, and there are no spaces between words. Thus, some of the same problems exist for both speech perception and lexical access.

▪ Perceiving Speech

The hearer plays the role of the inspector in the metaphor by Charles Hockett cited in Chapter 5 (Hockett 1955: 210). The phonetic "eggs" have been mangled and mixed together by articulatory processes; it is the hearer's task to identify from the resulting mess of the **speech signal** what the original phonetic elements were. There are three features of

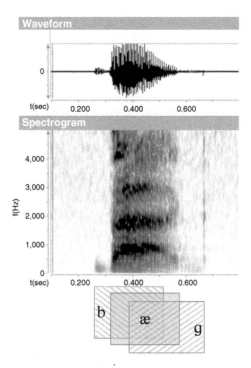

Figure 6.2 Illustration of parallel transmission of phonetic information. The figure is an adaptation of Figure 5 in Liberman (1970: 309).

the speech signal that the speech perception system must deal with: the signal is continuous, it transmits information in parallel, and it is highly variable.

We have pointed out elsewhere (briefly in Chapter 1 and in more detail in Chapter 5) that the speech signal is **continuous**: there are no spaces between consonants and vowels, or even between words. A central objective for the mechanisms involved in speech perception is to segment a continuous signal into discrete units: phonemes, syllables, and, ultimately, words. Because of coarticulation, the speech signal is characterized by the **parallel transmission** of information about phonetic segments (Liberman et al. 1967). Figure 6.2 illustrates how information about the three phonological units in the word *bag* is distributed across the word. In the recording whose waveform and spectrogram appear in the figure, the vowel has a duration of approximately 250 milliseconds, of which approximately 50 to 75 milliseconds carry information about all three phonological units. Properties of the word-initial /b/ spill into the vowel and persist through the beginning of the word-final /g/. Properties of /g/ begin at the offset of /b/ and continue through the second half of the vowel. The vowel /æ/ influences the pronunciation of the entire word, and carries acoustic information about both of the consonants in the word. This is an example of parallel transmission, of how the speech signal transmits information about more than one phonological unit simultaneously. The speech perception system must sort out all that information and figure out what the units are.

A third feature of the speech signal is its **variability**, or **lack of invariance**. The abstract mental representation of a phonological element does not vary. However, a speech sound may vary greatly each time it is actually produced. Many factors contribute to the fact that the same consonant or vowel, the same syllable, and even the same word are never pronounced exactly the same.

First, there is variability among speakers. Human anatomy is broadly similar, but there is individual variation in every aspect of our physique, which includes the organs involved in speech production. As a consequence, many aspects of the signal are intrinsically different for different speakers, including fundamental frequency and the spectral properties of consonants and vowels. In fact, a person's voice is as unique an identifier as are the person's fingerprints or retinas.

Second, there is variability within speakers. People sometimes speak fast, and other times slowly; they sometimes speak with chewing gum in their mouths; they mumble; they shout; they speak while being overcome with feelings of sadness or joy. All these variables affect the speech signal, and can make the acoustic signal associated with a single word very different each time it is uttered, even by the same speaker.

A third factor that makes the signal variable is ambient noise. Rarely do we speak to each other in noise-free environments. Other voices and other sounds (like music or traffic) can alter the speech signal dramatically. The same utterance will sound different in a small quiet room, in a large loud room, or coming from the room next door. The same voice could sound very different in person and on the telephone, and telephone transmissions will vary further depending on the connection and the equipment being used.

A fourth factor affecting variability in the signal is the context. The articulation of phonemes is affected by the phonemes around them, as illustrated in Chapter 5, and as just described with respect to parallel transmission. In addition to effects caused by coarticulation of phonological units, sentence context and neighboring words can also affect the pronunciation of individual lexical items.

The existence of all of these factors affecting the signal suggests that the accurate recognition of phonemes from the speech signal is nothing short of miraculous. In actuality, accurate decoding of speech is the norm, rather than the exception, because the speech perception mechanism operates in ways that overcome the variability of the signal. How does the speech perception mechanism overcome variability, to identify the phonological units that the signal carries? Speech perception relies on the relationships among acoustic elements, such as the fact that the F_1 for /a/ is high relative to the F_1 for /i/ and /u/, no matter who is speaking. Speech perception also exploits the reliability of certain acoustic cues as associated with distinct phonological units, some of which we discussed in Chapter 5. Stops are associated with a few milliseconds of silence, followed by a burst and a formant transition into the following vowel, glide, or liquid. Fricatives have high-frequency noise. Nasals have an attenuated signal. Glides, liquids, and vowels have clear formant structure. Though these are hardly invariable cues, they provide a great deal of guidance during speech perception.

Since the hearer is also a speaker, he can compensate for much of the variability produced by speaker characteristics, like speech rate and shouting. People use knowledge of their speech production in their perception of the speech of others: "to perceive an utterance is to perceive a specific pattern of intended gestures" (Liberman and Mattingly 1985). Some interesting evidence of how production influences speech perception comes from a speech shadowing study cited by Raphael, Borden, and Harris (2006: 264). In this experiment (Chistovich et al. 1963), the investigators asked participants to shadow speech (that is, to repeat words presented auditorily as fast as they could). Shadowers were able to produce consonants before all of the relevant acoustic cues for those consonants had been heard, suggesting that they were being guided by their production routines. More recently, Shockley and colleagues (Shockley, Sabadini, and Fowler 2004) have demonstrated that shadowers imitate with high fidelity phonetic details of the words they have just heard, and argue that this perception-driven response is due to a more general tendency of speakers to accommodate their speech (accent, rate, loudness, etc.) to that of the speech they are hearing from their interlocutors. These adjustments have important social consequences: they are ways that help speakers and hearers to get on the same "wavelength." The hearer also adapts rapidly to abnormal situations. For example, speech with a non-native-like accent, and sometimes speech produced by young children, can be difficult to decode, but this difficulty is overcome relatively quickly. Clarke and Garrett (2004) demonstrate that processing is slowed down for English native speakers listening to speech in English produced with a non-native (Spanish or Chinese) accent, compared to speech produced with a native accent. This slow-down, however, is reduced within one minute of exposure to the accented speech.

How much a hearer can adapt to abnormal situations can be affected by many variables. Speech presented in noise, for example, is under-stood more easily (and more efficiently) by native than non-native speakers. One study compared monolingual speakers of English, bilin-guals who were native speakers of Spanish and acquired English early (as infants or toddlers), and people who were native speakers of Spanish and acquired English as a second language after adolescence (Mayo, Florentine, and Buus 1997). Participants were asked to listen to pre-recorded English sentences, presented with or without noise, and to indicate what they thought the last word of each sentence was. The preceding context made the target words, at the end of each sentence, either predictable (*The boat sailed across the bay*) or unpredictable (*John was thinking about the bay*). Monolingual participants were best at toler-ating high levels of noise and using the context to predict what they heard, followed by early bilinguals. The participants with the worst performance were those who acquired English after adolescence. These findings suggest that age of acquisition is an important determinant in how accessible high-level information (top-down information, which we will discuss later in the chapter) is for a hearer. The study also dem-onstrates that perceiving speech involves much more than just experi-encing the acoustic signal.

The phonemic inventory and speech perception

Accurate speech perception is efficient and effortless because hearers rely on what they know about the language they are processing. One of the primary sources of information is knowledge of the phonemic inventory – as described in Chapter 2, this is the set of phonemes that are contrastive for the language.

As an example, let us consider how the dramatic variability in the acoustic signal for the consonant /d/, depending on the vowel that fol-lows, is overcome by what an English speaker knows about /d/ as a phoneme. In Chapter 5, we noted that formant transitions depend on both the place of articulation of the consonant and the articulation of the vowel that follows it; formant transitions are essentially the acoustic

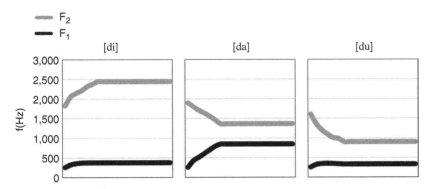

Figure 6.3 F_1 and F_2 measurements for three syllables, [di], [da], and [du], uttered by a female speaker of American English. The measurements show the transitions and steady-state formants for those three syllables. Notice that, in all three syllables, F_2 moves away from the same frequency.

traces of movement of the articulators, from the consonant to the vowel. Figure 6.3 shows the first and second formants (including their transitions) for three syllables, [di], [da], and [du].

Clearly, the formant transitions do not look anything alike, from one to the next syllable – nor do the consonants sound anything alike, if we eliminate the vowel. If we take a recording of [di], [da], and [du] and delete the three vowels (easily done with the help of a computer), we do not hear [d] three times. Instead, we hear little chirps with different tones for each of the three trimmed syllables. So where is the [d]? It is in the hearer's mind, and not in the physical signal. The speech signal containing the three syllables carries information allowing the hearer to reconstruct the three consonants that the speaker articulated, but the physical signals associated with the three syllables beginning with [d] do not contain three identical acoustic events corresponding to the phoneme we hear as [d]. Put another way, the hearer perceives different acoustic events as belonging to the same category.

The phenomenon of **categorical perception** (Liberman et al. 1957) helps explain the powerful effect that knowledge of the phonemic inventory has on speech perception. We will illustrate this phenomenon using the voicing contrast in stop consonants, since this has been extensively studied (and is very well understood). Recall from Chapter 5 that the primary acoustic difference between a voiceless and a voiced stop ([p] versus [b], for example) is **voice onset time (VOT)**. VOT is the time

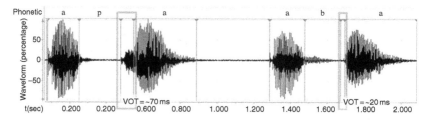

Figure 6.4   Waveform for [apa] and [aba], as produced by a female speaker of American English. The regions between the release of the stop and the onset of voicing are marked by a gray rectangle; approximate measurements for that region (VOT region) are indicated. The visible noise inside the VOT for [p] is aspiration.

that elapses between the release of the closure and the onset of voicing for the following vowel. For [b], voicing begins either the moment the closure is released (for a VOT of 0 milliseconds) or within the first 30 milliseconds after release of the closure. In contrast, [p] has a VOT between 40 and 100 milliseconds. Figure 6.4 illustrates how VOT is measured.

VOT offers an excellent example of variability in the speech signal. Unlike the phonological feature of voicing, which is binary (a sound is categorized as either voiced or voiceless), VOT is a *continuous variable*: stops have VOTs that can vary between 0 and 100 milliseconds – there are literally hundreds of different possible VOTs for stops. Yet, in the mind of the average English speaker, stops are either voiced or voiceless. People perceive the VOT continuum categorically, ignoring differences between sounds drawn from each of the perceived categories. How these categories are set depends crucially on the phonemic inventory of the language; more on this in a moment.

One way to study categorical perception is to synthesize a series of sounds that vary along a continuum of interest (like VOT), play those sounds for people, and ask what they think they have heard. Speech synthesis software can be used to generate a vowel preceded by a stop consonant with a VOT of 0 milliseconds, another with a VOT of 10 milliseconds, and so on. Everything about the signal will be identical, except the VOT. Different techniques exist to assess what participants think they heard. In some experiments, participants hear pairs of sounds and judge whether the pair is the same sound repeated or two different sounds; in other experiments, participants hear three sounds, and judge whether the third sound is the same as the first or the second. Some

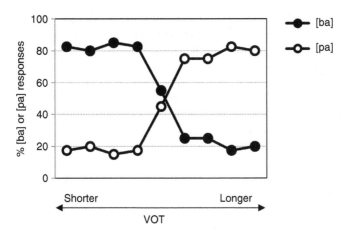

Figure 6.5 Hypothetical results of a categorical perception experiment, for participants listening to nine syllables in a VOT continuum, and asked to indicate whether they have heard [ba] or [pa]. The horizontal x-axis plots responses for each of the 9 syllables, varying from short VOT (left) to long VOT (right). The vertical y-axis indicates the percent of [ba] or [pa] responses for each signal.

experiments measure judgment responses and reaction times. Other experiments additionally collect information about brain activity while participants are listening to sequences of sounds and making judgments about them, or track participants' eyes as they listen to sequences of sounds and use a mouse to click on a display where they can indicate their choice.

The graph in Figure 6.5 illustrates what the results might look like for a very simple categorical perception experiment. In this hypothetical experiment, people are asked to listen to a single sound and make a binary choice about what they think they heard. The graph displays the percent of participants who heard [ba], and the percent who heard [pa], for each of 9 signals that varied in VOT in increments of 10 milliseconds. Shorter VOTs are on the left, longer VOTs are on the right.

For the four signals on the left, with shorter VOTs, the signal is heard as [ba] about 80 percent of the time; in contrast, for the four signals on the right, with longer VOTs, the signal is heard as [pa] about 80 percent of the time. Notice that only one of the signals – the fifth signal, in the middle of the chart – is responded to at chance level (both [ba] and [pa] responses are close to 50 percent); this is referred to as the *cross-over point* in the acoustic continuum.

Our hypothetical experiment illustrates a crucial aspect of categorical perception: physically different acoustic signals are categorized by the perceptual system as belonging to the same phonemic category. The difference in VOT between the first and fourth signals is greater (30 milliseconds) than between the fourth and sixth signals (20 milliseconds), yet the first and fourth signals are perceived as the same sound, while the fourth and sixth are perceived as different sounds.

Does this mean that the speech perception system cannot reliably distinguish between small differences in VOTs? An experiment in which participants' judgments about sameness were timed sheds some light on this question. Tash and Pisoni (1973) report that participants took slightly longer to say that two dissimilar members of the same category were the same (e.g., signals with VOTs of 40 versus 60 milliseconds) than to say that two identical members were the same (e.g., two signals with VOTs of 40 milliseconds, or two with VOTs of 60 milliseconds). The auditory system is evidently sensitive to small differences in VOT, but the speech perception mechanism conflates the acoustically different signals and perceives them all as the same phoneme.

Such decisions made by the speech perception mechanism are guided by knowledge of the language being heard – specifically, knowledge about the phonemes of the language. English makes a two-way phonemic distinction in stop consonants, as illustrated by the minimal pair *bat–pat*. (Recall from Chapter 2 that English has both aspirated and unaspirated voiceless stops in its repertoire of sounds, but [pʰ] and [p] are in complementary distribution: the former occurs initially at the beginning of stressed syllables, like *pat*, the latter in consonant clusters beginning with [s], like *spat*. Acoustically, an aspirated voiceless stop has a longer VOT than an unaspirated voiceless stop, as shown in Figure 6.4.) Differently from English, Thai makes a three-way distinction in its stop consonant phonemic inventory, and has near-minimal triplets like the following: *bâ*, pronounced [ba], means 'crazy'; *pâ* [pa] means 'aunt', and *pʰâa* [pʰa] means 'cloth' (Ladefoged 2005: 138). Because of these differences in the phonemic inventory for the two languages, English and Thai hearers perceive signals from the same VOT continuum very differently (Lisker and Abramson 1964). English-speaking participants divide the VOT continuum into two categories; Thai-speaking participants divide the same VOT continuum into three categories.

The biases that knowledge of a language confer on a hearer – making speech perception effortless, despite the variability in the signal – have consequences in the context of second language acquisition. Simply put, it is unavoidable, especially in early stages of second language acquisition, to listen to a new language with the "ears" of one's first language. As a result, new phonemic contrasts will be difficult to perceive. For example, English speakers have a hard time "hearing" the three-way contrast among Thai stops – particularly the unaspirated–aspirated contrast – even after instruction about it (Curtin, Goad, and Pater 1998). Catherine Best and colleagues propose that discriminating speech sounds in a second language crucially depends on how well they can be perceptually "assimilated" into the existing phonemic categories of the first language (Best, McRoberts, and Goodell 2001). In a similar vein, James Flege has argued that non-native characteristics in the speech of bilinguals are usually linked to interference from prior learning of phonetic categories in the first language (Flege 2003).

VOT is not the only acoustic continuum that is perceived categorically. Another similar phenomenon is observed with place of articulation. In Chapter 5 (see Figure 5.7), we discussed how F_2 transitions differ, based on place of articulation of a stop consonant. The F_2 transition of a naturally produced or computer-generated consonant can be manipulated using speech synthesis tools. With place of articulation continua, categorical perception effects are also observed: most signals in the continuum are grouped together into one or another category, and only a few signals (those at the cross-over points) are responded to at chance level. In a later section, we will describe a study that uses stimuli drawn from a place of articulation continuum.

Constructive speech perception and phonological illusions

Another important property of the speech perception system is that it is **constructive**. This means that the speech perception system takes information anywhere it can find it to construct a linguistic percept of the acoustic signal. As mentioned earlier, different phonemes have unique acoustic properties. The hearer also actively uses knowledge of the phonemic inventory, along with internalized information about how speech is produced.

Some interesting facts about the constructive nature of the speech perception system come from the study of phonological illusions, much as the study of optical illusions provides insights about visual perception. One such illusion – the **McGurk effect** (McGurk and MacDonald 1978) – illustrates how visual and auditory information together affect the construction of a phonological percept. If you watch a video of a person mouthing [ga ga ga ...], together with the audio track of a person saying [ba ba ba ...], you will hear neither [ba] nor [ga] – but [da]. Depending on the combinations used, the visual will override the audio, the audio will override the visual, or – as in our example – the audio and the visual will combine into a new "sound." Since it is a true illusion, you will perceive it the same way even if you know that the audio and the video do not match. Most stunning about the version of the illusion described here is that if you close your eyes, you will clearly hear [ba], and if you turn down the volume you will clearly "see" [ga], so it is not the case that the individual signals are inadequate.

The McGurk effect is compelling, but it is not really all that surprising. We all perceive speech better if the speaker is in view. If people are asked to report speech that has been made difficult to understand by embedding it in noise, comprehension is improved if participants can see the speakers (Macleod and Summerfield 1987). Also, the lip-reading abilities of many deaf people are quite remarkable. This is another example of a point made earlier, that knowledge of the way speech is produced is one type of information available to our speech perception system.

Another kind of illusion that illustrates the constructive nature of speech perception, **phoneme restoration**, was discovered by Warren (1970). Warren took a recording of the sentence *The state governors met with their respective legislatures convening in the capital city*, removed the [s] from the word *legislatures*, and replaced it with a recording of a cough of exactly the same duration as the excised [s]. Listening to this sentence, people reported that the [s] was present in the signal, and that the cough was in the background. Moreover, listeners tended to hear the cough either before or after the word *legislatures*, and not in the middle of it. This is a phenomenon known as *perceptual displacement*, which will come up again in Chapter 7. If a stimulus arrives while a perceptual unit is being processed – here, the word *legislatures* – the stimulus will be perceived as occurring either before or after the perceptual unit.

Another example of phoneme restoration involves inserting silence into words. With a recording of a word like *slice*, we can add silence between the [s] and the [l]. When the interval of silence is just the right duration – about 30 or 40 milliseconds – English speakers systematically hear *splice*. (As the interval of silence gets longer, the illusion disappears.) Remember that silence is a key acoustic indicator of the presence of a voiceless stop – any voiceless stop. How come, then, we don't hear *sklice* or *stlice*? Speech perception is constructive; the hearer uses knowledge of language to rule out *stlice* (on phonotactic grounds, since [stl-] is an impossible syllable onset for English) and *sklice* (if not on phonotactic grounds, then surely because [skl-] is such an infrequent onset – occurring in rare and oddly spelled words like *sclerosis* – that it is dispreferred relative to the more frequent [spl-]).

The phoneme restoration illusion is stronger when the sound being replaced and the sound used to fill in the gap are close acoustically (Samuel 1981); for example, replacing an [s] with a cough – a sound with lots of high-frequency noise – is more effective than replacing an [s] with a tone, and it doesn't work if the [s] is replaced by silence. The illusion is also stronger with obstruent consonants than it is with vowels. The effectiveness of phoneme restoration depends as well on whether the word carrying the missing sound is presented in isolation or inside a sentence. The phenomenon of phoneme restoration demonstrates the perceptual system's ability to "fill in" missing information, while actively trying to recover meaning from an acoustic signal: what we hear is sometimes not what we perceive.

The explanation for the effectiveness of phonological illusions lies in the operation of the lexical retrieval system. It locates words using as much acoustic information as is available. After a word has been retrieved, its full phonological representation is checked against what has been heard. This is called **post-access matching**. If the match is good enough, the word is accepted as correct and the full phonological representation from the lexicon becomes the percept. This process allows even a degraded acoustic signal to provide enough information to allow retrieval to take place; the phonological details are then filled in by the phonological information associated with that lexical item. Taking this view into account, plenty of acoustic information was available in the above examples for the words *legislatures* and *splice* to be accessed and to survive the post-access check. Thereafter, the [s] in *legi_latures* and the [p] in *s_lice* were "heard" based on the invariant phonemic information obtained from the lexicon, rather than from the initial acoustic signal. The fact that people can perceive the phonetic structure of nonsense words (e.g., *plice*) demonstrates that speech perception based solely on the acoustic signal is indeed possible, with no assistance from the lexicon (by definition, nonsense words are not stored in the lexicon, so they cannot engage post-access matching). However, the existence of phonological illusions, like phoneme restoration, demonstrates how the perceptual system can cope when it encounters inadequate acoustic information. In fact, all of these illusions demonstrate the constructive nature of all speech perception, not just perception in the laboratory or perception in the absence of adequate acoustic information. Consider the phenomenon of categorical perception. If we did not perceive divergent acoustic signals categorically, we could not communicate by speech. Categorical perception is the speech perception system's way to convert a variable acoustic signal into a phonological representation.

Slips of the ear (Bond 2005) bear some resemblance to phoneme restoration effects. Consider the person who "heard" *She had on a French suit*, from a signal produced by a speaker who intended to say *She had on a trench suit*. Slips of the ear are also called *mondegreens*, after a famous mishearing of a line in a ballad:

(1)   They hae slain the Earl Amurray,
       And Lady Mondegreen.

(In the original song, the second line is *And laid him on the green*.) An important difference between slips of the ear and phoneme restoration effects is that the former are often the result of inattentiveness to the signal, while the latter can be truly illusory. Certain types of phoneme restorations are provoked even when the hearer is paying close attention and knows that the signal has been altered. Slips of the ear, in contrast, are frequently the result of the hearer being distracted. Slips of the ear are more likely when the signal is noisy (which explains why song lyrics are so susceptible to being misheard) or when the signal is ambiguous (e.g., hearing *traitor* instead of *trader*, since the two words are identical when pronounced with a flap between the vowels, or hearing *fine me* instead of *find me*, since the /d/ in *find* is likely to be elided due to coarticulation).

Hearers can be very tolerant of the sometimes rather bizarre meanings that result from slips of the ear (Bond 2005). Consider, for instance, the strange but funny mishearing of a Beatles' song lyric: *the girl with colitis goes by* (the original lyric is *the girl with kaleidoscope eyes*). Bizarre meanings aside, slips of the ear, similarly to slips of the tongue, tend to result in "heard" sentences that conform to the grammatical properties of the language. For example, Bond cites the following mishearing of *A fancy seductive letter*:

(2)   A fancy structive letter

The signal very likely contained sufficient information for the hearer to recover a voiced [d] (in the word *seductive*), though the vowel in the first syllable was perhaps reduced enough so as to be inaudible. Yet the hearer did not "hear" *[sdʌktɪv], a form that violates the phonotactic constraints of English.

Bottom-up and top-down information

An influential concept in psycholinguistics (and in psychology in general) is the distinction between bottom-up and top-down processing. Psycholinguistic processes are, at their core, information processing routines; we can ask to what extent these processes are triggered automatically based only on the acoustic signal (bottom-up) or are aided by contextual information, either in the communication situation or within the sentence being processed (top-down).

Let us illustrate with an example. Suppose a friend walks up to you and says "Cat food," clearly and distinctly. You will, effortlessly, be able to decode the acoustic signal and retrieve the uttered words from your lexicon. In this situation, **bottom-up information** guides your processing: details of the acoustic signal help you build a phonological representation. Once you have retrieved the words, you might think that your friend saying *Cat food* out of the blue is a bit odd – or not.

Consider a different scenario: you and your roommate have a cat, and you are headed to the supermarket. Your roommate hollers from the kitchen (where the dishwasher is running noisily), "Fluffy's bowl is empty! Be sure to buy some cat food!" The acoustic information that reaches your ear is highly degraded; maybe you catch *Fluffy, bowl, buy*. You guess that *cat food* is somewhere in the sentence. You have understood this version of *cat food* (which you didn't even really hear) by using **top-down information**. This is information that is not part of the acoustic signal – contextual information that helps you understand what your roommate said absent a clear acoustic signal. In this case, part of the information guiding your processing was carried by the signal – the words you did catch, especially your cat's name. But other information well beyond the signal helped you too: usually you're the one who buys Fluffy's food and your roommate knew that you were going shopping. All of this conspires to allow you to understand *cat food* as a likely candidate for what your roommate might have been saying.

When bottom-up information inadequately specifies a word or phrase, top-down information can allow the hearer to select among a range of possibilities. If bottom-up information is adequate, however, top-down information will not be necessary. Recall from Chapter 3 that people with Broca's aphasia are good at understanding conversational speech but poor at understanding sentences for which they have to do a detailed analysis. The suggestion is that they are using contextual (top-down) information to understand what is said to them.

An experiment by Pollack and Pickett (1964) provides additional evidence for the interaction of top-down and bottom-up information. Pollack and Pickett asked participants to listen to single words excised from the sentences they had been produced in. Participants did not do very well understanding the words presented in isolation, but when the same words were presented inside their corresponding sentences, participants understood the words without difficulty. Evidently, the words alone provided inadequate information for bottom-up processing to proceed successfully; the surrounding context, though, provided just the right amount of top-down information.

Some experiments have focused on how specific aspects of the context – in this case, semantic information – affect speech perception (Garnes and Bond 1976; Borsky, Tuller, and Shapiro 1998), offering yet another illustration of how bottom-up and top-down processing depend on both the signal and the available context. In the experiment by Garnes and Bond, the investigators created a series of stimuli along a place of articulation continuum ranging from [beɪt] to [deɪt] to [geɪt]. (Remember that the place of articulation continuum involves differences in formant transitions of the stop consonants.) There were "perfect" versions of the stimuli for each of [b], [d], and [g], but there were also versions of the stimuli that were right in between [b] and [d], and [d] and [g] – "indefinite" signals, like the stimulus at the cross-over point in the VOT continuum in Figure 6.5, which is ambiguous between [ba] and [pa]. The stimuli were embedded in sentence contexts like the following:

(3)   a.   Here's the fishing gear and the …
      b.   Check the time and the …
      c.   Paint the fence and the …

Clearly, the most plausible continuation for the first carrier phrase is *bait*, for the second, *date*, and for the third, *gate*. Participants were simply asked to report which word they thought they had heard in the final position of the sentence.

Not surprisingly, when the signal was a "perfect" [beɪt], participants reported hearing *bait*, regardless of sentence context, even though in some cases the resulting sentence was somewhat senseless (e.g., *Check the time and the bait*). The same happened with "perfect" instances of [deɪt] and [geɪt]. However, when the signal was "indefinite" – for instance, a stimulus beginning with a consonant at the cross-over point for [b] and [d], a word acoustically ambiguous between *bait* and *date* – it was reported as the word that fit the context: it was heard as *bait* if carried by the phrase in (3a), but as *date* if in (3b). Experiments like this offer important insights about speech perception: clear and unambiguous segmental information in the signal is decoded precisely as it is presented, with bottom-up processing, even if this leads to implausible meanings; but indefinite or ambiguous information is processed by using whatever contextual information might be available, thus recruiting top-down processing.

Suprasegmental information in the signal

In the preceding sections we have focused on how segments (consonants and vowels) are recovered from the speech signal. We now turn to how suprasegmental information is recovered, and how that contributes to lexical retrieval. (In Chapter 7 we will discuss how suprasegmental information in the signal can influence syntactic parsing.) Suprasegmental information is signaled in speech with variations in duration, pitch, and amplitude (loudness). Information like this helps the hearer segment the signal into words, and can even affect lexical searches directly.

In English, lexical stress serves to distinguish words from each other (as we discussed in Chapter 2); for example, compare *trusty* and *trustee*. Not surprisingly, English speakers are attentive to stress patterns during lexical access (Cutler and Clifton 1984). In Mandarin Chinese, tone is lexically specified (another point illustrated in Chapter 2), and so to recover words from the speech signal, Mandarin speakers are attentive not only to segmental information but also to suprasegmental information (Fox and Unkefer 1985).

Suprasegmental information can be used to identify the location of word boundaries also. In languages like English or Dutch, monosyllabic words are durationally very different than polysyllabic words. For example, the [hæm] in *ham* has longer duration than it does in *hamster*. An investigation by Salverda, Dahan, and McQueen (2003) demonstrates that this durational information is actively used by the hearer. In this study, Dutch speakers were asked to listen to sentences (for example, the Dutch equivalent of *She thought that that hamster had disappeared*) while looking at displays (for this sentence, a display containing a picture of a ham and a picture of a hamster, along with other distracter pictures). Their task was to look for a picture that matched a word in the sentence they were listening to, and manipulate that picture using a computer mouse. Eye movements were tracked during the entire procedure. Participants were sensitive to whether the [hæm] they heard was monosyllabic or embedded in the bisyllabic word, even before the rest of the sentence was heard. For example, for a sentence containing *hamster*, there were more looks to the picture of a hamster than to the picture of a ham, very soon after the onset of the ambiguous segments [hæm], and before the disambiguating segments [stɚ]; participants evidently used suprasegmental information (syllable duration) to process the lexical material. Salverda and colleagues use evidence like this to argue that durational cues can signal to the hearer that there is no word boundary after [hæm] in a sentence containing *hamster* but that there is a word boundary in a sentence containing *ham*.

The durational variation described for Dutch and English has to do with the basic rhythm of these languages: Dutch and English are stress-timed languages. Recall from Chapter 2 that stress-timed languages emphasize syllables that are stressed (those syllables are longer, louder, and higher in pitch, relative to other syllables). Some of the characteristics of a stress-timed language are that they permit syllables with consonant clusters in coda position and that they reduce vowels in unstressed syllables (Ramus, Nespor, and Mehler 1999). Speakers of stress-timed languages are very sensitive to stress patterns. One such pattern for English is that content words (especially nouns, as described in Chapter 2) tend to start with a stressed syllable. In an experiment asking people to identify words in a stream of speech, a procedure called *word spotting*, English speakers found it more difficult to find a word like *mint* in a sequence with two stressed syllables, like *mintayve* – pronounced ['mɪn'tʰeɪv] – than in a sequence with a stressed syllable followed by an unstressed syllable, like *mintesh* – pronounced ['mɪntəʃ] (Cutler and Norris 1988).

Differently from English and Dutch, languages like Spanish, French, or Italian have regular durations, syllable to syllable, regardless of whether the syllables are stressed, and so they are classified as syllable-timed. Speakers of syllable-timed languages use syllable information in segmenting speech (Cutler et al. 1986). As mentioned in Chapter 2, languages like Japanese are mora-timed, and so speakers of Japanese are sensitive to moras when segmenting the speech signal (McQueen, Otake, and Cutler 2001).

■ The Role of Orthography

As we move into the next major topic for this chapter, lexical retrieval, we should address an important question that has probably crossed your mind: what about reading? People living in literate societies spend much of their time decoding language in written form. How different is decoding words in writing from decoding words in speech? Researchers concerned with how written language is decoded have found that phonology plays a crucial role in decoding words while reading, but so does orthography (Frost and Ziegler 2007). The **orthography** of a language is its writing system, including the characters (graphemes) it uses and the set of conventions for spelling and punctuation.

The basis of reading is the ability to decode individual words; this involves matching each orthographic symbol (each grapheme) with a phoneme. Programs for literacy and reading readiness that focus on training in phoneme-to-grapheme correspondences have been very successful. This fact provides evidence of how closely linked reading is to phonology. The form-priming experiments described later in this chapter offer more evidence of the fact that phonological forms are recovered for words, even when we are reading them. The involvement of phonology in reading has been confirmed even for languages with writing systems that represent morphemes rather than sounds, like Chinese (Perfetti, Liu, and Tan 2005). Thus, retrieving words presented in writing involves reconstructing their phonological representations.

There is also some evidence that people's knowledge of orthography can mediate how they access their lexicon. For example, one study found that speakers of French were less likely to be able to identify the phoneme /p/ in words like *absurd* than *lapsus*, because in the former, pronounced [apsyrd], the /p/ is spelled with the letter *b* (Halle, Chereau, and Seguí 2000). Another study measured how well Hebrew–English bilinguals performed in a phoneme deletion task, involving monosyllabic words that sound exactly alike in the two languages, like [gʌn] (*gun* in English, "garden" in Hebrew) or [bʌt] (*but* in English, "daughter" in Hebrew) (Ben-Dror, Frost, and Bentin 1995). Importantly, English uses three letters (each corresponding to one of the phonemes) to represent these words, but Hebrew only represents the consonants: גן (*gn*) for "garden" and בת (*bt*) for "daughter". Participants were asked to listen to the words and delete the first sound; words in each language were presented separately. Native English speakers (for whom Hebrew was a second language) performed very well; however, native Hebrew speakers (for whom English was a second language) frequently committed an interesting error, related to the way Hebrew is written: rather than just deleting the initial consonant, they deleted the initial consonant plus the following vowel. Studies like this show that how one's language is written can affect phonological awareness; indeed, it has been shown that literacy itself has a strong effect on a person's ability to consciously manipulate phonemes (Morais et al. 1979).

As you continue reading this chapter, bear in mind that both orthography and phonology mediate access to the lexicon; the two systems interact bidirectionally (Frost and Ziegler 2007). The sections that follow will describe experiments performed predominantly using written stimuli, but generally assume that a phonological representation is built from those stimuli.

Accessing the Lexicon

The speaker enters the lexicon using information about meaning so she can retrieve the phonological structure of the appropriate words to convey the meaning she is constructing for a sentence. The hearer's (or reader's) task is the opposite. He uses a phonological representation (decoded using information from the acoustic signal) to retrieve information about meaning. The hearer looks for a lexical entry whose phonological representation matches the one he has heard. When there is a match, a word is retrieved, and information about the word's meaning and structural requirements is then available. As pointed out in Chapter 5, the speed of lexical retrieval is remarkable – it takes a mere fraction of a second to find a word in a lexicon consisting of some 80,000 items. The lexicon is searched by meanings in production and by phonological forms in perception. Evidence about both the process of retrieval and the way the lexicon is organized is provided by studies that examine how lexical access is affected by meaning and form relations among words, as well by variables such as phonotactics, word frequency, and lexical ambiguity.

A technique widely used to investigate lexical access is the **lexical decision task**. Participants are briefly shown a string of letters and asked to push one button if the letters constitute a word in their language, and a different button if they do not. Responses in a lexical decision task tend to be very rapid, ranging between 400 and 600 milliseconds. In a lexical decision experiment, participants will see equal amounts of words and non-words, and within the many words

Table 6.1 Word list for simulated lexical decision task. For each string, write Y if it is a word of English, N if it is not.

CLOCK ☐	DOCTOR ☐	ZNER ☐	FLOOP ☐
SKERN ☐	NURSE ☐	TABLE ☐	FABLE ☐
BANK ☐	TLAT ☐	URN ☐	MROCK ☐
MOTHER ☐	PLIM ☐	HUT ☐	BAT ☐

they will see throughout the experiment, a subset of those is of interest to the investigator: those words contain a contrast being investigated in the experiment.

To simulate how a lexical decision task works, consider the 16 letter strings in Table 6.1, and write Y or N next to each one, to indicate for each whether it is a word of English. Try to write your responses as quickly as possible.

You probably wrote N next to six of the letter strings, and might have even noticed that you responded to three of them very quickly – TLAT, ZNER, and MROCK – and to the other three somewhat more slowly – SKERN, PLIM, and FLOOP. All six strings are non-words in English, but the first three violate the phonotactic constraints of the language. **Impossible non-words**, like TLAT, ZNER, and MROCK, are rejected very rapidly in a lexical decision task. It is as if the lexical retrieval system were carrying out a phonological screening of sorts, not bothering to look in the lexicon when the string is not a possible word in the language. In contrast, **possible non-words**, like SKERN, PLIM, and FLOOP, take longer to reject, as if the retrieval system conducted an exhaustive, ultimately unsuccessful, search for their entries in the lexicon.

Experimental evidence for the distinction in lexical access between possible and impossible non-words is abundant; one interesting example is a brain imaging study that used positron emission tomography (PET) to measure blood flow changes in the brain while people were presented with real words (BOARD), possible non-words (TWEAL), impossible strings of characters (NLPFZ), and strings of letter-like forms – "false fonts" (Petersen et al. 1990). Petersen and colleagues found that the same areas of the brain are activated in response to real words and possible non-words, and that these areas are different from those activated in response to impossible non-words and "false fonts" strings.

Of the real words in Table 6.1, you probably responded faster to the more frequent ones (like CLOCK and BANK) than to the less frequent ones (like HUT and URN). The **lexical frequency** of a word can be measured by counting how many times a particular word occurs in a large corpus for that language. Lexical frequency is correlated with lexical decision times and with responses to other types of lexical access tasks: more frequent words are responded to faster (Forster and Chambers 1973; Forster 1981). Words that are used often are evidently more available to the lexical retrieval system.

Another property of words that has been used to study lexical retrieval is lexical ambiguity. Lexically ambiguous words are words that have more than one meaning. Some research has examined whether such words have more than one lexical entry, and whether having more than one lexical entry can lead to retrieval advantages. Consider the word *bank*, which as a noun can be a money bank, a river bank, or a snow bank; *bank* can also be a verb. Some lexically ambiguous words have multiple meanings that are completely unrelated (e.g., the noun *punch* can refer to a type of drink, or to a blow with the fist, or to a piercing instrument); such ambiguous words are called *homonyms*. Other ambiguous words have meanings that appear to have a systematic relationship to each other (e.g., the noun *eye* refers to an organ used for vision, or to the opening in a needle, or the aperture of a camera); these words are *polysemous*. Rodd, Gaskell, and Marslen-Wilson (2002) compared these two types of ambiguity in a series of lexical decision experiments, and found that ambiguous words with related senses (polysemous words like *eye*) are retrieved faster than ambiguous words with unrelated senses (homonyms like *punch*). Homonyms have multiple meanings that compete against each other, resulting in delayed recognition. In contrast, the semantic relationships between the multiple senses of polysemous words facilitate their retrieval.

One final variable we will discuss affecting lexical access routines is **priming** (Meyer and Schvaneveldt 1971). Priming is actually a very general property of human cognition: a stimulus you just experienced will affect how you respond to a later stimulus – and this associative response is true not just with linguistic stimuli, but with stimuli of any type (pictures, smells, non-linguistic sounds, etc.). In the list in Table 6.1, the words DOCTOR and NURSE are related semantically, and the words TABLE and FABLE related phonologically. Reading the words in each pair consecutively might have influenced how quickly you responded to the second member of the pair.

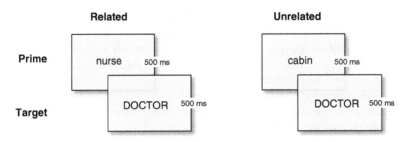

Figure 6.6 Example of two prime–target pairs in a lexical decision experiment. The primes are in small letters, the targets in capital letters. The figure simulates the display sequence: the prime appears by itself and remains on the screen for a few hundred milliseconds; then the target appears. On the left, the prime and target are semantically related; on the right, they are unrelated. Notice that the primes, *nurse* and *cabin*, are matched in length (both are five characters long); primes are also usually matched by frequency and other variables.

How does priming work? When you encounter a stimulus of a given type, you activate its mental representation, but as you search for the unique mental representation for the stimulus, you activate associates for that stimulus, as well. Priming, then, is residual activation from previously experienced stimuli.

In a lexical decision experiment concerned with measuring priming effects, a **prime** word is presented for a brief amount of time; it then disappears and a **target** word takes its place; Figure 6.6 illustrates this graphically. (In many priming experiments, primes are presented in small letters, while targets are presented in capitals, and participants are asked to make lexical decisions only on words presented in capital letters.) The experiment includes primes that are related to the target (e.g., for a target like DOCTOR, a related prime would be "nurse"), as well as primes that are unrelated to the target. Responses to the target will be faster when it is preceded by a related than by an unrelated prime.

Many studies have used semantic priming techniques to study to what extent semantic representations are shared between translation-equivalent words in bilingual lexicons. This research has confirmed that when a prime and a target are in different languages, a semantic relation between them facilitates retrieval of the target word; for a French–English bilingual, access to *cat* is facilitated by both *dog* and *chien* (Kroll and Sunderman 2003). The strength of the priming can be asymmetric: priming is typically stronger from the bilingual's dominant language (which is usually, though not always, the bilingual's first language) than from the non-dominant language. The idea is that the dominant (or first language) lexicon is bigger, since it was learned first, making the links to (non-linguistic) conceptual representations stronger for words in the dominant language than in the non-dominant language (Kroll and Dijkstra 2002).

Sometimes words that have the same (or very similar) form between two languages are not related semantically at all. A pair of languages can have *interlingual homographs* (words that are written the same way between the two languages), like *coin* in English and *coin* ('corner') in French, as well as *interlingual homophones* (words that sound the same in the two languages), like *aid* in English and *eed* ('oath') in Dutch. Notice that these two examples are pairs of words that are not translation equivalent, but rather interlingual "false friends." False friends have become useful in research that examines to what extent bilinguals are able to inhibit one language while retrieving lexical entries in a unilingual mode. In research like this, bilingual participants perform lexical decisions in one language only, and the experiment compares reaction times to interlingual homographs and frequency-matched controls, for example, on the assumption that false friends will result in processing cost if the other language is not inhibited. Generally, studies such as this have found that interlingual homographs take as long to process as control words, suggesting that the bilinguals' other language is inhibited during unilingual processing; however, other experiments using priming techniques (discussed in more detail in the following section) have demonstrated that words with orthographic and semantic overlap in the two languages can affect processing time (Dijkstra 2005). One such study (Beauvillain and Grainger 1987) asked participants to make a lexical decision on word pairs consisting of one word in French (like *coin*) followed by a word in English (like *money*). Beauvillain and Grainger found that when the prime and target were semantically related, in English, reaction times on the target word (*money*) were faster, suggesting that even though the prime had been accessed in French, the corresponding English lexical representation had been activated as well.

Types of priming

The examples we have given above are of **semantic** or **associative priming**. In this type of priming there is a meaning relationship between the prime and target word. Other aspects of words also produce priming

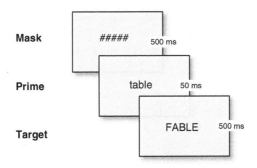

Figure 6.7   Example of a prime–target pair in a masked priming experiment.

effects. There is, for instance, **form priming**, in which the prime and the target are not related semantically, but are related in their phonological form: for instance, *table* will prime *fable*, and *able* will prime *axle*.

An experimental method called **masked priming** (Forster and C. W. Davis 1984) demonstrates that the prime word may be presented so briefly that it is not consciously processed, but will still result in the priming effect. In this technique, the prime is "sandwiched" between a mask ("#####", for example) and the target, as illustrated in Figure 6.7. The mask and the target each remain on the screen for 500 milliseconds, typically, but the prime only flashes on the screen for the impossibly brief time of 50 milliseconds. This is not enough time for the word to register consciously – people generally report seeing a flicker between the mask and the target, but they have no memory of having seen an actual word. However, it is apparently enough time for the stimulus to prime the following target. Masked priming technique has been used to study both form priming (C. J. Davis 2003) and semantic priming (Carr and Dagenbach 1990).

Masked priming can be very useful to study the relationship between words in two languages, in bilinguals, because a task involving some aspect of lexical access can be presented to participants as being only in one language, but masked primes can be presented in the other language. One such experiment, by Sánchez-Casas, C. W. Davis, and García-Albea (1992), examined the relationship between a special type of translation-equivalent words: cognates. **Cognates** are word pairs, like *rico–rich* in Spanish–English, which share not just semantic representations but also have a common stem and are phonologically very similar. In their study, Sánchez-Casas and colleagues presented Spanish–English bilinguals with a task in which targets in Spanish were preceded by masked primes in either Spanish or English. The prime was either identical to the target (*rico–rico*, *pato–pato*), an English cognate of the target (*rich–rico*), an English non-cognate (*duck–pato*), or a control non-word (*rict–rico*, *wuck–pato*). Sánchez-Casas and colleagues found that responses to target words were as fast with cognate primes as with identical primes, and both of these were faster than either non-cognate primes or non-word primes. These findings suggest that cognate words for bilinguals have a special kind of morphological relationship that is represented in the lexicon differently than are words that are translation-equivalents (Sánchez-Casas and García-Albea 2005).

Bound morphemes

In Chapter 2 we discussed bound morphemes, which are affixes attached to word stems to form new words. There are *inflectional morphemes*, like the *–s* attached to nouns to make them plural (*car*/*cars*) or the *–ed* attached to verbs to make them past tense (*kiss*/*kissed*). There are also *derivational morphemes*, which can change the meaning of a word, and sometimes the grammatical class of the word as well. For instance, the suffix *–er* can be attached to a verb, changing it into a noun meaning a person who performs the activity of that verb (*play*/*player*). An important question about bound morphemes is whether words created by adding morphemes to them are stored separately in the lexicon or whether derived forms are created when they are produced. With respect to lexical retrieval, if a derived form is stored as a whole, it will be retrieved as a single word. If the derived form is created by adding a morpheme to a stem, the morpheme must be removed before the stem is accessed. This is called **morpheme stripping** (Taft 1981).

There is general agreement among psycholinguists that inflectional morphemes are stripped before their stems are accessed (Marslen-Wilson 2005). Of course, the meaning of the stripped morpheme contributes to the meaning of the sentence that it appears in. Derivational morphemes, however, differ in their productivity. The agentive suffix *–er* can be attached to almost any verb. In contrast, morphemes like *–tion* in words like *derivation* are not only less productive, they also change the pronunciation of the stem. Bradley (1980) reports a series of experiments demonstrating that words derived by affixing productive morphemes are not stored lexically, but are subject to morpheme stripping; in contrast, words containing less productive morphemes are stored in the lexicon, so they do not require morpheme stripping.

▓   The cohort model of lexical access

Models about lexical access help us understand more about the rapid and unconscious retrieval of words from the lexicon. One such model, the **cohort model of lexical access** (Marslen-Wilson and Tyler 1980; Marslen-Wilson 1987) accounts for many facts about lexical retrieval and helps summarize a number of facts related to lexical access described in the preceding sections. A word's **cohort** consists of all the lexical items that share an initial sequence of phonemes. According to the cohort model, acoustic information is rapidly transformed into phonological information, and lexical entries that match the stimulus phonologically are *activated*. After the first syllable of a word is received, all the lexical entries in its cohort will be activated; after the second syllable is received, a subset of those will remain activated (when an entry ceases to match, it deactivates). Finally, at some point – before the end of the word, if the target word is unambiguous – a single lexical entry will be uniquely specified, and it will be retrieved. This is called the **recognition point** for the word, and on average it occurs within 200 to 250 milliseconds of the beginning of the word. Of course, if a word is ambiguous and has more than one lexical entry, there will be no recognition point before the end of the word, so all entries that are pronounced the same will be retrieved.

The fact that words can be retrieved before they are completed has been demonstrated by Holcomb and Neville (1991) in an event-related potentials (ERP) experiment. Recall from Chapter 3 that there is a brain response, the N400, associated with the presence of semantic anomaly in a sentence. Holcomb and Neville (1991) showed that the N400 begins long before the entirety of a semantically anomalous word has been heard. According to the cohort model, an initial cohort of phonologically similar words is activated and, by the word's recognition point, one is selected and integrated into the representation of the sentence being constructed. If this results in a semantic anomaly, given the context, an N400 wave is the neurophysiological result.

The cohort model predicts that the initial part of a word will be more important for lexical access than its end, a prediction that has been confirmed by a number of different kinds of experiments. Mispronunciations at the beginnings of words are detected more accurately than are mispronunciations at the ends of words (Cole, Jakimik, and Cooper 1978). The phoneme restoration effect is also more robust when the missing phoneme is in the middle or at the end of a word rather than at the beginning (Marslen-Wilson and Welsh 1978). Final consonants are also much more frequently involved in slips of the ear than are initial consonants (Bond 2005).

The cohort model (as well as other similar ones about lexical access) assumes that every word in the lexicon has some resting level of activation. Stimulation by matching phonological information increases a word's level of activation. When activation reaches some threshold level, the word is retrieved and is then available for use for subsequent processing (be this making a lexical decision, or incorporating the word into an ongoing sentence). The notion of activation helps account for the observed frequency effects in lexical retrieval. High-frequency words have a higher resting level of activation than do low-frequency words. Since retrieval depends on a lexical item reaching some threshold of activation, high-frequency words will reach that threshold faster than low-frequency words. The phenomenon of priming is also accounted for by the concept of activation. A prime increases the activation of words related by either form or meaning, enhancing their retrieval.

A factor that affects retrieval times for words is **neighborhood density**. A word's **neighborhood** consists of all the lexical items that are phonologically similar. Some words have larger cohorts than others: the word *cot* has many words that are phonologically similar to it, so it is said to come from a dense neighborhood; in contrast, the neighborhood for a word like *crib* is more sparse. Words with larger phonological neighborhoods take longer to retrieve than those from smaller neighborhoods (Connine 1994). The finding is reasonable: more phonological information is required to specify uniquely a word from a dense neighborhood than from a sparse neighborhood.

Another factor that has been found to affect retrieval is the similarity between the phonological information in the input and the phonological representation of the word in the lexicon. A priming experiment by Connine, Blasko, and Titone (1993) explored this factor, by using non-words to prime actual words. Connine and colleagues created what they called minimal and maximal non-words, by replacing the initial phoneme of words by a phoneme that was minimally or maximally different from the original. For example, based on *doctor*, *toctor* is a minimal non-word (/t/ and /d/ are both alveolar stops), while *zoctor* is a maximal non-word (/z/ is a fricative, while /d/ is a stop). Both base words (*doctor*) and minimal non-words (*toctor*) facilitated retrieval of semantically related targets (like *nurse*), but maximal non-words (*zoctor*) did not have this priming effect. Recall that when we discussed phonemic restoration, we pointed out that the acoustic representation of the deleted phoneme must be similar to the actual phoneme for restoration to take place. This is because lexical retrieval (and post-access matching) will not be triggered if the acoustic signal is too different from the stored phonological representation of the word. Similarly, minimal non-words will trigger lexical retrieval, but maximal non-words will not.

Interlingual form relationships between words have been found to affect lexical access in bilinguals, evidence that both languages are active at all times. Phonotactic constraints of one language, for example, have been found to affect lexical decisions on non-words in another (Altenberg and Cairns 1983). A study by van Heuven, Dijkstra, and Grainger (1998) examined whether lexical decision times would be affected by neighborhood density, when the neighborhood included words from two languages. The participants were Dutch–English bilinguals, who performed lexical decision tasks on words either from only one language or from both languages. The experiment used words with large neighborhoods in one language but small neighborhoods in the other, as estimated by a corpus analysis; for example, *bird* has more neighbors in Dutch than in English, while *busy* has more neighbors in English than in Dutch. Van Heuven and colleagues found that making a lexical decision about a word in one language was affected by the number of neighbors that word had in the other language: response times to words in one language were systematically slowed down when the number of orthographic neighbors in the other language was large. This effect was absent in a monolingual control group making lexical decisions on English words with large or small neighborhoods in Dutch.

Lexical Access in Sentence Comprehension

Because one of the primary interests of this book lies in understanding how lexical retrieval relates to sentence comprehension, it is important to know to what extent these characteristics of lexical items operate as sentences are being processed. A typical approach to this question is to ask whether the presence of a lexical item with a particular property facilitates or impedes the processing of a sentence. The effects on sentence processing of both word frequency and ambiguity have been studied.

Lexical frequency

Early research on the effects of word frequency in sentence processing used a procedure called the **phoneme monitoring task** (Foss 1969). Participants listen to a pre-recorded sentence over headphones and are told to push a button when they hear a word beginning with a particular phoneme. The time is measured between the onset of the phoneme in the recording and the moment the participant pushes the button. This reaction time reflects people's ability to perceive and respond to the target phoneme, with an important added feature: the reaction time will vary depending on the cognitive effort involved in processing the sentence at the moment the phoneme was heard. Phoneme monitoring exploits a very general psychological principle known as **resource sharing**. If you are engaged in a complex cognitive activity, your motor responses will be delayed. For instance, if you are doing something difficult like multiplication problems in your head, it will take you slightly longer to push a button in response to a stimulus (like a light or a tone) than it would if you were not doing the multiplication problems.

In one of the experiments reported by Foss (1969), participants were told to monitor for words beginning with [b] (like *bassoon*), while listening to sentences like (4a) or (4b):

(4) a.   The traveling bassoon player found himself without funds in a strange town.
     b.   The itinerant bassoon player found himself without funds in a strange town.

The difference between these sentences is the word preceding *bassoon*: high frequency in (4a), low frequency in (4b). Foss reports that participants were slower to respond to *bassoon* following the low frequency *itinerant* than the high frequency *traveling*. Low-frequency words increase sentence processing complexity, a finding that fits well both with the lexical decision findings discussed above (more common words are retrieved more rapidly from the mental lexicon) and the observation in Chapter 5 that hesitations are more likely before low-frequency words.

Lexical ambiguity

As described in the preceding section, word frequency has an effect in sentence processing similar to its effect in lexical decision tasks. Now we turn to lexical ambiguity. How ambiguity is dealt with in sentence processing is of central concern in psycholinguistics, because ambiguity is rampant in human language. The majority of the 1,000 most common words in English are multiply ambiguous. Yet, people are rarely aware of making decisions about word meaning, and getting the correct meaning given a specific sentence context tends to be very easy. The only exception to this is the **garden path sentence**, an example of which is in (5):

(5)   The two masked men drew their guns and approached the bank, but the boat was already moving down the river.

Such misleading sentences are called "garden paths" because they lead the hearer "down the garden path," first to an incorrect representation, then to the realization that the sentence makes little sense, finally to a stage of reanalysis which may or may not lead to the correct interpretation. When you read the sentence in (5), you probably interpreted *bank* as referring to a financial institution. When you got to *the river*, you might have realized that you were wrong about your initial assessment of *bank*, inferring that whoever wrote that sentence had probably meant *river bank*. Thus, you were "led down the garden path." The selection of the incorrect meaning of an ambiguous word can also lead to entertaining results. (In fact, it is the basis of all puns.) Newspaper headlines often contain amusing ambiguities:

(6)   New vaccine may contain rabies.

(7)   Prostitutes appeal to Pope.

Only in cases like these does one become aware of the presence of an ambiguous word in a sentence being processed, yet every sentence of any length likely has several ambiguities. People usually resolve these ambiguities correctly without creating either a garden path sentence or an amusing one. The existence of garden path sentences like (5) demonstrates that at some point following the ambiguous word, a single meaning has been selected. When and how is that single meaning selected, and why is it so often the correct one?

A phoneme monitoring experiment by Cairns and Kamerman (1976) compared sentences with ambiguous and unambiguous words. Participants were asked to listen for [d] while listening to recordings of one of the following sentences:

(8)   a.   Frank took the pipe down from the rack in the store.
       b.   Frank took the cigar down from the rack in the store.

Both *pipe* and *cigar* are high-frequency words, but only *pipe* is ambiguous. Cairns and Kamerman report that phoneme monitoring reaction

200 THE HEARER: SPEECH PERCEPTION AND LEXICAL ACCESS

times were longer following the ambiguous *pipe* than following the unambiguous *cigar*, indicating that the ambiguous word required additional processing resources. When processing sentences, all meanings of an ambiguous word need to be considered.

Cairns and Kamerman (1976) included another pair of sentences in their experiment; in these, the target phoneme was located a few syllables down from the ambiguous and unambiguous words:

(9) a. Frank took the pipe from the dollar rack in the store.
     b. Frank took the cigar from the dollar rack in the store.

For the pair of sentences in (9), phoneme monitoring times did not differ. The additional complexity produced by the ambiguous word is over just a few syllables later. This suggests that when an ambiguous word is encountered while processing a sentence, all of its meanings are retrieved, but very quickly one of the meanings is selected. On what basis is one meaning selected over the other?

To answer this question, David Swinney developed an account of lexical ambiguity processing, using empirical evidence from a technique called **cross-modal priming**. In a cross-modal priming experiment, participants are asked to make lexical decisions on words presented visually while they are listening to sentences presented auditorily. Sometimes the word that appears visually is a close associate of a word contained in the sentence presented auditorily. The logic of cross-modal priming is that ambiguous words will prime only those associates of the meaning or meanings that are currently active. For example, suppose you are listening to a sentence like the following:

(10) The man was not surprised when he found several bugs in the corner of his room.

The ambiguous word *bug* can mean either an insect or a covert listening device. If the insect meaning is active, then related words like *ant* should be primed. If the other meaning is active, then related words like *spy* should be primed. In one experiment, Swinney (1979) had participants listen to sentences like (10). At the offset of the word *bugs*, one of three words was displayed for lexical decision: *ant*, *spy*, or *sew* (this third word was unrelated to either of the meanings of *bug*). Participants responded faster to both *ant* and *spy* than to *sew*. This finding confirmed that all meanings of an ambiguous word are initially accessed while a sentence is being processed.

What about context? In sentences like (10), there is no prior context to disambiguate the lexical ambiguity. But consider a sentence like (11):

(11)   The man was not surprised when he found several spiders, roaches, and other bugs in the corner of his room.

Will all meanings of *bug* still be retrieved? With sentences such as (11), Swinney (1979) found that both *ant* and *spy* were still primed, when presented at the offset of *bugs*.

A final manipulation in Swinney's (1979) investigation involved pre-senting the lexical decision targets *ant*, *spy*, and *sew* a few syllables after the offset of *bugs*. When the targets appeared between *the* and *corner*, the contextually related target *ant* was primed, but not the contextually unrelated target *spy* (or the fully unrelated target *sew*). Similar to Cairns and Kamerman's findings (with sentences like (9)), a single meaning for the ambiguous lexical item had been selected only a few words downstream, in this case, the contextually related meaning.

Accessing the lexicon while processing sentences, then, begins with phonological information activating all matching lexical entries, and is followed by selection among those entries of the one that best fits the current sentence. When the context offers a bias for one of the activated entries, the context-appropriate word is selected. When the context does not provide a bias, the most frequent meaning is selected.

Accordingly, the initial retrieval of all possible meanings is exclu-sively a bottom-up process. Information contained in the phonological representation of the word directs activation of all potential candidates for retrieval: every lexical entry matching that phonological structure is activated. Selection, however, involves top-down processing. The hearer recruits any and all information available to direct the selection process: the context inside the sentence, context provided by the sen-tences preceding the current sentence, knowledge about the speaker, real-world knowledge, and so on. Thus, processing lexical ambiguity is another excellent example of the general observation that top-down processes are recruited when bottom-up processes prove to be insuffi-cient. Bottom-up processes do not uniquely specify a single lexical entry, so top-down processes take over.

▓ Summing Up

We have described how hearers use information carried by an acoustic signal to determine the phonological form of an utterance and retrieve lexical items. The phonological representation is constructed from the signal, using multiple sources of information. Evidence that demonstrates how this works includes phonological illusions like the McGurk effect and phoneme restoration.

We also reviewed evidence about how the phonological representation being constructed guides lexical access, activating all potential matches. Research on how words are retrieved offers insights about both how the lexicon is accessed and how words in the lexicon are organized, both phonologically and semantically, with respect to each other, both within a single language (in monolinguals) and between languages (in bilinguals).

Finally, we explored how lexical access works while words are retrieved during sentence comprehension. Low frequency words increase processing cost, because they take longer to retrieve. Ambiguous words increase processing cost, because incorporating a word into a sentence requires selecting a context-appropriate meaning.

Recovering a phonological representation and lexical retrieval are the two steps in sentence processing that are the precursors to syntactic processing, or parsing, the topic of the next chapter.

New Concepts

bottom-up information	phoneme monitoring task
categorical perception	phoneme restoration
cognates	possible non-words
cohort	post-access matching
cohort model of lexical access	prime
constructive speech perception	priming
cross-modal priming	recognition point
form priming	resource sharing
garden path sentence	semantic (associative)
impossible non-words	priming
lexical access	slips of the ear
lexical decision task	speech perception
lexical frequency	speech signal
masked priming	continuous
McGurk effect	parallel transmission
morpheme stripping	target
neighborhood	top-down information
neighborhood density	variability, lack of invariance
orthography	voice onset time (VOT)

Study Questions

1. Why is coarticulation so important for speech perception?

2. When comparing the syllables [di], [da], and [du], what is meant by the statement that the initial consonant [d] exists in the speaker/hearer's mind but not in the physical speech signal?

3. What are the sources of variability in speech? How does speech perception overcome acoustic variability to create a mental percept?

4. Explain categorical perception, making reference to Figure 6.5. How does the hearer's linguistic competence influence his perceptual categories?

5. What does it mean to say the perceptual system is constructive? How do phonological illusions support this claim?

6. What are some ways that speech perception in a second language differs from speech perception in the native language of a monolingual?

7. What are some of the differences between languages in the way that suprasegmental information is used during speech perception?

8. What is the role of phonology during reading? What is the role of orthography? Do these two systems operate independently?

9. What is the difference between bottom-up and top-down processing? When do psycholinguists think that top-down processing is used by the hearer? Is this a conscious decision on the part of the hearer?

10. How does the frequency and ambiguity of lexical items affect subjects' performance on a lexical decision task? Do these variables have the same effect when words are processed in sentences?

11. What are "garden path" sentences? Why are they of interest to psycholinguists?

12. Lexical processing in sentence comprehension involves two operations: retrieval and selection. How do Swinney's cross-modal priming experiments demonstrate these processes with respect to ambiguous lexical items?

7 The Hearer: Structural Processing

In order to understand the message carried by a sentence, the hearer must reconstruct the structural units that convey the intended meaning. Recall from Chapter 5 that the speaker creates mental representations of those elements: a set of words syntactically related to each other. As we discussed in Chapter 6, the hearer uses knowledge of language and information in the acoustic signal to reconstruct a phonological representation that is then used to retrieve a set of lexical items from the internalized lexicon. Identifying the syntactic relations between the perceived set of words is the essential next step, which eventually leads to recovering the basic meaning the speaker intended. Reconstructing the structure of a sentence, the focus of this chapter, is a job undertaken by the **structural processor**, or **parser**.

A review of the basic operations of the syntax will assist in understanding the operation of the parser:

- it creates basic structures;
- it combines simple sentences into complex ones; and
- it moves elements of sentences from one structural position to another.

The parser needs to identify the basic components of sentences (elements like subjects and predicates, prepositional phrases, relative clauses, and so on). It can only do this if it is able to dismantle complex sentences into simple clauses. And it must also be able to identify elements that have been moved and link them up with the gaps they left behind in their original structural positions.

In the sections that follow, we explore what psycholinguists have discovered about the way the parser builds structure during sentence processing. We first take on the question of the psychological reality of sentence structure and provide evidence for the claim that the clauses that make up complex sentences are processed as individual units. We then discuss how studying structural ambiguities has shed light on how the parser operates, examining some of the basic strategies the parser follows when building syntactic structure. We then consider the different types of information that the parser can exploit to determine the syntactic relations among words.

■ The Psychological Reality of Syntactic Structure

Sentence processing involves recovering abstract mental structures based solely on the hearer's knowledge of language, since the signal itself carries no information about syntax. In writing, commas and periods help to indicate when clauses begin and end; in speech, prosody sometimes carries information about certain types of syntactic constituents (we will discuss this later on). But for the most part, syntactic units – from subject NPs to predicate VPs, and everything in between – are not labeled as such in the signal. Yet we think that hearers (and readers) systematically compute syntactic structure while processing sentences. How do we know this is so?

Early experiments studying sentence comprehension measured how processing sentences affected performance in other cognitive tasks, like memory and perception. In such experiments people would be asked to memorize lists of words, or to listen to lists of words presented in noise; the investigators would measure to what extent performance was impaired under different conditions. One experiment (Miller and Selfridge 1950) compared how well people memorized word lists like the following:

(1) a. hammer neatly unearned ill-treat earldom turkey that valve outpost broaden isolation solemnity lurk far-sighted Britain latitude task pub excessively chafe competence doubtless tether backward query exponent prose resourcefulness intermittently auburn Hawaii uninhabit topsail nestle raisin liner communist Canada debauchery engulf appraise mirage loop referendum dowager absolutely towering aqueous lunatic problem
    b. the old professor's seventieth birthday was made a great occasion for public honors and a gathering of his disciples and former pupils from all over Europe thereafter he lectured publicly less and less often and for ten years received a few of his students at his house near the university

The systematic finding in experiments like this was that unstructured sets of words, like the 50 words in (1a), were much harder to recall than structured sets, like the 50 words in (1b) (Miller and Selfridge 1950). A greater percentage of words was recalled from the structured than from the unstructured sets of words. A straightforward explanation of this effect proposes that syntactic structure is psychologically real. Recalling strings of words is easier if the words are related to each other syntactically. The psychological reality of sentence structure is pervasive and profound, even though syntactic structure itself is abstract and not as consciously available as words are.

An alternative hypothesis is that recall in experiments like the one just described is facilitated, not by syntactic structure, but by the semantic relations among words: after all, the passage in (1b) means something, while the one in (1a) does not. Can people compute syntactic relations in the absence of meaning? Consider the opening verse of the poem "Jabberwocky," written by Lewis Carroll in 1872:

(2)   'Twas brillig, and the slithy toves
      Did gyre and gimble in the wabe:
      All mimsy were the borogoves,
      And the mome raths outgrabe.

When you read or hear Jabberwocky language – language consisting of pseudowords placed in grammatical syntactic frames – you cannot help but compute the syntactic relations, even though you may have no idea what the words actually mean. You (tacitly) know that *toves* is the head noun of the subject NP in the first clause, that *gyre* and *gimble* are verbs, and that *in the wabe* is a locative PP indicating where the toves gyred and gimbled. This has been demonstrated by a number of investigations of how people process Jabberwocky language. One experiment used functional magnetic resonance imaging (fMRI) to examine brain activity in people listening to speech input with or without meaning, with or without syntax (Friederici, Meyer, and Cramon 2000) – sentences like the following:

(3) a. The hungry cat chased the fast mouse.
     b. The mumphy folofel fonged the apole trecon.
     c. The cook silent cat velocity yet honor.
     d. The norp burch orlont kinker deftey glaunch legery.

(The materials actually used were in German; these examples are the English translations provided by Friederici et al.) The study found that certain areas of the brain, in the left inferior frontal cortex, are exclusively recruited when processing input that contains syntactic relations – sentences like (3a) and (3b) – compared to simple word lists – like (3c) and (3d).

   This and many other experiments examining brain activity during sentence processing indicate that syntactic processing has not only psychological reality but also specific physiological correlates. Investigations examining event-related potentials (ERP) have discovered components specifically related to processing syntax, some of which we discussed briefly in Chapter 3. Two such components are the very early left anterior negativity (ELAN) and the left anterior negativity (LAN). In both of these components, there is increased negativity with syntactically anomalous sentences. The ELAN is very early (around 150–200 milliseconds after the onset of the anomaly), and is a response to syntactic structure that cannot be computed, like the example in (4a), compared to (4b) (Neville et al. 1991):

(4) a. *Max's of proof.
     b. Max's proof.

The ELAN response is obtained both with regular sentences and sentences with Jabberwocky words (Hahne and Jescheniak 2001). The

ELAN, thus, is the brain's response to **word category errors**, that is, when the category of a new word does not fit into the current structure being built by the parser. The brain responds slightly differently to **morphosyntactic violations**:

(5)   a.   *The elected official hope to succeed.
      b.   The elected official hopes to succeed.

Subject–verb agreement violations, like the one in (5a) compared to (5b), elicit a LAN, involving negativity around 300–500 milliseconds after the onset of the anomaly (Osterhout and Mobley 1995).

Ungrammaticality, like word category errors and morphosyntactic violations, also elicits a P600 – an ERP component involving positivity at around 600 milliseconds (Osterhout and Holcomb 1993). We will see later in this chapter that the P600 is also a characteristic brain response to garden path sentences (introduced in Chapter 6), which are grammatical but hard to process for structural reasons. All of these ERP components are different from the N400 component, which is elicited by semantic anomalies. That the brain should have such specific responses to different types of syntactic anomalies, which in turn differ from responses to semantic anomalies, is strong evidence of the psychological reality of syntactic structure building during sentence comprehension.

The clause as a processing unit

Recall from Chapter 2 that a clause consists of a verb and its arguments. (In the tree-diagramming notation introduced in Chapter 2, a clause is an S-node.) A given sentence can include an independent clause and one or more dependent clauses. Each clause corresponds to an integrated representation of meaning and an integrated representation of structure, so clauses are reasonable candidates for processing units. Clauses correspond to manageable units for storage in working memory during processing. In Chapter 5, we described research in sentence production suggesting that clause-sized units are used in planning. It is not surprising that clauses – units containing a verb plus its arguments – also play a role in perceptual processing.

Decades ago *click displacement studies* confirmed the idea that clauses constitute processing units (Fodor and Bever 1965; Garrett, Bever, and Fodor 1966). These studies worked on the principle of perceptual displacement that was briefly mentioned in Chapter 6, in the context of phoneme restoration. The phenomenon is simple: a stimulus can sometimes be displaced, and perceived as having occurred either before or after a perceptual unit of processing. Consider, as an example, a study by Fodor and Bever (1965) in which people heard sentences like the following:

(6) a. In her hope of marrying Anna was surely impractical.
    b. Your hope of marrying Anna was surely impractical.

Notice that in (6a) there is a **clause boundary** separating the words *marrying* and *Anna* (the dependent clause in (6a) is similar to the adverbial clauses briefly described in Chapter 2); in contrast, in (6b) the words *marrying Anna* are part of the same syntactic constituent (here, *marrying Anna* is a construction containing a verb that has been turned into a noun, through a process called nominalization; *your hope of marrying Anna* is the (complex) subject of the sentence). A clause boundary is the location where a new clause begins.

In this experiment, a brief tone sounding much like a click was superimposed on the tape, coinciding with the middle of the word *Anna*. Importantly, the two versions of the sentence were created by splicing in an identical recording for the parts containing identical words, so that any prosodic (intonation or phrasing) differences between the two sentences would be eliminated. Participants reported hearing the click very differently in the two sentences. They said the click occurred before *Anna* in (6a), but after *Anna* in (6b). This is an elegant demonstration of the psychological reality of sentence structure: participants heard physically identical stimuli but responded to the click differently depending on the abstract structure of the sentence. The finding is inexplicable if people do not construct internal representations of the abstract structures of the sentences they hear, even though these structures have no physical reality. The experiment also illustrates that the constituents of the abstract structures – an adverbial clause in (6a), a complex subject in (6b) – form integrated processing units.

If the parser breaks up complex sentences into clause-sized units, as the click displacement studies suggest, then sentence processing should be easier when clause boundaries are easier to locate. Consider the following example:

(7) a. Mirabelle knows the boys next door.
    b. Mirabelle knows the boys are rowdy.

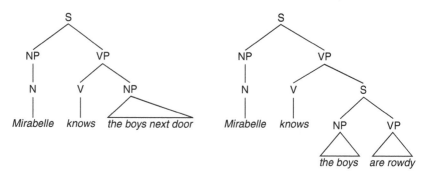

Figure 7.1   Diagrams for sentences (7a) and (7b). This figure repeats Figure 2.10 from Chapter 2.

The simple sentence in (7a) consists of a single clause, while the complex sentence in (7b) contains two clauses – an independent clause (*Mirabelle knows* [*something*]) and a sentential complement (*the boys are rowdy*); Figure 7.1 provides diagrams for the two sentences.

The work of the parser is, logically, facilitated when important syntactic constituents, like clauses, are marked explicitly in the signal. Clause boundaries can be marked by function words (like *that* or *who*), by punctuation (commas or periods), and by prosody (pitch movements or pauses). In (7b), the boundary between the two clauses is not marked. Compare it to the following, where the complementizer *that* identifies the beginning of the new clause:

(7)   c.   Mirabelle knows that the boys are rowdy.

Many investigations – Hakes (1972), for example – have demonstrated that more computation resources are recruited in processing sentences like (7b) than sentences like (7c). Sentences with marked clause boundaries incur less psycholinguistic processing cost than do sentences with unmarked clause boundaries.

Structural ambiguity

Deconstructing the incoming signal into individual clauses and computing their internal structure is not the only task that the parser faces during sentence processing. It must deal with the **structural ambiguity** of many sentences. In earlier chapters we discussed **globally ambiguous** sentences, like the following:

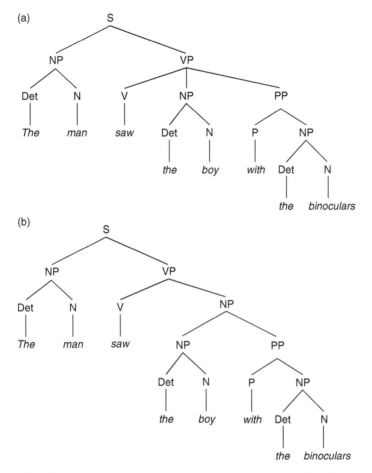

Figure 7.2 Diagrams for the two syntactic structures associated with the structurally ambiguous sentence in (8). This figure repeats Figure 1.2 from Chapter 1.

(8)   The man saw the boy with the binoculars.

Such sentences have two alternative syntactic structures: for the sentence in (8), the PP *with the binoculars* is either a modifier of *boy* or an argument of the verb *saw*; the two structures are diagrammed in Figure 7.2. Globally ambiguous sentences can be very informative about how people process sentences; as it turns out, people generally fail to notice the global ambiguity and have one preferred interpretation. So ambiguity per se does not always incur processing costs, as we will see later.

Global ambiguities provide insight into sentence processing, and so do **local ambiguities**. We have already seen a locally ambiguous constituent, in the sentence in (7b), where the NP *the boys* could initially be either the object of *knows* or the subject of a new clause. The ambiguity is local, because information coming later in the sentence serves to **disambiguate**. As soon as you get to the next word (*are*), the first structural alternative is ruled out.

Local ambiguities are everywhere. To illustrate this for yourself, try to complete the phrase below as many different ways as you can think of:

(9)   The student told the professor that …

There are many possible continuations; all of the following are structurally very different:

(9)   a.   … he wanted a better grade.
       b.   … taught the course that he wanted a better grade.
       c.   … really unbelievable story.

In (9a), *that* is a complementizer; introducing a sentential complement; in (9b) *that* is a relativizer introducing a relative clause. In (9c), *that* is a demonstrative adjective introducing a noun phrase.

Sometimes local ambiguities are resolved very quickly and go completely unnoticed. This is probably the case for the local ambiguity in (7b). Other times, however, a local ambiguity can lead to a **garden path**, as in the sentence below (Bever 1970):

(10)   The horse raced past the barn fell.

(Before you continue reading, try to identify the local ambiguity in (10); it will help you explain why the sentence is a garden path.)
The structure in (10) includes a **reduced relative clause**, a construction we discussed in Chapter 2, with examples like the following:

(11)   Danielle emailed me a photograph of the Corvette raced at the Daytona Speedway.

In (11), the reduced relative clause is *raced at the Daytona Speedway*. In (10), the reduced relative clause is *raced past the barn* – reduced from *which was raced past the barn*. As noted in the previous section, the parser's work is facilitated when a new clause is marked explicitly by a

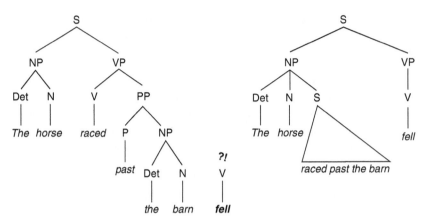

Figure 7.3   Diagrams illustrating the way the garden path sentence in (10) is parsed. The left panel shows the structure that corresponds to taking the verb *raced* as a simple past. This analysis leads to a garden path: when *fell* is reached, there is no place to incorporate it. The right panel shows the intended structure, where *raced* is a past participle inside a reduced relative clause modifying *horse*. (The triangle in the diagram indicates that internal structure has been omitted.)

function word – for example, a complementizer (like that in (7c), above) or a relative pronoun (like *who* or *which*). Part of the difficulty with (10) has to do with the fact that the relative clause boundary is not marked explicitly. But the real difficulty is caused by the local ambiguity encountered at *raced*. In the correct interpretation of the sentence, *raced* is a past participle. In the interpretation of the sentence that leads to a garden path, *raced* is taken to be a simple past form. Overwhelmingly, people initially take *raced* to be a simple past verb, and this gets them into trouble: when they reach the verb *fell*, they have no way to incorporate it into the ongoing structure. Figure 7.3 illustrates this process. This effect is only observed when the simple past tense and the participle form of a verb are the same. For some verbs, the participle and the simple past are different; (10) is not a garden path sentence if the participle *ridden* is substituted for *raced*.

Building Structure

In order to recreate the structure of a sentence, the parser must rapidly and efficiently compute the hierarchical relationships among words, which come to it in a linear sequence. It does this while coping with the fact that at almost any point in the sentence it might have two (sometimes more) structural options to choose from. How does the parser build structure?

One source of information is the grammar: syntax and morphology help the parser identify nouns and verbs and place them inside constituents that are grammatical for the language being processed. (We discussed earlier the fact that ungrammaticality triggers different types of brain responses.) Another source of information is the lexicon: the lexical entry for a retrieved word is rich with information about possible structural frames for that word. (A section later in this chapter examines in detail how lexical information affects structure building.) A third variable is the way the parser itself operates, following a handful of routines that help it build structure using minimal computational resources, as proposed by the **garden path model** of sentence processing (Frazier and Fodor 1978; Frazier 1987). We will discuss three general strategies associated with minimal effort: minimal attachment, late closure, and active gap filling. According to the garden path model, the parser makes immediate decisions about locally ambiguous constituents, always opting for the analysis that requires fewer computational resources. Sentences with structures that cannot be processed using these general strategies will lead to a garden path, which is costly to recover from.

The garden path model is far from being the only model proposed to account for how people build syntactic structure (van Gompel and Pickering 2005), but it does provide a useful vocabulary with which to describe the basic phenomena that have led psycholinguists to posit the existence of a parser that operates independently of the grammar. The grammar constrains the parser's structural analyses (for example, the parser will not build a parse that produces an ungrammatical sentence). However, the grammar does not have preferences about structural ambiguities, nor does it contain information about the resources necessary to process particular sentences. The grammar is part of the hearer's linguistic competence, while the parser is a component of linguistic performance.

The parser's preference for simple structures

The parser has a very general preference for simple structures. This preference is captured variously in different sentence processing models; in the garden path model, simple structures are preferred because of **minimal attachment**. By application of this strategy, lexical material is incorporated into the ongoing parse by building the minimal, or simplest, structure. One way this preference is reflected in sentence processing in English is in the parser's preference for sequences consisting of a subject, a verb, and an optional object. Recall that SVO is the canonical, or default, word order of English.

Let us examine how minimal attachment works to predict processing cost for the sentence in (7b). The first word, *Mirabelle*, is a good candidate for a subject for the sentence. The second word, *knows*, is a good candidate for a verb. On encountering *the boys*, the parser applies minimal attachment and takes it to be the direct object of *knows*. This, as we know, is the incorrect structure for the sentence – as the parser would figure out as soon as it reached the next word, *are*.

At this point, the parser needs to undo the original (minimal) structure, and **reanalyze** the sentence. Reanalysis is sometimes easy, as in the case of (7b), but it is sometimes very hard, as in the severe garden path in (10). Generally, processing cost is low if the minimal structure is the correct analysis (like with (7a)), or if there are cues to prevent an incorrect minimal structure (like with (7c)).

The parser's preference for minimal structures consisting of a subject, a verb, and an optional object helps explain the severe difficulty people encounter with the garden path in (10), as well as some funny newspaper headlines, like the following:

(12)   British Left Waffles on Falkland Islands

(13)   Teacher Strikes Idle Kids

In both of these, the parser initially takes the first word to be the subject and the second to be a verb, leading to unexpected (and unintended) meanings. In (12), the headline is about indecisive talk on the part of the left-wing political party in Britain about the situation on the Falklands (and not about breakfast foods being left behind). In (13), the headline describes how a teacher work stoppage has left schoolchildren idle (and not about an abusive teacher).

Minimal attachment has entailments for the processing of ordinary sentences. One entailment is that certain structurally ambiguous sentences will have a preferred interpretation – the interpretation that involves the minimal structure. Here is an example:

(14)   The student told the professor that everyone hated a lie.

This sentence has two possible structures associated with it (they are diagrammed in Figure 7.4). The preferred interpretation – probably the

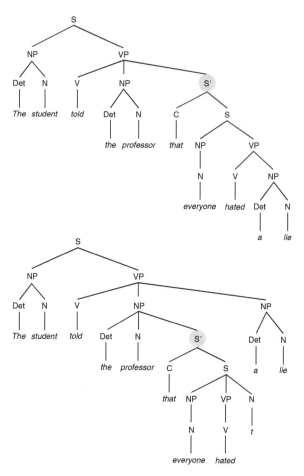

Figure 7.4 Two possible structures for the ambiguous sentence in (14). In the top panel, *that everyone hated a lie* is a sentential complement of the verb *told*. In the bottom panel, *that everyone hated* is a relative clause modifying *professor*. The top nodes for the sentential complement and the relative clause are shaded. The preferred structure is (a).

one you thought of first – has a structure in which *that everyone hated a lie* is sentential complement of the verb *told* (to paraphrase: *The student told the professor: "Everyone hates a lie"*). The less preferred structure is one in which *that everyone hated* is a relative clause modifying *professor* (to paraphrase: *The student told a lie to the professor that everyone hated*). In this second interpretation, *The student told the professor a lie* is the main clause and the relative clause is embedded under the NP headed by *professor*.

Exactly how does minimal attachment work in this example? The complementizer *that* signals a clause boundary; the new clause can be a relative clause or a sentential complement. The verb *told* requires two arguments: what was told and who it was told to. Who it was told to is *the professor*. What was told can be expressed with a sentential complement. A sentential complement clause is opened, then, and is minimally analyzed as containing a subject (*everyone*), a verb (*hated*), and an object (*a lie*). The preferred structure is a result of the combination of structural requirements of the verb and the minimal attachment strategy.

One way psycholinguists have studied garden path sentences is by tracking people's eye movements as they read sentences (Staub and Rayner 2007). In a garden path sentence, eye movements change measurably at the point where a parsing error is identified. It is important to use such sensitive methods, because sometimes garden path effects are so mild that they are not experienced consciously. Such an experiment (Frazier and Rayner 1982) examined how people read sentences like the following:

(15)   The second wife will claim the entire family inheritance belongs to her.

Notice that the structure in (15) is just like the structure in the example (7b) discussed above: the NP *the entire family inheritance* is the subject of an embedded sentential complement. On initial analysis, however, the parser takes that NP to be the direct object of *claim*, and when it reaches the verb *belongs*, it realizes something has gone wrong. Frazier and Rayner reported that eye movements move along smoothly until the reader reaches the word *belongs*. At this point, readers have longer fixations, and are more likely to make eye movements to earlier parts of the sentences, than they would with control sentences that do not induce this garden path.

The preference for minimal attachment is also evident when people are processing sentences in their second language. For example, Juffs (1998) compared reading times of native English speakers to those of second language learners whose first language was Chinese, Korean, Japanese, or a Romance language (like Spanish or French). The participants read materials like the following:

(16)   a.   The bad boys watched during the morning were playing in the park.
       b.   The bad boys seen during the morning were playing in the park.

These sentences have a structure similar to the sentence in (10): they contain a reduced relative clause modifying the subject noun, *watched during the morning* and *seen during the morning*. However, only (16a) should provoke a garden path, because *watched* can be a simple past or a past participle, but *seen* cannot be a simple past. Juffs found that the second language learners, like native speakers, were misled by the local ambiguity, as reflected in reading time patterns that were similar across the different groups of participants. Both native and non-native speakers experience a garden path effect with sentences that contained ambiguous verbs like *watched*, but not with sentences with unambiguous participles like *seen*.

Attaching new constituents

So far we have described how the parser deals with local ambiguities for which one of the structures is syntactically simpler than the other. For such local ambiguities, the parser chooses the simpler alternative, by application of minimal attachment. There are some ambiguities whose alternative structures are equally syntactically complex. Such ambiguities can be resolved by a structure building strategy called **late closure**. This strategy prompts the parser to integrate new words received from the lexical processor into the syntactic constituent that is currently being processed. Put another way, the parser has a preference to attach new material to more recent constituents rather than constituents that are farther away (*Recency Preference*, Gibson et al. 1996), because this is a computationally easier alternative. The name of the strategy is traced back to an early formulation (Frazier and Fodor 1978), which proposed that the parser keeps the constituents it is working on open as long as possible.

The application of the late closure strategy is behind many unintended interpretations of sentences in the popular press, like the following two headlines:

(17)   Physicists are thrilled to explain what they are doing to people.

(18)   Two Sisters Reunited after 18 Years in Checkout Counter

In both of these, the final prepositional phrase attaches inappropriately to a recent constituent, resulting in a funny interpretation. For (17), applying late closure results in an interpretation that suggests physicists are using human subjects in their laboratories; for (18), you might wonder what store has checkout lines with a wait of up to 18 years.

Late closure can account for the processing cost associated with sentences like the following:

(19)   John said that he will take out the garbage yesterday.

(20)   Alma was looking for a gift for a boy in a box.

In (19), the parser wants to incorporate *yesterday* into the more recent verb phrase, headed by *will take*, but there is a temporal incompatibility: *yesterday* requires a verb in past tense. In (20), the parser wants to incorporate *in a box* inside the more recent NP, *a boy*, but runs into trouble with the resulting implausible meaning (boys are generally not boxed up). Both of these sentences are costly because they involve attaching to a non-recent node, in violation of late closure.

The structure illustrated by the following sentence has posed an intriguing puzzle to psycholinguists interested in understanding how the late closure strategy works:

(21)   Someone shot the maid of the actress who was on the balcony.

In (21), the relative clause, *who was on the balcony*, is ambiguous: the person who was on the balcony could be *the actress* or *the maid*. Late closure predicts a preference for modification of the more recent noun, *actress*; this is called the **low attachment** interpretation, because the relative clause attaches to the structurally lower of the two possible attachment sites. Indeed, this is what a number of studies have found: the ambiguous relative clause is preferably attached low, as a modifier of the more recent noun (Traxler, Pickering, and Clifton 1998; Fernández 2003). It turns out, however, that the preference for low attachment can be weakened by many factors, including a long relative clause (Fernández 2003), an animate noun heading the NP (Desmet et al. 2006), certain prepositions between the two nouns (De Vincenzi and Job 1993), and by the presence of a comma before the relative clause (Carreiras 1992).

In a seminal study of this construction, Cuetos and Mitchell (1988) found that Spanish speakers prefer the **high attachment** interpretation of (21), in which the relative clause modifies *maid*. This was an important finding because psycholinguists had wondered whether low attachment was a universal processing strategy, as minimal attachment appears to be. If Spanish speakers prefer to attach relative clauses high, they do not apply late closure with this construction, hence late closure might not be universal. Subsequent work has pursued this cross-linguistic difference, and found that many languages pattern like Spanish, exhibiting a preference for high attachment of relative clauses.

Bear in mind that a late closure preference for low attachment is still observed, in languages like Spanish, for the translation-equivalents of sentences like (19), so even if Spanish speakers prefer the high attachment interpretation of (21), they obey late closure with other constructions. The cross-linguistic differences in relative clause attachment preferences clearly suggest that there is something special about the construction in (21). It is less clear, however, what is special about the construction. Some research has pursued the idea that prosody drives relative clause attachment preferences (we will discuss this later in the chapter). Other research has examined the use of pragmatic reasoning considerations to determine the preferred meaning (Frazier and Clifton 1996). Yet other work has tried to map preferences in perception with preferences in production (Desmet, Brysbaert, and De Baecke 2002), based on the hypothesis that the parser's preferences in perception can be "tuned" by the overall preferences people have in production (Mitchell and Cuetos 1991).

Even though the nature of the cross-linguistic differences in relative clause interpretation is not yet clearly understood, the finding by Cuetos and Mitchell triggered research about how bilinguals and second language learners process syntactic ambiguities in their two languages. The cross-linguistic difference lends itself easily to interesting questions about bilingual language processing: do bilinguals have similar relative clause attachment preferences in both of their languages? Some studies have found that bilinguals follow the preferences of their dominant language (Fernández 2003) or their first language (Frenck-Mestre 1999). Other work has found that bilinguals have preferences that match those of the language more frequent in their environment (Dussias 2003). Yet other research findings indicate that second language learners have no measurable preferences when interpreting relative clauses, leading to the suggestion that the structure built while parsing in a second language can be "shallower" (less detailed) than that computed for a first language (Clahsen and Felser 2006); the idea is that second language learners do not specify the attachment of the relative clause, and this is reflected in their failure to exhibit a preference for the high or the low attachment interpretation.

Some research has examined the question of whether people always build detailed syntactic representations of the sentences they are processing. This work is partly motivated by the fact that during rapid verbal interactions, in normal conversation, there may not be sufficient time for the parser to successfully reanalyze a garden path sentence, or to consult the information necessary (e.g., real-world knowledge) for successful interpretation. The pressing needs of making the next contribution to an ongoing conversation could then preempt complete processing of complex structure. Experiments by Fernanda Ferreira and colleagues (Ferreira and Patson 2007) suggest that, sometimes, people build syntactic representations that are just "**good enough.**" Consider the following examples:

(22)   a.   While Mary bathed the baby played in the crib.
       b.   *While Katie fixed the car hit a fire hydrant.

The sentence in (22a) is difficult to parse, because *the baby* is initially taken to be the direct object of *bathed*, rather than the subject of *played*. Ferreira and colleagues have found that participants asked to read such sentences, when asked about the correct interpretation, respond in ways that suggest they did not ultimately build a correct structure. For example, if asked *Did Mary bathe the baby?* they will incorrectly answer *Yes* (Ferreira, Christianson, and Hollingworth 2001). Apparently, the parse in which *the baby* is the direct object of *bathed* persists. Other experimental results support this idea: participants will correctly judge ungrammatical sentences like (22b) only about one-third of the time (Ferreira and Patson 2007). Notice that (22b) is ungrammatical because the verb *fix* requires a direct object, and the verb *hit* requires a subject; there is only one NP, *the car*. Compare (22b) to the grammatical sentence, *While Katie fixed her hair the car hit a fire hydrant.*

Filling gaps

Another function of the syntax is to move elements of a sentence around, obeying universal restrictions on movement and language-particular rules. An element that has been moved is called a **filler**, and it has left a **gap** at its original position. In order to create structures that represent sentence meaning, when it encounters a filler, the parser must identify the location for its gap. In the following sentences, *which car* is the filler:

(23)   a.   Which car did Mike drive?
       b.   Which car did Mike force off the road?
       c.   Which car did Mike force Mary to buy?

Finding the gaps can be a very simple process, as with (23a) or (23b), where the gap is obviously in the direct object position, right after the verb, *drive* and *force*, respectively. Matching fillers and gaps can get increasingly complicated, though, when there are multiple possible locations for the gap. Consider (23c), for example, where a possible spot for a gap is after the verb *force*. However, that position is already occupied, by *Mary*. The presence of this noun produces what has been termed the **filled gap effect**: processing a sentence like (23c) is slightly costlier than a sentence like (23b).

The filled gap effect apparently arises because when the parser encounters a filler, like *which car* in the sentences in (23), it immediately begins searching for a gap to insert the filler into. Frazier and Clifton (1989) have called this the **active filler strategy**. In a sentence like (23c) this strategy is thwarted because *Mary* occupies the first possible position for a gap. The parser must continue to search for an unfilled gap, which it eventually locates in direct object position, after *buy*.

A different kind of situation arises when there is a position that will allow – but not require – a gap, as in the following example (Fodor 1978):

(24)   We didn't know which book the teacher read to the children from.

In (24), the verb *read* can be transitive (appearing with a direct object) or intransitive (without a direct object). People typically perceive a sentence such as this as a garden path sentence: they initially fill the direct object gap and don't know what to do when they get to the preposition *from*. Fodor (1978) explains the fact that such a sentence produces a garden path effect by postulating a **first resort strategy for gap filling**. This strategy interacts with the active filler strategy and causes the parser to fill the first gap that it encounters. An ERP experiment by Garnsey, Tanenhaus, and Chapman (1989) confirmed this, using sentences like the following:

(25)   The businessman knew which article the secretary called at home.

Participants exhibited a large N400 after *called*, indicating that they had filled the gap with an implausible filler, *article*, obeying the first resort strategy even though the result is an implausible sentence.

Gap filling has been studied using the cross-modal priming technique. The idea is that when a filler is inserted into a gap, an abstract "copy" of the filler is actually inserted into the mental representation of the sentence at the gap position. This is known as **reactivation** of the filler. If reactivation indeed takes place, words related to the filler should be primed at gap positions. Swinney et al. (1988) used cross-modal priming to demonstrate reactivation of fillers in sentences such as the following:

(26)   The policeman saw the boy that the crowd at the party accused of
       the crime.

They found that words related to *boy* were primed at the gap following
accused, indicating that *boy* had been reactivated in the gap. At that point
there was no priming of words related to either *policeman* or *crowd*, demonstrating that only the relevant filler was reactivated. Cross-modal priming has been used to study the ability of people with Broca's aphasia to fill
gaps during sentence comprehension (Zurif et al. 1993). Broca's patients
do not show the priming effects at gaps as people without aphasia do,
suggesting that they are unable to build as complete a structural representation as people without their particular type of brain damage. Being
unable to build filler-gap chains badly impairs agrammatic aphasics' ability to understand complex sentences, even if their lexical storage and
retrieval systems are intact. This finding fits well with the idea that people
with Broca's aphasia have special problems when processing sentences in
which elements have been moved (Grodzinsky 1990).

Locating pronominal referents

The process of identifying the noun phrases to which pronouns refer is
closely related to gap filling. Recall that the grammar treats various
types of pronouns differently: a reflexive pronoun, like *himself*, must
refer to a noun phrase in its clause; a personal pronoun, such as *him*,
must refer to a noun phrase outside its clause. With those grammatical
restrictions in mind, consider the following sentences:

(27)   a.   The boxer told the skier that the doctor for the team would
            blame himself for the recent injury.
       b.   The boxer told the skier that the doctor for the team would
            blame him for the recent injury.

In (27a) *himself* must refer to *doctor* and not to either *boxer* or *skier* because
only *doctor* is in the same clause with the reflexive pronoun. In (27b),
however, *doctor* cannot be the referent of *him* because it is in the same
clause. Either *boxer* or *skier* are grammatical referents of *him* in (27b).
Using a cross-modal priming task, Nicol (1988) demonstrated that, in
fact, only *doctor* is reactivated by *himself* in (27a), and both *boxer* and
skier, but not *doctor*, are reactivated in (27b). This result is an elegant
demonstration of the fact that the parser respects restrictions imposed
by the grammar on sentence representations.

Cowart and Cairns (1987) also showed that the mechanism assigning pronoun reference is sensitive to structure. In one of their experiments, the pronoun requiring a referent was *they*, in sentences like the following:

(28)   a.   If they want to save money, visiting uncles ...
       b.   If they want to believe that visiting uncles ...

Cowart and Cairns found that *they* was understood as referring to *visiting uncles* in sentences like (28a), where coreference is grammatical, but not in (28b), where the structural relationship between *they* and *visiting uncles* prohibits their being coreferential. Structurally allowed coreference was assigned even when pragmatic information might rule out a coreferential relationship, as in the following sentence:

(29)   Whenever they lecture during the procedure, charming babies ...

Evidently, when the processor encounters *they* in (29), it immediately begins searching for a referent, selecting the first structurally available plural noun phrase, *charming babies*, despite the fact that babies delivering lectures is a fairly implausible scenario. In this sense, reference assignment is much like building a minimal filler-gap chain: the first available solution is accepted, constrained only by grammatical principles. Considerations of plausibility or real-world knowledge do not guide initial assignment of pronouns to referents or fillers to gaps.

Information Used to Build Structure

We have described garden path effects of different types in the preceding sections, under the general premise that the parser prefers to build structures with minimal effort. If the minimal structure turns out to be correct, everything runs smoothly. If the simple structure turns out to be incorrect, though, there is processing cost, because the sentence must be reanalyzed until the correct structural analysis is found.

Some of the most exciting work on sentence processing is concerned with identifying the types of information available to the parser, information that might help it avoid garden paths. We have already shown how lexical information is an important variable helping the parser make structural decisions; more examples of this line of research are discussed below. We will also examine investigations of how prosody in the speech signal affects parsing decisions. We will conclude the chapter with some discussion of research that examines the extent to which the parser is influenced by non-linguistic variables – including the visual context, discourse context, and real-world knowledge.

Lexical information

The direct input to the parser is a set of words ordered linearly (one after the other); the parser's job is to figure out how these words are related hierarchically. Lexical material comes to the parser with an abundance of information, not only semantic, but also morphosyntactic. Lexical entries contain information not only about the subcategorization frames of verbs (i.e., the arguments that a verb can take), but also about how frequently particular verbs are followed by specific types of arguments. To what extent does the parser use this information to make parsing decisions?

Let us consider a construction we have already discussed in some detail. The structure in (7b) is repeated here, with different lexical content:

(30)   Mary understood the problem had no solution.

The sentence contains a local structural ambiguity: *the problem* could be the direct object of *understood*, or the subject of a new clause. By minimal attachment, the direct object interpretation is initially preferred, but this leads to a garden path when we reach the word *had*.

The local ambiguity in (30) has to do with the fact that the subcategorization frame for *understand* permits a direct object as well as a sentential complement as arguments. Other verbs, like *think*, are different, and allow sentential complements (*Mary thinks she knows the truth*) but not direct objects (**Mary thinks the truth*).

In addition to these subcategorization frame restrictions, the lexical entry for a verb contains information about which of a verb's possible arguments are more frequent. For example, both *understand* and *admit* take direct objects or sentential complements, but a direct object is a more frequent argument for *understand*, while a sentential complement is more frequent for *admit*.

Garnsey et al. (1997) developed a large database of verbs, with information about which of the verb's arguments was more frequent – the **verb's argument bias**. The experiments in this study used two different techniques to measure difficulty: eye movements while participants were reading sentences presented one by one on a computer screen, and reading times for sentences presented one word at a time (a technique called self-paced reading). Garnsey and colleagues showed that strong garden path effects resulted with direct object biased verbs, like *understand* (*Mary understood the question had no solution*), but not with sentential complement biased verbs, like *admit* (*Mary admitted the question had no solution*).

The parser's use of verb argument bias information has also been examined in ERP experiments. Recall from Chapter 2 that different types of ERP responses are associated with syntactic anomalies (which elicit a P600) and semantic anomalies (which elicit an N400). Osterhout (1994) measured ERP responses to sentences with clausal complements, like the following:

(31)   a.   The doctor hoped the patient was lying.
       b.   The doctor believed the patient was lying.
       c.   The doctor charged the patient was lying.

The three verbs in these sentences are different from each other: *hope* subcategorizes for a sentential complement only (it cannot take a direct object); *believe* can take a direct object or a sentential complement, but it is biased toward a direct object; and *charge* can take a direct object or a sentential complement, but it is biased toward the sentential complement.

Osterhout observed a pronounced P600 effect (indicating that participants were experiencing a syntactic anomaly) in sentences like (31b): the direct object bias of the verb caused people to analyze *the patient* as the direct object, only to find they were wrong when they got the next words, *was lying*. The sentences with *hoped* (31a) and *charged* (31c) did not elicit a P600, presumably because *the patient* was not initially processed as a direct object.

Experiments like these demonstrate that verb bias information is used by the parser to make decisions about what structure to build. Recall from Chapter 2 that a lexical entry for a verb also includes selectional restrictions for that verb. Garnsey and colleagues (1997) also investigated the effect of selectional restrictions on sentence processing, by manipulating the semantic possibility that a given NP could serve as the object of the verb in question. For example, for a verb like *understand*, *snow* is not as good a direct object as *message* (see (32)); similarly, for a verb like *admit*, *airplane* is not as good a direct object as *mistake* (see (33)); and for a verb like *fear*, *dress* is not as good a direct object as *tantrums* (see (34)). Remember that *understand* is direct object biased, while *admit* is sentential complement biased; *fear* is an unbiased verb, occurring with equal frequency with direct objects or sentential complements.

(32) a. The frustrated tourists understood the snow would mean a late start.
    b. The frustrated tourists understood the message would mean they couldn't go.

(33) a. The ticket agent admitted the airplane had been late taking off.
    b. The ticket agent admitted the mistake had been careless and stupid.

(34) a. Mary Ann's mother feared the tantrums would get worse and worse.
    b. Mary Ann's mother feared the dress would get torn and dirty.

Garnsey and colleagues found that the semantic match between the verb and the following NP did not affect the garden path effect of direct object bias verbs, like *understand*. The object bias of the verbs was so strong that the following NP was analyzed as a direct object whether or not it was semantically compatible; sentences like (32a) and (32b) always produced garden paths.

In contrast, NPs following verbs with sentential complement bias were never analyzed as direct objects, regardless of their semantic compatibility with the verb; sentences like (33a) and (33b) never produced garden paths.

Selectional restrictions did have a dramatic effect with unbiased verbs. Sentences like (34a) produced garden paths, compared to sentences like (34b). The emerging picture is one in which the parser uses subcategorization and verb bias information exclusively to make structural decisions, but if that information does not lead to a particular preference, semantic information is consulted as the "tie-breaker".

Another effect of verbal information on the parser arose when we discussed the sentence in (8). We demonstrated that a garden path sentence does not result if the participle form of the verb is not the same as its simple past. Taking this idea a step further, MacDonald, Pearlmutter, and Seidenberg (1994) examined whether the frequency with which a verb appears as a participle could control whether it will create a garden path sentence in a reduced relative construction. For example, consider *carried* versus *raced*. Both are verbs in which the simple past tense and the participle forms are identical. *Raced*, however, only appears as a participle 8% of the time, whereas *carried* appears as a participle 52% of the time (Francis and Kucera 1982). MacDonald and colleagues (1994) demonstrated that verbs such as *raced* are more likely to produce garden path effects than verbs such as *carried*. Presumably it is easier for the parser to construct a reduced relative structure when it encounters a verb that is more likely to be a participle.

One final type of lexical information we will consider is the thematic information associated with verbs. The arguments of a verb relate to the structures in which it can appear, but the thematic roles of an argument refer to the semantic relationship between the argument and the verb. For example, consider the verb *open* in the following sentences:

(35) a. John opened the door.
      b. The key opened the door.
      c. The door opened.

In all three sentences, the verb *opened* requires a subject argument: *John* in (35a), *key* in (35b), and *door* in (35c). Thematically, these three noun phrases play very different roles: *John* in (35a) is the agent (the person who opened the door); *key* in (35b) is the instrument (that which was used to open the door); and *door* in (35c) is the theme (something was done to it). To examine whether thematic information can help the parser avoid garden paths, Trueswell, Tanenhaus, and Garnsey (1994) compared sentences such as the following:

(36) a. The defendant examined by the lawyer turned out to be unreliable.
      b. The evidence examined by the lawyer turned out to be unreliable.

The verb *examine* needs an agent as its subject, which means that its subject must be animate. *Evidence*, an inanimate noun, is not a good agent for *examine*, but it is a good theme for the verb. Having access to this thematic information prevents the parser from taking *examined* in (36b) as the matrix verb, and a garden path, which is produced by (36a), is avoided – as confirmed by evidence reported by Trueswell and colleagues.

Prosody

Recall from the beginning of the chapter that clause boundaries marked by function words – like *that*, for example – reduce processing cost. Subcategorization information and argument bias information can also help the parser avoid garden paths. Additional help can come in the form of the prosody of the utterance. Prosody is the intonation and phrasing of a sentence. Intonational boundaries are signaled by pitch excursions (rises or falls, or combinations of the two), fluctuations in duration (a word has a slightly longer duration at the end of an intonational phrase than when it appears in the middle of an intonational phrase), and pauses.

The contribution of prosody to parsing has been examined for many of the ambiguities described in this chapter. In this section, we discuss only two examples. Consider the following globally ambiguous sentence:

(37)   They invited Sue and Jim and Amanda got rejected.

The sentence has a different meaning, depending on how the three proper names are grouped. If there is an intonational boundary after *Sue*, one person was invited and two people got rejected. If there is an intonational boundary after *Jim*, two people were invited and one person got rejected. Indeed, participants in listening experiments interpret the sentence differently, depending on whether there is an intonational boundary after *Sue* or after *Jim*; this has been observed in English (Clifton, Carlson, and Frazier 2006) and in Bulgarian (Stoyneshka, Fodor, and Fernández 2010).

The contribution of prosody to the interpretation of relative clause attachment ambiguities has also been studied. The general finding is that, for a sentence like (21), repeated below, an intonational boundary after *maid* greatly increases the likelihood of a low attachment interpretation, while an intonational boundary after *actress* mildly increases the likelihood of a high attachment interpretation (Fernández 2007; Teira and Igoa 2007).

(21)   Someone shot the maid of the actress who was on the balcony.

Stoyneshka and colleagues (Stoyneshka, Fodor, and Fernández 2010) included sentences like the following in their investigation of Bulgarian:

(38)   Подцениха адвоката на певицата, който/която купи имението.
       Podtseniha advokata na pevitsata kojto/koiato kupi imenieto.
       '(They) underestimated the lawyer of the singer who bought the estate.'

The relative pronoun in Bulgarian is marked for gender: *kojto* is masculine, *koiato* is feminine, so depending on which relative pronoun appears in the sentence, the relative clause attaches high (to the masculine noun *advokata*) or low (to the feminine noun *pevitsata*). The audio recordings included intonational boundaries after *advokata* or *pevitsata*, and had one additional important manipulation: the part of the relative pronoun that revealed it as being masculine or feminine was spliced out and replaced with a brief segment of white noise. Participants were asked to report whether they heard *kojto* or *koiato*. (This technique to elicit participants' responses exploits the phoneme restoration effect described in Chapter 6. It was the procedure Stoyneshka and colleagues used to elicit data for the Bulgarian equivalents of sentences like (37), as well.) As expected, the prosody biased the interpretation of the ambiguity, and replicated the finding in other experiments: that an intonational boundary after the first noun, masculine *advokata*, greatly increases low attachments eliciting the perception of *koiato*, while an intonational boundary after the second noun, feminine *pevitsata*, mildly increases high attachments eliciting the perception of *kojto*.

Non-linguistic information

An important question about garden path sentences is whether they can be avoided if there is non-linguistic information, such as plausibility based on real-world knowledge, associated with them. After all, garden paths are not experienced on a regular basis (unless, of course, you are a regular participant in a sentence processing laboratory). A number of researchers have posed this question, and examined to what extent non-linguistic information affects the way the parser operates.

An investigation by Rayner, Carlson, and Frazier (1983) focused on real-world knowledge. As an example, you probably agree that performers routinely receive flowers, while florists routinely send them; this information is not stored lexically, but forms part of what you know about the real world. With those facts about performers and florists in mind, consider the following:

(39) a. The performer sent the flowers was very pleased.
      b. The florist sent the flowers was very pleased.

Does your real-world knowledge help you avert a garden path effect with (39a), but not with (39b)? This was the logic of the experiment by Rayner and colleagues: if the structural processor has access to knowledge that in the real world performers tend to receive flowers rather than send them, the garden path effect will be reduced in (39a), compared to (39b).

In the eye tracking data reported by Rayner and colleagues (1983), both of these sentences showed strong garden path effects, indicating that the parser had gone right ahead with a minimal attachment analysis despite the unequal plausibility of performers and florists sending flowers. Real-world information did, however, assist participants when they were asked to paraphrase the sentences they had just heard. The *performer* sentences were easier to paraphrase than the *florist* sentences. This secondary finding is something we will come back to in Chapter 8: incorporating the meaning of a sentence into long-term memory representations might be more reliable if the meaning fits well within what we know about the real world.

It could well be that real-world knowledge is not easy to access with sentences in isolation, without any context. A series of experiments by Rayner, Garrod, and Perfetti (1992) measured readers' performance with garden path sentences of different types, and manipulated discourse context. The target sentences (with ambiguities that might trigger garden paths) were presented surrounded by contexts that supported or did not support the minimal attachment readings of the local ambiguities. The target sentences were also sometimes in discourse focus in the passages. (Discourse focus is discussed in more detail in Chapter 8.) Rayner and colleagues found that the discourse context did not help the parser avoid garden-pathing. However, when the target sentences were in discourse focus, reanalysis was easier: participants were able to recover faster from the initial incorrect parse. These combined findings resemble those from the experiment described above (Rayner, Carlson, and Frazier 1983): the parser is not able to use real-world knowledge and discourse context immediately, but it can take it into consideration when reanalyzing the sentence, and when committing its meaning to memory.

Many recent experiments have devoted attention to the effects that the visual context has on parsing decisions. These studies use what is referred to as the **visual world paradigm**, in which people's eye gazes are tracked as they work with a visual display (consisting of objects or pictures), following directions presented auditorily. Consider the following sentences:

(40) a. Put the apple on the towel in the box.
      b. Put the apple that's on the towel in the box.

In (40a), but not in (40b), the prepositional phrase *on the towel* is locally ambiguous: it could be the destination for *apple*, or it could be a modifier of *apple*.

An experiment by Spivey and colleagues tracked participants' eye movements, as they followed instructions like those in (40), for manipulating objects in a display in front of them (Spivey et al. 2002). The display might contain a single apple on a towel (in which case only one referent is available for *the apple*), or two apples – one of which was on a towel (in which case two referents are initially available for *the apple*). The displays always also included an empty towel, and an empty box. (We discussed this experimental set-up, the visual world paradigm, in Chapter 4.)

The eye movement data reported by Spivey and colleagues show that the visual context has an immediate effect on how lexical material is incorporated into a syntactic parse. With the one-referent displays, participants initially looked at the empty towel when listening to (40a), showing that they initially interpreted the ambiguous prepositional phrase in (40a) as a destination for the apple. This difference was not observed with the two-referent displays, because in those (in which there were two apples, only one of which was on a towel), *on the towel* was initially taken to be a modifier of *apple*, allowing them to rapidly select between the two possible referents. Irrelevant to the visual aspect of this experiment, but interesting, is the fact that, when hearing (40a), participants were able to shift from a destination meaning of the prepositional phrase to the modifier interpretation upon hearing *in the box*. It is this meaning shift that young children cannot make.

▨ Summing Up

The preceding sections have described how the parser builds a structural representation of the lexical material recovered by the lexical processor. Syntactic structure is computed, following strategies for minimal effort, and by using a limited amount of information. The syntax of the language is consulted, as is information in the lexical representations for the words at issue. Also available for use by the parser is the prosody contained in the phonological representation, and information provided by the visual context. Information that goes beyond these very immediate sources – for example, knowledge about the real world – appears to be less accessible to the parser, but it may well influence what is done with the meaning of the sentence as it is incorporated into long-term memory.

The lexical processor, together with the parser, creates a representation that is sufficient to reconstruct the basic meaning of the sentence encoded by the speaker. Once that basic meaning is determined, the sentence can be stored in memory, understood as part of a narrative, or treated as part of a conversation. How people store sentences in memory and use them in conversations is the subject of the next chapter.

New Concepts

active filler strategy	local ambiguity
clause boundary	low attachment
disambiguation	minimal attachment
filled gap effect	morphosyntactic
filler	violations
first resort strategy	parser (structural processor)
gap	reactivation
garden path	reanalysis
garden path model	reduced relative clause
global ambiguity	structural ambiguity
"good enough" representations	verb argument bias
high attachment	visual world paradigm
late closure	word category errors

Study Questions

1. Ask several friends to memorize the two word lists in (1). From which list are more words recalled, (1a) or (1b)? Why?

2. How do experiments using Jabberwocky language demonstrate that people compute syntactic structure automatically?

3. How does the click displacement study by Fodor and Bever (1965) demonstrate that the clause is a unit in sentence comprehension?

4. What is a clause boundary? What are two reasons the parser's task is made easier by the marking of clause boundaries? How can clause boundaries be marked?

5. Describe the minimal attachment strategy and show how this preference on the part of the parser can result in a garden path effect.

6. Describe the source of the structural ambiguity of the sentence *Physicists are thrilled to explain what they are doing to people.* Why is the funny interpretation also the preferred interpretation?

7. Explain the difficulty of the sentences (i) *The soldiers marched into the desert surprised the Persian forces* and (ii) *When Madonna sings the song is always a hit.* How are they illustrative of important parsing preferences?

8. Consider the experiment by Garnsey et al. (1997). Why did direct object biased verbs result in garden path effects, but not verbs biased toward clausal arguments? What kind of an effect did selectional restrictions have on the verbs that were unbiased for argument type?

9. How does prosodic information help the parser avoid garden paths?

10. The first resort strategy for gap filling is another example of a strategy that facilitates the speed and efficiency of parsing, although it can result in analyses that need to be reprocessed. Describe the strategy and explain why this statement about it is correct.

11. How does the online discovery of referents for pronouns demonstrate that the parser creates structure and obeys grammatical constraints?

12. Review all the kinds of information the parser uses to avoid creating an analysis that will result in a garden path effect. What kind of information does it not use? Why does the inability to use certain kinds of information actually increase the speed and efficiency of sentence processing?

8 Remembering Sentences, Processing Discourse, and Having Conversations

The preceding three chapters have presented the processes engaged during the production and perception of sentences. We have focused on sentences produced or perceived in isolation. Yet sentences hardly ever occur under such conditions. While a sentence, uttered or written, may be comprehensible by itself, the effect it might have on a listener or reader – or on a speaker or writer, for that matter – will invariably differ depending on a number of factors. Among these are: the context the sentence occurs in, the state of mind of the perceiver or producer, the purpose of the interaction, and the mode (oral or written) of the interaction. As an example, consider an utterance like *Thanks a lot!* The speaker might be grateful or resentful, sincere or sarcastic, and multiple variables will affect what the set of words is intended to convey, beyond its literal meaning, as well as what effect the utterance will have on both speaker and listener.

In this chapter we examine discourse processing, an area of psycholinguistics that draws from research in sociolinguistics, anthropological linguistics, and the philosophy of language. We will begin by surveying the range of discourse domains that the human language processing mechanism is exposed to, identifying some of the basic phenomena studied under the domain of discourse processing. We will then discuss some of the critical differences between processing individual sentences and processing sentences linked together inside a discourse. We will consider the ways that working memory and long-term memory are used in discourse processing. This will be followed by a section describing the linguistic units and the psychological processes that play a central role in making the sentences within a discourse coherent. We will conclude with a section on the principles that guide how people have conversations, as one example of the many types of discourse that follow such principles.

■ Discourse: Beyond the Sentence

In both semantics and pragmatics, the term **discourse** is used to refer to sets of sentences that have some sort of connection to each other. Other terms used to refer to the same concept (by linguists, psycholinguists, and scholars in a number of other fields) include **text** and **narrative**. When people engage in sustained linguistic interaction, they are creating discourse. Letters, emails, stories, lectures, meetings, debates, instant messaging sessions, and face-to-face conversations are all examples of types of discourse. The primary objective in such exchanges is usually to communicate, to transmit information; we will see later in this chapter that sometimes the primary objective is to socialize or bond.

In this chapter we will try to provide examples from a number of different **discourse domains**, to illustrate an important point: the principles that are at play in the organization of discourse are vastly similar, whether the discourse is written (a letter) or oral (a conversation); whether the exchange is conducted in real time (an instant messaging session) or asynchronously (an electronic discussion board); and whether the interlocutors are in immediate proximity to each other (a face-to-face conversation) or located in different parts of the planet (a long-distance telephone call). Different discourse domains will sometimes call for domain-specific linguistic behaviors. For example, you probably talk to your friends differently than the way you talk to your professors. If you speak more than one language, you also probably have a very good sense about which of your languages is the best one to use, depending on your interlocutor (i.e., the person you are talking to), the topic of the conversation, the reason for your interaction, and so on. The discourse domain will also dictate the way to express certain elements within a discourse that might not be domain specific. For example, both an instant messaging session and a business letter are expected to have elements to indicate when the discourse is coming to a close, but it would be very strange to close an instant messaging session with *Very truly yours*, and it would be equally odd to close a business letter with *TTYL :)*.

The **topic** of a given discourse segment – as well as its **participants**, its **context**, and its **function** – will determine the amount of knowledge necessary for successful engagement with it. Think of the types of sentences you are likely to encounter while reading a passage about particle physics, or the current baseball season, or phonological representations. The sentences in each passage will necessarily include domain-specific terminology (e.g., *gluon, shortstop, phoneme*), and will likely use or allude to domain-specific extra-linguistic symbols (e.g., diagrams of sub-atomic particles, hand gestures used by umpires, syllable structure trees). Reading each of these passages successfully, then, will require much more than the ability to decode the letters on the page and grammatical competence in the language of the passage, to reconstruct the meaning of the individual sentences. Reading these passages will also require some familiarity with the way that the experts in these fields talk and think about their subject matter, i.e., literacy in the **semiotic domain** of the passage (Gee 2003). (The term *semiotic* expands the notion of a discourse domain to include non-linguistic symbols.) Depending on your own expertise in each of these semiotic domains, you may be able to extract more or less information from each of those hypothetical passages.

Do experts really process language differently from novices? Beilock and Lyons (2008) report some findings that might help answer this question. They acquired fMRI scans of people listening to sentences like the following:

(1) a. The individual pushed the doorbell.
     b. The hockey player received the pass.

There were three types of participants in this experiment: hockey experts (athletes in a first division league), hockey fans (who reported having extensive experience watching hockey, but were not athletes themselves), and hockey novices (who reported neither playing nor watching hockey). Participants had to listen to the sentences and respond to pictures presented that matched or did not match the message conveyed by the sentence. For sentences like (1a), all participants were slower to make a judgment when the sentence did not match the picture than when it did; everyone has experience with pushing door-bells. But for sentences like (1b), the hockey athletes and fans showed the mismatch effect, while the hockey novices did not, suggesting that the experts' experience with hockey led to a very specific mental simulation of the actions described by the hockey-related sentence. This was confirmed by the neuroimaging data, which showed activation of the motor-planning areas of the brain in the hockey athletes and fans (but not the novices) listening to the hockey-related sentences: the experts were simulating the action talked about in the hockey-related sentences.

Understanding discourse – be it written or spoken – is linked only minimally to the words we might be looking at or listening to, though it goes without saying that being able to process individual words and individual sentences is an absolutely necessary prerequisite for the type of processing we will discuss in this chapter. The information we extract from those printed or spoken words becomes represented mentally in an elaborate matrix of existing knowledge, attitudes, and emotional biases we might have about the topic, the writer or speaker, the reason we are reading or conversing, and so on. To understand discourse, we take the basic meanings of the individual sentences and integrate them into a coherent framework by discovering the links between and among the meanings of the sentences that make up the discourse. This goal requires an intricate orchestration of a number of different processes, which include committing elements of the preceding sentences to memory, finding references for anaphoric elements in current or upcoming sentences, and building inferences. The sections that follow address each of these processes in turn.

Working Memory and Sentence Processing

While a sentence is being processed, words are held in **working memory**. This is a storage system where information is retained for very brief periods of time before it is sent on in a recoded form to long-term memory. The famous psycholinguist George Miller discovered that people can remember approximately five to nine bits of information for short periods of time. He coined the term **chunks** to refer to these information bits. In an article titled "The magical number seven plus or minus two," Miller (1956) reported experiments demonstrating that people can recall five to nine single letters, short words, or short sentences – five to nine chunks of information. For these chunks to be held in working memory, they must first be recoded into analyzed units (recall from Chapters 6 and 7 that words and sentences must be reconstructed from an indeterminate signal). This, as we have already seen, is the primary task of the sentence comprehension system. Working memory, then, provides a finite amount of (temporary) storage space which can get used up if the processing system is being asked to do too much at once, or if the processing system is performing just one task that is very resource demanding. Think of how a computer is limited by its technological specifications, like its clock speed and amount of random-access memory. If these working-memory-like resources are all used up, the computer will slow down or maybe even crash.

The role of working memory in sentence processing has been investigated in many ways. Early studies (Foss and Cairns 1970; Wanner and Maratsos 1978) showed that requiring participants to recall word lists impaired their ability to process sentences. Similarly, Slowiaczek and Clifton (1980) demonstrated that silent reading comprehension is impaired if readers are distracted by a verbal task, like counting or repeating a short phrase (e.g., *Coca-Cola cola*). A number of studies have shown that compromising working memory resources (e.g., by a distracting task), affects processing more with sentences of greater complexity, such as those with subject–object relative clauses (2a), than with less complex sentences, such as those with the analogous subject–subject relative clause (2b):

(2) a. The reporter that the senator attacked admitted the error.
     b. The reporter that attacked the senator admitted the error.

We have been discussing working memory in spatial terms, particularly when making the analogy between the temporary storage that humans and computers use during processing. Research that examines the role of working memory in language processing uses what is called **working memory span** to understand how working memory supports or limits processing. Working memory span is measured in different ways, including tests that measure digit span, reading span, and operation span. In a reading span test, for example, people read a sequence of sentences, presented one after the other, and have to remember the last word of each sentence. The first trial is a sequence of two sentences, and subsequent trials increase the number of sentences by one. Participants who recall more words have higher working memory spans. These types of tests are essentially ways to estimate the temporary storage space; they differ depending on the type of chunks they measure (numbers, words, and so on).

Researchers have investigated the language processing abilities of people with varying working memory spans. For instance, Just and Carpenter (1992) showed that people with low memory spans have more difficulty with subject–object relative clauses than do people with high memory spans. In order to understand a sentence like (2a), a person must maintain *the reporter* in working memory so it will be available to fill the gap following *attacked*. The better the memory span, the more available the filler will be. Carpenter, Miyake, and Just (1994) reported studies showing that following access of all the meanings of an ambiguous lexical item, people with high memory spans were able to maintain them in working memory for longer periods of time than people with more limited spans. As a result, high-span people are less adversely affected by lengthy delay of disambiguating information than are low-span people.

During discourse processing, working memory plays a key role by providing the platform for the ongoing computations that perform all of the operations we have discussed in Chapters 6 and 7: pre-lexical recognition, lexical access, and the integration of lexical elements into a syntactic frame, as individual sentences are processed. Thus, working memory is associated with obtaining the basic building blocks of sentence meanings. But discourse processing requires access to other resources, so that individual sentences can be retained and integrated with other information. This information is stored in long-term memory, which, as we will see, is crucial for actually putting individual sentence meanings to use.

Memory for sentences

Three important things happen to sentences when they get stored in **long-term memory**. First, information about structure and even individual lexical items is lost, while meaning is retained. Second, meanings of many sentences are combined, so individual sentences no longer have independent representations. Third, inferences are added to representations of meaning. Any human-to-computer analogy for memory stops working at this point. When you save a word processing document, or a sound clip, or an image file on your computer's hard drive – its long-term memory – it is saved in an intact form, and it does not change while it is in long-term storage (unless malware corrupts or destroys your files). If computers worked like human long-term memory, a document you saved yesterday and will not open until tomorrow could be altered by a document you create today.

A well-known early experiment on memory for sentences demonstrated that information about form (structure) is not retained, while information about content (meaning) is (Sachs 1967). Participants listened to a narrative containing the sentence in (3), followed by a probe sentence, one of the three sentences in (4); participants were to judge whether they had heard the probe sentence in the narrative.

(3)   He sent a letter about it to Galileo, the great Italian scientist.

(4)   a.   He sent a letter about it to Galileo, the great Italian scientist.
      b.   He sent Galileo, the great Italian scientist, a letter about it.
      c.   Galileo, the great Italian scientist, sent him a letter about it.

To respond to the probes, participants in the experiment would have to search their memory representation of the narrative, attempting to match the probe with part of that representation. Notice that the first probe is identical to the sentence that actually appeared in the passage; the second probe changes the structure, but not the meaning; the third probe changes both the structure and the meaning. Participants tested immediately after hearing the sentence in the passage were very accurate at identifying only (4a) as having been heard in the passage. However, participants who were tested after a brief time interval (less than a minute) would report having heard both (4a) and (4b), suggesting that they did not retain the exact form of the sentence in memory, but held on to the meaning.

There is compelling evidence that, when people are asked to recall a sentence heard just a few moments before, the sentence is regenerated rather than merely recalled verbatim; in other words, people use active lexical representations plus sentence production mechanisms to reconstruct the syntax of the recalled sentence. Potter and Lombardi (1990) devised an experimental paradigm to test this idea. They presented sentences, like the example in (5), word by word (using a technique called *RSVP*, or *rapid serial visual presentation*), and participants read them silently for recall.

(5)   The knight rode around the palace searching for a place to enter.

Before or after the word-by-word presentation of the sentence, participants had a distracter task. They saw a sequence of six words – five in
lower case, the last one in capital letters – and had to say whether the
final word was one of the preceding five. In some trials, the word list
contained a "lure" word, that is, a synonym of one of the words in the
sentence to be recalled; for the example in (5), among the five lower-
case words was the word *castle*, as a synonym of *palace*. Potter and
Lombardi (1990) found that participants frequently substituted, in
recall, the plausible lure nouns for nouns actually occurring in the stimulus sentence, producing sentences like *The knight rode around the castle
searching for a place to enter.*

Lombardi and Potter (1992) replicated this finding with verbs, and
further demonstrated that the structure of the recalled sentence is generated on the spot. One of the structure types tested by Lombardi and
Potter is the dative alternation illustrated in (6):

(6)   a.   The rich widow is going to give a million dollars to the
            university.
        b.   The rich widow is going to give the university a million
            dollars.

Notice that replacing *donate* for *give* results in a grammatical sentence in
(6a) but not in (6b); this is because the verb *give* permits the alternation
in (6b), while *donate* does not. For the trials with non-alternating lures
like *donate*, participants were extremely unlikely to change the basic
structure with sentences like (6a). But when the stimulus sentence was
(6b), and an alternating lure intruded, participants were extremely
likely to change the basic structure in their response, from the alternating structure in (6b) to the non-alternating *The rich widow is going to
donate a million dollars to the university.*

Investigations like these demonstrate that people retain a representation of the meaning of sentences they hear, but not the exact form. It is a
perfectly reasonable finding, since sentence structure exists only to
determine the basic meaning of a sentence. Once that task has been
accomplished, sentence structure is useless and need not be stored in
memory. People recall the gist (general meaning) of what they have heard,
but not the surface form. Bilinguals who listen to radio stations in both
their languages report that they often remember the content of a particular news report but do not recall which language they originally heard
it in. Likewise, bilinguals might remember the gist of a conversation

had with another bilingual, but might not be able to recall with precision which language the conversation was in. Experiments eliciting autobiographical memories from bilinguals suggest that the language of a memory is reconstructed on recall (Schrauf and Durazo-Arvizu 2006) – much like the structure of a sentence is also reconstructed.

Trying to recall the precise form of something just said is, in fact, pretty difficult. One exception is sentences that carry so-called *high interactive content* – for instance, *Do you always put your foot in your mouth?* or *Can't you do anything right?* (Keenan, MacWhinney, and Mayhew 1977). The exact form of sentences with great interpersonal import is more likely to be recalled than the exact form of neutral sentences.

Creating long-term representations of meaning

Another reason it is difficult to remember exactly what was said is because individual sentence meanings are integrated to create more global representations of meaning. A great deal of research has demonstrated that the memory system is very good at integrating and synthesizing information, but is not good at keeping individual bits of information distinct from others. In a much-cited investigation, Bransford and Franks (1971) presented participants with sentences that represented only partial meanings of a complete idea, and later asked those participants whether they had heard sentences that conveyed the complete idea. For example, participants were trained on sentences containing one (7a), two (7b), or three (7c) propositions. Each participant heard a few sentences of all three types:

(7) a. The ants were in the kitchen.
         The jelly was on the table.
         The jelly was sweet.
         The ants ate the jelly.
     b. The ants ate the sweet jelly.
         The sweet jelly was on the table.
     c. The ants ate the jelly which was on the table.
         The ants in the kitchen ate the sweet jelly.
     d. The ants in the kitchen ate the sweet jelly which was on the table.

Importantly, all four pieces of information were never contained in one sentence, as in (7d). Following presentation of the sentences, participants were asked to indicate which ones they had heard. They could not distinguish between sentences they had actually heard and different sentences with the same information in different configurations. In fact, recognition ratings varied as a function of sentence complexity, with sentences like (7d), which none of the participants had heard, systematically receiving the highest recognition ratings, and sentences like those in (7a), which everyone heard, receiving the lowest recognition ratings. This experiment is an elegant demonstration that sentences are not stored individually in memory, but information from related sentences are combined to form a single coherent representation.

Unlike the sentence processing system, the memory system uses a wide range of different types of information. It recruits **real-world knowledge** and it makes **inferences** that it stores right along with the information it actually received. For example, if we are listening to a story and we hear (8a), we might infer something about the instrument that was being used – a hammer, most likely; our real-world knowledge tells us hammers are used to pound nails. We are less likely to make such an inference if instead we hear (8b).

(8) a. He was pounding the nail when ...
     b. He was looking for the nail when ...

A study by Johnson, Bransford, and Solomon (1973), investigating **instrumental inferences**, asked participants to say whether they had heard the word *hammer* when listening to passages containing either (8a) or (8b). Participants who heard (8a) reported having heard the word *hammer*, while participants who heard (8b) did not.

Along similar lines, Bransford, Barclay, and Franks (1972) demonstrated that people add **spatial inferences** to their memory representations of sentences. Participants in this study heard a sentence such as one of the following:

(9) a. Three turtles rested on a floating log and a fish swam beneath them.
     b. Three turtles rested beside a floating log and a fish swam beneath them.

Notice that our knowledge of spatial relationships tells us that if turtles are resting on a log, as in (9a), and a fish is swimming beneath the turtles, the fish is also swimming beneath the log, but that this is not so if the turtles are resting beside the log, as in (9b). Participants who heard (9a) could not report whether they had heard that sentence or a different sentence shown in (10a). In contrast, participants who had heard (9b) could easily report that they had not heard (10b).

(10) a. Three turtles rested on a floating log and a fish swam beneath it.
      b. Three turtles rested beside a floating log and a fish swam beneath it.

These experiments examining the way people make inferences illustrate another reason why it is virtually impossible for people to recall exactly what has been said to them. Not only do people integrate a wide variety of meanings; they also add to their memory all the inferences they have made at the time they originally heard the speech.

Notice that inferences are not part of the basic meaning constructed by the sentence processor. Jenkins (1971) demonstrated this in a study in which he presented participants with the two types of *turtle* sentences in (9a) and (10a), and asked, *Did the fish swim beneath the turtles?* The correct answer in either case is *yes*, but the answer is based on the basic meaning of (9a) and the inferred meaning of (10a). It took people significantly longer to answer *yes* with (10a) than with (9a). Information that had to be inferred was not available as quickly as information contained in the basic meaning of the sentence.

All of these facts about memory for sentences have important entailments for so-called "eye witness" testimony – or in this case "ear witness" testimony. Elizabeth Loftus has spent her career investigating aspects of memory that may have legal implications (Loftus 2003). One of her experiments (Loftus and Palmer 1974) demonstrated not only the role of inferences in memory but also the endless possibilities for manipulating the memories of others. Two groups of people saw a film of an automobile accident. One group was asked *How fast was the Buick going when it hit the Ford?* The participants estimated 34 mph. A second group was asked *How fast was the Buick going when it smashed into the Ford?* These participants estimated 41 mph. The difference between the estimates of the two groups was statistically significant. A week later the same two groups of participants were asked whether there had been any broken glass at the scene of the accident (in actuality there had been none). Only 14 percent of the people initially asked the question using the word *hit* said there was broken glass, but 32 percent of the people who heard the question with *smashed into* erroneously recalled broken glass. The group who had heard *smashed* had been led to store in memory a more violent representation of the original scene than did the other group.

The famous Swiss psychologist Jean Piaget grew up believing that his earliest childhood memory was of being rescued from kidnappers by his nanny. Years later he discovered that she had made up the story to curry favor with his parents. His memory of this event was completely constructed, based on a story he had been told repeatedly (Piaget 1962: 187–8). If you want to find out about people's earliest memories, you should be careful not to rely on memories of events they have been told about, seen pictures of, and so on. Human memory is not a simple recording device. It is a complex and dynamic system that constructs memories based on many factors, only one of which is what was actually experienced.

▓ Discourse Processing

We mentioned earlier that a discourse is an organized sequence of connected sentences. Understanding discourse, then, involves taking basic meanings of individual sentences and integrating them into a semantically and pragmatically coherent framework. In order to do this, links must be discovered between and among the sentences of a discourse, and this new information then integrated into existing knowledge. These links made between and among sentences are both semantic and referential, and are sought out by using logic and consulting real-world knowledge. The goal of discourse integration requires at least two major processes: *anaphoric reference* and *inference*. Although these two processes interact in many cases, we will discuss them separately.

▓ Anaphoric reference

An **anaphor** is a linguistic device that refers to someone or something that has been mentioned in the previous context. An anaphor can be either a pronoun or a definite noun phrase (a noun phrase introduced by a definite article), like the italicized elements in the following two examples:

(11)   John came home yesterday for spring break. *He* spent the afternoon telling Dad all about college life.

(12)   I got a new puppy yesterday. *The little darling* slept with me last night.

In order to understand these brief discourses, the anaphors (*he* and *the little darling*) must be matched with their **referents** (*John* and *a new* *puppy*, respectively). In this section, we explore some of the factors that influence a person's ability to locate referents for the anaphors encountered in different types of discourse. Let us first explain why pronouns and definite noun phrases are anaphors.

Pronouns are anaphors because they cannot be interpreted without locating an antecedent for them; they have no independent meaning, except as indicated by their gender, number, or case, all given by their grammatical form. As discussed in earlier chapters, there are grammatical principles that restrict the referents for pronouns (for example, we know that *he* in (11) cannot be *Dad*). But understanding pronouns correctly requires locating the intended referent from among the set of grammatically possible ones (*he* in (11) could be John's brother, or John's neighbor, or John's dad's best friend, but we can be pretty sure that the intended referent for *he* is indeed *John*, because that interpretation makes the entire discourse more coherent). Pronominal reference is an aspect of linguistic performance for which, unlike sentence processing, all kinds of non-linguistic knowledge is recruited.

Definite noun phrases are anaphors for a different reason. They are anaphoric because the use of the definite article *the* presupposes that the referent of that noun phrase is already in the discourse. The first mention of an entity is introduced with an indefinite article (as in *a new puppy* in (12)). Later reference to the same entity requires the use of the definite article. The entailment for the hearer is that when a noun phrase with a definite article is encountered it must refer back to an earlier instantiation of the same referent: it is anaphoric. (An exception to this is the use of the definite article to refer to a species, as in *The snowy owl is a diurnal bird of prey*.)

The use of an anaphor in discourse has two purposes. First, it anchors a sentence to prior representations in the discourse. Second, the anaphor creates a semantically **coherent** text, promoting resolution for its referent in such a way as to produce the most semantically plausible meaning possible. For example, the pronouns in the second sentence of each of the following two discourses are resolved very differently (Garrod and Sanford 1994):

(13)   a.   Bill wanted to lend his friend some money. *He* was hard up and really needed it.
       b.   Bill wanted to lend his friend some money. However, *he* was hard up and couldn't afford to.

The ambiguous singular masculine pronoun, *he*, could grammatically refer to either *Bill* or *his friend*, since both of those can be construed as having any male referent. A combination of semantics and real-world knowledge serves to determine the referent of *he* in each of those discourses: *his friend* in (13a) and *Bill* in (13b).

Identifying the reference of pronouns is driven in part by the urge in discourse processing to arrive at the most plausible and coherent interpretation. Stevenson and Vitkovitch (1986) demonstrated that assigning *Henry* as the antecedent of *he* is faster for (14a) than (14b):

(14)   a.   Henry jumped across the ravine and he fell into the river.
       b.   Henry jumped across the ravine and he picked up some money.

In both cases, *he* could refer to any male individual, but the context supplies *Henry* as a possible antecedent. However, the contexts differ in an important respect: it is easier to imagine falling into the river than picking up money as being a consequence of jumping across a ravine. Thus, identifying *he* as *Henry* produces a more semantically coherent interpretation in (14a) than in (14b).

An important factor in the assignment of anaphoric reference is **discourse focus**. In general, a referent is more available if it is focused, and there are many ways this can be accomplished. Recency is one way to achieve focus: in general, a near referent will be located more quickly than a more distant referent. In an eye tracking study, Ehrlich and Rayner (1983) demonstrated that when an antecedent was distant, readers spent a longer amount of time fixating the region immediately after the pronoun than when an antecedent was near. Similarly, Clark and Sengul (1979) showed that the immediately prior sentence has a privileged status in terms of the availability of a referent for an anaphor. They took three-sentence sets, such as the following:

(15)   A broadloom rug in rose and purple colors covered the floor. Dim light from a small brass lamp cast shadows on the walls. In one corner of the room was an upholstered chair.

The three sentences were presented for silent reading to different groups in different orders. A target sentence like (16) followed the three context sentences, containing a definite NP (*the chair*) whose antecedent had appeared in one of the context sentences (in this example, *an upholstered chair*):

(16)   The chair appeared to be an antique.

Reading times for the target sentence (16) were much faster when the context sentence containing *an upholstered chair* was the third sentence in the context, compared to when it was in either the second or the first sentence. There was a much smaller difference between the availability of the referent from the first sentence to the second sentence than between either of the two earlier sentences and the third sentence. A subsequent experiment demonstrated the same effect even if the second and third sentences were joined as two clauses in a single sentence. This shows that the clause preceding the anaphor is privileged for referent location, not the entire sentence.

Other factors contribute to long-term focus throughout a text. Main characters in a novel, for example, are more likely to be in focus and more available for anaphoric reference than are minor characters. Characters introduced by their proper names are more likely to be main characters and in focus than those introduced by less specific role descriptions. This was investigated in a reading time study by Sanford, Moar, and Garrod (1988), who presented readers with brief discourses like the following, which contained a named (*Mr. Bloggs* or *Claire*) and an unnamed character (*the manager* or *the secretary*):

(17)   Mr. Bloggs was dictating a letter. The secretary was taking shorthand. It was getting to be late in the afternoon. He/she was beginning to feel hungry.

(18)   The manager was dictating a letter. Claire was taking shorthand. It was getting to be late in the afternoon. He/she was beginning to feel hungry.

An anaphor in the last sentence referred to either the male or the female antecedent. The materials were presented sentence by sentence, and whole sentence times were recorded. The final sentence took less time to read if it contained an anaphor with a named character as the antecedent – *he* for (17), and *she* for (18).

Another focusing device is position in a prior sentence, with the subject being in focus position. Antecedent location is facilitated if the pronoun refers to the subject of a previous sentence. Hudson, Tanenhaus, and Dell (1986) compared reading time for sentence pairs like the following:

(19)   a.   Jack apologized profusely to Josh. He had been rude to Josh yesterday.
       b.   Jack apologized profusely to Josh. He had been offended by Jack's comments.

In (19a), the antecedent for the pronoun *he* is *Jack*, the subject of the preceding sentence, while in (19b), the antecedent for *he*, *Josh*, is embedded inside a prepositional phrase in the preceding sentence. The sentences in (19a) were read faster than the sentences in (19b), a demonstration that subject position focuses discourse elements.

Independent of discourse focus, Matthews and Chodorow (1988) showed that when antecedents and pronouns are in the same complex sentence, the structure of the sentence affects how quickly the antecedent can be located. A more deeply embedded antecedent, such as the object of a prepositional phrase, takes measurably longer to locate than one that is closer to the surface, such as a subject or object noun phrase.

Locating the referents for anaphors is essential to building a connected, semantically coherent, and pragmatically felicitous mental representation of a sequence of sentences that makes up a discourse. The more available a referent, in terms of recency and general importance in the text, the greater the facility with which it will be discovered and integrated into one's ongoing representation of the text.

Making inferences

Memory for sentences – and memory for just about everything else – is enhanced by inferences, which are stored in memory alongside information extracted directly from sentences that were actually experienced. The formation and storage of inferences is a central feature of discourse processing. Even the shortest stretches of discourse require the reader to make inferences in order to connect the sentences into a coherent structure. Roger Schank called inferencing the "core of the understanding process" (Schank 1976: 168).

In an earlier section in this chapter, we discussed how instrumental and spatial inferences are added to memory representations of sentences one encounters. Inferences are also involved in the location of referents for anaphors. Haviland and Clark (1974) examined how people generate **bridging inferences** to connect sentences in discourse. This type of inference is illustrated in the following example, which requires an inference about *the beer* being part of *the picnic supplies* for coherent comprehension:

(20)   We checked the picnic supplies. The beer was warm.

Processing is facilitated or impaired depending upon the ease with which hearers will be able to make such inferences, and if too many inferences are required, the discourse can sound decidedly odd.

The bridging inference in (20) is easier than the one required to find the referent for *the fire* in (21), for *him* in (22), or for *the woman* in (23):

(21)   A careless tourist threw a lighted match out of his car window. The fire destroyed several acres of virgin forest.

(22)   A: My daughter just got engaged.
       B: Do you like him?

(23)   We went to a wedding. The woman wore white.

Notice that sociocultural norms and the real-world knowledge of the interlocutors clearly impinge on the success (or failure) of inference-making. This is evident for the discourse in (23), since not all brides wear white, and not all weddings have brides.

Inferences can do more than locate referents for definite noun phrases. They can also enhance their meaning. Consider the meaning of a noun phrase such as *the container*, which is a very general term with a non-specific meaning. When used in a sentence, though, *the container* can take on more specific meaning. Compare, for instance, *The container held the soup* with *The container held the gas*. By inference, the former is an open small bowl or cup whereas the latter is a closed large metal cylinder. Anderson et al. (1976) called this increased specificity of meaning the *instantiation of general terms*. These researchers demonstrated how instantiation of the more specific meaning is stored in memory. In their experiment, participants heard a list of sentences, which included either (24a) or (24b):

(24)   a.   The woman was outstanding in the theater.
       b.   The woman worked near the theater.

Participants' memory was probed using either *the woman* or *the actress*. *The woman* was an equally good memory probe for both sentences, and *the actress* was no better for participants who had heard (24b). However, *the actress* as a probe enabled the participants who had heard (24a) to recall it twice as often as they did following the probe *the woman*. This finding is particularly important because it illustrates that instantiation is not simply the result of a simple association between, in this case, *the woman* and *the theater*. The inferences that allowed *the actress* (which had not even appeared in the sentence) to be a good memory probe were very specific to the participants' real-world knowledge about the relationship that likely exists when a woman is said to be *outstanding in the theater*.

Bridging inferences are **backward inferences** in the sense that they require the hearer to review previous information in a discourse to provide coherence with a current item. For example, it is not until one encounters *the beer* in (20) that one infers that the picnic supplies contained beer. **Forward** or **elaborative inferences** are those made immediately after a piece of text is encountered, whether or not it is needed for coherence. We would make a different elaborative inference about what happened next for each of the following two sentences:

(25) a. Alex accidentally dropped his wine glass on the carpet.
      b. Alex accidentally dropped his wine glass on the stone patio.

The inferences that lead to the instantiation of general terms are examples of elaborative inferences. It is unclear under what circumstances people create elaborative inferences, but it is almost certain that they do so often. Since elaborative inferences are not necessary for discourse coherence, they are not as vital to text comprehension as bridging inferences are. Singer (1994: 488) reported an experiment in which participants were asked to verify a statement such as *A dentist pulled the tooth* after hearing one of the following three types of contexts:

(26) a. The dentist pulled the tooth painlessly. The patient liked the new method.
      b. The tooth was pulled painlessly. The dentist used a new method.
      c. The tooth was pulled painlessly. The patient liked the new method.

In (26a), no inferences are required to confirm who did the tooth pulling, since the first sentence states explicitly that it was the dentist. In (26b), a bridging inference – that the dentist pulled the tooth – has to be made immediately in order to connect the two sentences in a semantically coherent way. In (26c), it is not necessary to create the bridging inference that a dentist pulled the tooth. If the inference were made that a dentist was the puller of the tooth, it would have been an elaborative inference, not a necessary one. (The sentences are coherent only with the inference that the patient was the possessor of the tooth, but that is irrelevant to this study.) Notice that for (26a) and (26b) the initial memory representation for the pair of sentences must include the information chunk that the dentist was the tooth puller. At issue in this study, therefore, was whether the elaborative inference in (26c) was also part of that initial representation. It turned out that verification times were about the same following (26a) and (26b), but slower following (26c). The conclusion, then, is that bridging inferences are made immediately, while elaborative inferences are made only when the stored memory representation is probed for verification. A very interesting question is when and under what circumstances elaborative inferences are made in day-to-day discourse processing.

All inferences, whether bridging or elaborative, are based either on logic or on real-world knowledge, and one important ingredient for successful communicative exchanges is ensuring that the interlocutors share enough knowledge to make appropriate inferences. Many inferences are made on the basis of **scripts** (Schank and Abelson 1977), which are general scenarios about common sequences of activities. For instance, most people have a "restaurant script." If someone says that Fred went to a restaurant and ordered a steak, knowledge of the restaurant script allows you to infer that Fred ordered from a menu, was served by a waiter or waitress, ate what he ordered, received and paid a check, and so on. Part of learning a new job or how to function in a new institution (like college) involves acquiring scripts for how things are done there.

The closer people are socially and culturally, the more shared scripts they will have. This is why people who share little information will find communication more difficult than will those who share a great deal. The more information two people share, the more likely each of them will be able to judge correctly what is in the mind of the other and, therefore, what inferences that person can be relied upon to make. For instance, the inference we might make about the sentence pair in (23), above, is highly culture specific: Western brides traditionally wear white, but not brides in other cultures. We will return to this point later in this chapter.

In addition to facilitating the interpretation of discourse, inferences can convey information. Suppose you hear the following:

(27)   Nigel is coming home from school this weekend. The nerd will probably spend the entire weekend at the computer.

The anaphoric resolution of *Nigel* as the referent of *the nerd* conveys the speaker's opinion of Nigel. Similarly, suppose your friend told you the following:

(28)   My son-in-law is a neurosurgeon, but he's a really sweet guy.

You might infer that your friend believes neurosurgeons are usually not sweet. Somewhere in this book there might be a sentence like the following:

(29)   *John* is a good choice for the thematic role of agent because *he* is animate.

If you did not know before you read it, you could infer from (29) that it is, in general, good for agents to be animate. Vonk and Noordman (1990) suggest that inferences of this type are not made if a person is reading unfamiliar material. This is unfortunate, because it implies that students reading textbooks about unfamiliar material may read at too shallow a level, failing to make the type of inferences that would enhance their learning.

Much of the discussion to this point has used short stretches of discourse (two or three sentences long) as illustrative examples. In actuality, we are usually involved in processing – reading or hearing – long stretches of discourse: a conversation, a lecture, a five-part television mini-series, or a 500-page novel. In doing this, we are constantly building a representation of the meaning of the entire discourse. Each new sentence is integrated into that growing mental representation. The ease with which we can do this depends upon the relatedness of the individual sentences or information inside them to the global discourse structure that has been created (Hess, Foss, and Caroll 1995). The less related an individual sentence or sentence chunk is to the discourse structure that is being constructed, the more processing effort will be required to integrate it into the semantic representation of the discourse. Sentences that have been more difficult to integrate, or sentences that are less well integrated because of low relatedness, will be more available for recall after the processing is complete. The same effect holds for words that are difficult to integrate with the basic meaning of a sentence. Cairns, Cowart, and Jablon (1981) demonstrated this using a visual probe recognition task. Participants took longer to report that they had seen *camera* if it had appeared in a predictable context, like (30a), than in an unpredictable context, like (30b):

(30)   a.   Kathy wanted a snapshot of my baby, but she unfortunately forgot her camera today.
        b.   Kathy finally arrived at my baby shower, but she unfortunately forgot her camera today.

Presumably, the integration of *camera* is easier and more complete when it is easily connected by inference to the initial clause of the sentence than when the connection is more difficult to construct. But the difficulty in integrating an unrelated element makes it more salient.

It is always easier for people to build a semantic representation of a discourse that is about something they are already familiar with. The more they know about a topic (the more familiar they are with the semiotic domain), the easier it will be to make the bridging inferences they need to integrate each sentence into a global representation. It is also the case that when people read or hear new information, they integrate it, not only with the text that is currently being processed, but also with the knowledge structures they already have about that topic. This is why advanced courses are often easier than introductory ones. In an introductory course, students are likely to know very little about the topic they are learning, and thus they do not have a knowledge base to help them integrate the type of discourse they routinely face in academic contexts: readings and lectures. This problem is magnified by the fact that textbook authors and classroom lecturers are experts in the topic, and they are formulating their discourse building upon a background of knowledge that the student does not have. In an advanced course, in contrast, the course material might be more difficult because it is more advanced, but students have a larger knowledge base to support their processing of the material, and so the course might be perceived as being easier. You might have also noticed that reading the same book or watching the same movie at different times of your life leads to different insights (Wolf 2007). This is because you are integrating that same discourse into a long-term memory that is different at different times of your life. Your current knowledge and state of mind will necessarily affect the inferences and connections you make about any discourse you process.

◼ Having Conversations

When people use language, they produce discourse of various types: letters, stories, lectures, meetings, debates, and so on. We now turn to the principles that govern the use of language in the creation of discourse; the study of these principles is called pragmatics. Compliance with these principles is sometimes referred to as **communicative competence**. Pragmatic principles are very different from those that contribute to grammatical competence. Grammatical principles and rules, if violated, produce an ungrammatical sentence. Pragmatic principles relate to the **felicitous** (appropriate) use of sentences in discourse, and sentences that violate these principles are **infelicitous**. We will see that pragmatic principles govern how people use language to convey more – and often different – information than that contained in the basic meaning of sentences.

In the 1960s and 1970s, philosophers of language J. L. Austin (1962) and John Searle (1969) produced a great deal of the framework upon which the study of pragmatics is based. Austin and Searle characterized discourse as a series of *speech acts*, each of which has not only a particular linguistic form (*locution*) but also an intended function (*illocutionary force*) and an effect on the interlocutor (*perlocutionary force*). These distinctions help us understand the use of **non-literal language**. People often use language when the intended meaning is very different from the basic meaning based on the words and their structural organization. For example, in an **indirect request**, the illocutionary force of a speech act is a request, but its locution is a declarative sentence. For example, suppose you and your friend are in a room. You are near the window; she is not. She says, *Gee, it's getting warm in here*. That is a statement (its locution), but it is intended as a request (its illocutionary force), and the effect is supposed to be for you to open the window (its perlocutionary force). Sometimes a yes/no question (locution) is posed in a context in which it would be completely inappropriate to answer either *yes* or *no*. For instance, consider the question *Would you mind passing the salt?* It is not a question at all, but rather a request for action.

Sarcasm is another example of non-literal language use. For example, pretend that you and your friend went to a movie last night. He was so bored he slept through the last half. You know he slept, and he knows you know. So when you say, *Hey, you really enjoyed that movie last night!* both of you are aware that you mean exactly the opposite of the literal meaning of what you said. Prosody (tone of voice, sentence intonation, and word stress) can be a valuable signal of sarcasm or irony (Cheang and Pell 2008), but it is not the only way to signal non-literal language use. More important than any prosodic signal is the **shared knowledge** between the participants in a communicative exchange.

In an investigation of how non-literal language is processed, Gibbs (1986) demonstrated that sarcastic comments are processed just as rapidly as non-sarcastic comments embedded in brief passages, suggesting that the processes that lead to the identification of sarcasm as such are very rapid. Gibbs also found that processing sarcastic or ironic statements is facilitated if those remarks are echoic, that is, if they have been alluded to somehow, in the preceding context. In one of his experiments, Gibbs asked people to read passages like one of the following:

(31)   Gus just graduated from high school and he didn't know what to do. One day he saw an ad about the Navy. It said that the Navy was not just a job, but an adventure. So, Gus joined up. Soon he was aboard a ship doing all sorts of boring things. One day as he was peeling potatoes he said to his buddy, "This sure is an exciting life."

(32)   Gus just graduated from high school and he didn't know what to do. So, Gus went out and joined the Navy. Soon he was aboard a ship doing all sorts of boring things. One day as he was peeling potatoes he said to his buddy, "This sure is an exciting life."

The sarcastic remark at the end of (31) echoes something mentioned in the passage (*the Navy was not just a job, but an adventure*); the same remark at the end of (32) has no such previous mention. It took participants in this study significantly less time to read and make a paraphrase judgment of the target sarcastic phrase, *This sure is an exciting life*, when it was embedded in an echoic passage, like (31).

Another interesting aspect of pragmatics concerns the *presuppositions* of certain kinds of speech acts. The old joke *Have you stopped beating your wife?* is one example of this. It presupposes that the addressee has been beating his wife, and the presupposition cannot be denied by either a *yes* or *no* answer. Verbs like *know* and *realize* presuppose the truth of their complements. For example, notice that (33a) is a felicitous sentence only if it is true that Margaret was lying, while (33b) is felicitous irrespective of Margaret's mendacity:

(33)   a.   I realize Margaret was lying.
       b.   I believe Margaret was lying.

The structure of conversations

The process of having a conversation is a good deal more complex than one might have thought. Like other aspects of language use, many of the rules of conversation are applied unconsciously and are noticed only if they are broken. Conversations have structure. They have a beginning, during which one gets the other's attention and perhaps exchanges a few completely meaningless remarks such as *How are you?* (to which it is usually infelicitous to respond by saying anything other than *Fine, thanks*). There is a middle that can be of varying length and has internal structure, which will be discussed below. Finally, there is an end, signaled by a variety of pre-closing devices, such as summarizing the points in the conversation, reiterating the conclusion, or alluding to other demands on one's time. People tend to avoid brute force closings, such as *Gotta go now*, though what is considered a brute force closing depends very much on the context and the participants in a conversation.

Identifying the appropriate register (should you address your interlocutor as "Mr. Humperdinck" or as "Harry"?), dialect (should you ask for a "hot dog" or a "dirty water dog"?), or even language or languages (should you stick to English, or is it okay to intersperse some Spanish?) for a conversation is a choice that is made depending on the context and participants in a conversation. For bilinguals language choice is sometimes straightforward: when the interlocutor is monolingual, there is only one appropriate choice. But when two participants in an interaction speak the same two languages, multiple variables will guide **code choice**. A variable affecting code choice is discourse domain. For example, when speaking to other bilinguals, you might choose English in some discourse domains (e.g., to talk about something you have recently read about global warming, or to gossip about a co-worker), you might choose your other language in others (e.g., offering a friend tips about a favorite recipe, or sharing your insights about a recent election abroad), even though you might be perfectly capable of having those exchanges in either language. Certain conversational exchanges are typically expected to be in one but not the other language; for example, greetings and leave takings might always be in one language, discussions about work in another. Switching from one code to another inside the same discourse, then, serves important communicative functions. A code-switch could be a signal to include or exclude a participant in the conversation, or even to identify a specific participant as the addressee for a given message; a code-switch could also be used to emphasize something just mentioned in the other language, or to signal that the message contained in the switched-to code modifies or expands upon what was just said (Romaine 1995). Code choice, and code-switching, are thus elements that add structure to conversations, and form part of people's communicative repertoire.

Code choices are guided (tacitly) by the sociolinguistic norms of the bilingual community. In fact, in many bilingual communities the two languages have non-overlapping functions (Fassold 1984): one language might be used for discourse domains involving government, education, and business, while the other language is the language of choice for discourse domains involving household and personal matters. Language choice is further shaped by the individual bilingual's life experience and real-world knowledge base.

A study of Russian–English bilinguals by Marian and Kaushanskaya (2004) examines how the language of the discourse drives both linguistic and non-linguistic aspects of the discourse content. The study examined how autobiographical memories are retrieved and encoded, in two languages that are associated with rather different cultures: Russia is a collectivist culture, while the United States is individualistic. The investigators elicited narratives from a group of bilinguals in each of the two languages, and determined the extent to which the narratives revealed individualism or collectivism, by a number of measures. One of the measures was to what extent the narratives, in English and in Russian, used first person singular (*I*) or plural (*we*) pronouns to refer to past events. Another measure was an agency measure: the narratives were classified as telling about events in which only the speaker was involved as the main actor, only others were involved as main actors, or a combination of the speaker and others were involved. The narratives produced in English had fewer group pronouns and were more likely to have the speaker as the main actor, compared to the narratives produced in Russian, which had more group pronouns and were more likely to have others as main actors.

The most basic rule in conversations is that participants must **take turns**. There are a number of devices that signal when a person has come to the end of a conversational turn. There may be a fall in pitch or a drop in loudness; hand gestures could signal yielding of one's turn; and turns always end with the completion of a grammatical constituent: a phrase, clause, or sentence. Gaps between turns are relatively brief, with an average of 400 milliseconds when strangers are talking over the telephone. Moreover, there is some overlapping of speech – about 5 percent of the time in telephone conversations, with overlaps averaging 250 milliseconds (Ervin-Tripp 1993: 243–4).

A study conducted with speakers of ten different languages (Stivers et al. 2009) addressed the question of whether there are universal tendencies in turn-taking. The discourses analyzed were videotaped conversations that included a number of questions and their answers. All ten languages examined had a similar distribution of question-to-answer pause times, averaging around 200 milliseconds after the end of the question. Additionally, in nine out of the ten languages tested, if the questioner was gazing at the answerer, pause time was shorter. Data from all ten languages also indicate that speakers avoid overlap between turns. Stivers and colleagues report some minor variations in pause durations between languages. For example, Danish speakers had the longest pauses, Japanese speakers the shortest. Although these differences were very small (all differences fell within 100 milliseconds or less), it is plausible that people are sensitive to them.

As the conversation progresses turn by turn, it is each contributor's responsibility to construct messages such that the other person will understand what he intends to say. For example, a question like *Are they asleep?* posed by a parent to a babysitter need not have introduced the referent for *they*; the speaker infers that the hearer has the necessary knowledge to accurately identify the anaphor's referent. If comprehension fails, the conversational partner must indicate somehow that understanding has broken down (e.g., the babysitter, mystified, replies, *Who, the cats?*), and the speaker must **repair** the message. To do this successfully, the speaker must identify the cause of the breakdown (an ambiguous anaphor) and fix exactly that part of the message that was unclear (e.g., countering with something like *No, the kids!*). This process is not always simple: the need for message repair is sometimes quite subtle, signaled by a puzzled expression or a response that suggests less than total understanding. Successful message repair depends upon the speaker's ability to identify the locus of difficulty and reformulate the message appropriately. This often requires conscious awareness of the hearer's state of knowledge.

The philosopher Herbert Paul Grice characterized conversations as a form of cooperative activity. According to Grice, a **Cooperative Principle** is observed by participants in conversations for their contributions to be pragmatically felicitous (Grice 1975). Subsumed under the Cooperative Principle are four maxims (or rules of conduct) for cooperative conversations. These maxims may or may not be followed by participants in a conversation, but each participant will assume the other person is obeying them, and will thus formulate inferences based on that assumption. Since participants in a conversation expect their interlocutors to be cooperative, violation of a maxim will invite incorrect inferences.

One of the four Gricean maxims is the **Maxim of Relevance**, referring to relevance both to the conversational topic and to the previous conversational turn. Consider the following conversational exchange:

(34)   Ernest: Is the boss in?
         Grace: The lights are on.

Grace's reply to Ernest's question seems, on the surface, irrelevant. Ernest will assume Grace is obeying the Maxim of Relevance, and will successfully understand her response if he infers that the boss must be in, because the lights are on (presumably, in the boss's office). Shared knowledge between Ernest and Grace is the key to the success of this communicative exchange.

A second Gricean maxim is the **Maxim of Quantity**, by which people give their conversational partners exactly the amount of information that they need, with the right level of detail. If someone asks you where your brother is, the correct answer could be *In the United States* if he has been out of the country and you know that the person asking knows that, or it could be *At the office* if the person wants to get in touch with him. It would rarely be appropriate to cite the exact whereabouts of your brother (e.g., *In room 355 of Kissena Hall at Queens College*). If each participant in a conversation assumes that the other obeys the Maxim of Quantity, incorrect inferences can result from violation of the maxim. If someone asks whether you have any pets and you reply, *Yes, I have a beautiful black cat with gold eyes*, the person will infer that you have only one cat. If you really have two (or more) cats, or both a cat and a dog, you will not have lied, but you will have allowed the other person to make an inaccurate inference. It would probably be difficult, in such a circumstance, to convince the other person that you did not lie. Why? Because the person will store in memory not the exact words that you spoke, but the inferences that could be drawn from them.

The third Gricean maxim, the **Maxim of Manner**, requires conversational contributions to be organized in a sensible way. For example, if you are telling someone your life story, you will begin with childhood, move through adolescence, and proceed to adulthood, citing meaningful events in chronological order. If you are explaining to someone how to make your favorite recipe, you will likely organize your explanation with the earliest steps first, leaving the later steps for last. Notice that the order in which you introduce information using language also leads to inferences. In mathematics (and in formal semantics, incidentally), $A + B = B + A$. However, *She got married, and she got pregnant* does not mean the same thing as *She got pregnant, and she got married*.

The final **Maxim of Quality** simply states that participants in a conversation assume that the other is telling the truth and that conversational contributions are made with sufficient evidence. It follows, then, that comments that are only an opinion must be marked as such (e.g., *In my honest opinion, you don't need to dye your hair*). Citing the source of information is a way of signaling adherence to Quality (e.g., *I read in the* *paper this morning that ...*; *The weatherman said that ...*). The flip side of having sufficient evidence to make a statement is that if you ask a question you must not already know the answer. If someone already has information, then it is infelicitous to ask for it. It is very odd that adults violate this principle with children all the time. We have all heard a mother ask her child a question such as *Where did we go this afternoon?* when both mother and child know perfectly well they went to the zoo. Such questions are infelicitous in most discourse domains, but they are permitted (perhaps even expected) in specific contexts.

Using Language to Communicate

Conversation can serve a variety of purposes. It is usually thought of as a vehicle for communication, and it certainly is, but conversation is also our primary means of social interaction. A distinction has been made between **interactional** and **transactional discourse**, the purpose of the former being primarily social, the latter being true communication. True communication requires the participants to intend to change each other's mental state. Accidental communication – such as reading someone's "body language" (**paralinguistic cues**) or figuring out that a baby is hungry by the quality of its cry – does not count. Intent is key. Communication is actually an extremely complex cognitive activity, because it requires that one person evaluate another person's state of knowledge and then devise a message that will alter that state in exactly the desired way. Communication games, in which one person must communicate a route on a map or uniquely describe a complex pattern to another person, can be extremely difficult, even for an adult. As discussed earlier, successful conversation (even for purely social purposes) requires a great deal of shared knowledge and the ability to evaluate the mental states of others.

In order to communicate effectively, people must not only maintain a felicitous conversation (in Grice's terms), they must also make sure that their referents are available to their listener and that the listener will be able to make the inferences necessary to fill in the gaps of the dialogue. Wilkes-Gibbs and Clark (1992) suggest, in their **collaborative theory of reference**, that speakers and hearers adopt procedures to establish to their mutual satisfaction that they share knowledge about intended referents. Anderson and Boyle (1994) used a communication game to study some of the factors that contribute to the success of this enterprise. The game involved participants using pairs of complicated maps which differed slightly in that one map of the pair provided some landmarks that the other omitted. An "Information Giver" participant had a map with a route drawn on it, and had to instruct his partner, the "Information Follower," to replicate the route on her map. This setup allowed the researchers to study the characteristics of information introduction (by the Giver) and response (from the Follower) that lead to successful communication, as measured by the quality of fit between the Follower's final route and the Giver's original one.

A major finding of the study by Anderson and Boyle was that successful pairs of communicators tended to use questions to introduce reference to a new landmark. Thus, a successful Giver (knowing in advance that the maps do not match perfectly) would say, *Do you have a burnt forest?* before giving a direction that mentioned a burnt forest. Unsuccessful communicators would introduce new landmarks with statements such as *Now go down and around the burnt forest.* Some people used the question introduction strategy from the beginning; others acquired the strategy in the course of the game; some never got it and were dramatically less successful in describing their routes to their partners. Responses of the Followers also made a major contribution to the success of mutual communication. Following an instruction to *Go down and around the burnt forest*, if the Follower did not have a burnt forest, the Follower could give either an informative response (e.g., *I don't have a burnt forest, but I have a picnic site*) or an uninformative one (e.g., *OK* or *What kind of a forest?*). Successful communication was a function of both the quality of the Giver's instructions and the informativeness of the Follower's responses. Both were based on the ability to take the knowledge and informational needs of the other into account and to formulate messages that responded properly to both.

Throughout this chapter we have focused on conversations, in describing the principles that organize discourse, but we stress that the same principles generally apply in other **discourse modes**, both spoken and written. That is not to say that the discourse principles guiding speaking and writing are completely indistinguishable. Crystal (2003) identifies a number of criteria that distinguish speech from writing, all of which have some sort of connection to discourse processing. Speech – but not writing – is time-bound, spontaneous, face-to-face, loosely structured, socially interactive, and prosodically rich. Clearly, there are categories of speech that meet only some of these criteria (consider a well-rehearsed speech delivered over the radio, which is not spontaneous, or face-to-face, or socially interactive). There are also categories of written language – specifically, language produced with electronic media – that do not neatly match up with traditional writing. For example, a blog (short for "web log") is an electronic journal whose entries can be commented on by readers, thus making this form of writing highly interactive.

Perhaps even more interactive is the type of writing that takes place in wiki formats, where multiple authors (sometimes just a handful, other times – as in Wikipedia – hundreds of individuals) work asynchronously to create a text. Applying the criteria for distinguishing writing and speech to electronic media – including webpages, blogs, emails, and instant messaging – Crystal (2006) proposes that electronic texts are a unique medium of their own – a "third medium." Evidently, electronic media are subject to their own mode-specific discourse constraints.

Psycholinguists know a great deal about how people engage in spoken conversations and how people approach written texts such as novels and short stories. We know a great deal less about how people process language on the internet, and it remains to be seen to what extent new media lead to new types of literacy (Wolf 2007). Indeed, as people spend more time online (perhaps playing video games or visiting social networking sites), there are some reports of decreases in literary reading (that is, reading literature for pleasure; National Endowment for the Arts, 2004). At the same time, since the internet is predominantly a text-based medium, people are reading and writing more than ever before, even though they are reading and writing non-traditional texts: blog feeds and tweet streams, instruction manuals for video games, or comments reviewing products on e-commerce websites.

▪ Summing Up

It is clear that the use of language to interact, communicate, and interpret discourse is not the relatively context-free process that single-sentence processing is. Higher-level processing of discourse requires the recruitment of all of one's personal knowledge and the deployment of cognitive strategies that depend upon the assessment of the mental states of others. The principles of single-sentence processing are very different from those recruited during discourse processing. Higher-level processing principles are also more available to conscious awareness than are the more basic processing activities. While it is true that pragmatic principles governing the use of language are applied automatically, it is more possible to become aware of taking turns in conversation and making inferences than it is to become aware of lexical retrieval or the creation of sentence structure. Chances are you will not notice the next time your parser is garden-pathed, but the next time you encounter a sarcastic remark, you might notice that its surface form and its intended meaning are actually quite different.

New Concepts

anaphor
chunks
code choice
coherence
collaborative theory of
  reference
communicative
  competence
context
Cooperative Principle
discourse (narrative text)
discourse domains
discourse focus
discourse mode
discourse participants
felicitous
function
indirect request
infelicitous
inferences
  backward, bridging
  bridging
  forward, elaborative

instrumental
  spatial
interactional discourse
long-term memory
Maxim of Manner
Maxim of Quality
Maxim of Quantity
Maxim of Relevance
non-literal language
paralinguistic cues
real-world knowledge
referent
register. See discourse
repair
sarcasm
scripts
semiotic domain
shared knowledge
topic
transactional discourse
turn-taking
working memory
working memory span

Study Questions

1. When the basic meanings of sentences are stored in memory, what kind of information is lost? What kind of information is added?

2. What is an anaphor? Why are anaphors important in the comprehension and production of texts?

3. What factors affect how easily the referent for an anaphor can be located?

4. Explain the difference between elaborative inferences and bridging inferences, and try to come up with a couple of examples for each. How are they used in discourse processing?

5. Why are advanced academic courses frequently perceived as easier than introductory courses?

6. What are some of the communicative functions that can be served by code-switching, in a conversation with bilingual participants?

7. How does the use of non-literal language allow us to distinguish between locution, illocutionary force, and perlocutionary force?

8. What is the difference between an utterance that is ungrammatical and one that is infelicitous?

9. How does Grice's Cooperative Principle affect participants in conversations?

10. Distinguish between interactional and transactional discourse. How do they differ? Which seems to be more difficult for adults as well as children?

Epilogue

Producing and understanding a single sentence involves immensely complex cognitive operations. The fact that every adult human can do this, unconsciously and effortlessly, hundreds of times a day, and often in more than one language, is truly amazing. It is appropriate, however, at the completion of an entire book dealing with the details of language and its use, to step back and consider the power of language and its role in the human condition. Because we have language, we have the ability to convey information about a limitless range of topics across vast amounts of space and time. Language provides access to the historical narrative of our species. For good or for ill, it places us at the pinnacle of life forms. The linguist Emmon Bach (1974: 280) provides an eloquent comment on the study of human language: "And one of the most rewarding fruits of trying to answer questions about language, this most characteristic and mysterious of human gifts, is that we are led to other questions about the fundamental nature of man, this most fascinating, terrible, and noble of the animals."

Appendix: Experimental Designs in Psycholinguistics

Psycholinguistic experiments provide empirical tests of the ideas psycholinguists have about how language is acquired or processed. Throughout this book, we describe many different types of experiments, giving you only as much detail as necessary for you to understand not just the results but also the logic underlying the design. Just from reading the chapters, you can become familiar with a number of techniques, and you can develop a sense for how psycholinguists test hypotheses empirically. This appendix provides a little more background on experimental designs in psycholinguistics.

Basics

An experiment always involves a **comparison** of some kind, between elements of the same class but which vary with respect to some property. The comparison can be two or more linguistic units: e.g., two types of phonemes, two types of words, or two types of sentences. The comparison can also be between non-linguistic units: e.g., participants with different linguistic or socioeconomic backgrounds, or linguistic materials presented in different languages or different modes (visually or auditorily). Each of these is an example of a **variable** that can be tested experimentally. An experiment might be concerned with, for example, whether signals from an acoustic continuum are perceived differently than other signals in the continuum, whether words of some types result in faster lexical decision times than words of other types, or whether ambiguous sentences disambiguated one way are understood better than if they are disambiguated another way. Let us illustrate with a concrete example: an experiment designed to examine the effect of lexical frequency on sentence processing, using the phoneme monitoring technique. (An experiment like this is discussed in Chapter 6.) The variable of interest is lexical frequency, the contrast is between high-frequency and low-frequency words, and the procedure is phoneme monitoring. In this sort of experiment participants listen to recorded sentences and are asked to push a button when they hear a word beginning with a target phoneme. We want to know whether people are faster to respond to a word that begins with a /b/ if it follows a high-frequency word like *traveling*, than after a low frequency word like *itinerant*; here is an example:

(1) a. The traveling bassoon player found himself without funds in a strange town.
     b. The itinerant bassoon player found himself without funds in a strange town.

▪ Materials

Assuming we were designing such a study, the first step would be to construct a set of **materials** containing the contrast of interest. For our example, a set of sentences will have to be written, each in two versions, like the example in (1) above. In each of our sentence pairs, the high- or low-frequency words will have to be immediately followed by a word containing the phoneme that is being monitored. We will also want to match the length of the high- and low-frequency words as best we can. And, ideally, the high- and low-frequency words should not differ very much in meaning.

Having one or two sentence pairs that contain the contrast is not enough; though actual numbers vary, the typical materials set for a psycholinguistics experiment has approximately ten items per experimental condition, though the ideal number of items can vary depending on the task. (A lexical decision task, for example, typically uses many more items per experimental condition than a sentence-reading task.) Our experiment has two conditions (high-frequency and low-frequency words), so we would need to come up with some 20 basic items, each in two versions. We will have to write sentences that are unique, but that resemble each other with respect to extraneous characteristics that are not of interest, such as sentence length, sentence structure, lexical frequency of other words in the sentences, etc. The goal is to have participants' responses differ only because of the variable or variables we have manipulated. If extraneous characteristics of the materials also produce variability, then that variability, known informally as **noise**, can mask the variability we are interested in.

In our experiment we would not want a given participant to hear both versions of each of our sentences, or else the participant might figure out what the experiment is about, which might result in strategic behavior. To avoid this problem, we will recruit two groups of participants – from the same participant pool, so they are matched as well as possible on background variables beyond our control – and present each group with half of the sentences in one version (1a), the other half in the other version (1b). Other pairs of sentences will be constructed. The group who saw the "a" version of, say, sentence (1) will hear the "b" version of another sentence pair, and so on for ten versions of "a" sentences and ten versions of "b" sentences for each group. Distributing materials like this – called **counterbalancing** – is very common in psycholinguistic experiments. In the end, every participant will hear an equal number of sentences in each experimental condition, but the sentences with high-frequency words will be different sentences from those with low-frequency words. Thus, we will have responses for both versions of each sentence, only they will come from different participants. Each presentation of a sentence is called a **trial**.

Psycholinguistic experiments generally include two types of items: **experimental** (or **target**) **materials**, and **filler** (or **distracter**) **materials**. The target materials are the ones of interest for the experimental hypothesis, and usually make up a small subset of the complete set of materials. Filler materials, which are presented interspersed among the experimental materials, can constitute the majority of the trials presented during an experimental session. We include filler sentences for the same reason we don't want participants to hear both versions of the experimental sentences: to disguise the experimental hypothesis. Filler materials distract participants from becoming aware of the fact that they are hearing many sentences of the same type. If participants recognize what the experiment is about, they may adopt unwanted strategic behaviors when responding. Properly constructed filler materials help avert this problem. In a phoneme monitoring experiment, the fillers might contain the phoneme to be monitored after a variety of words and at different positions in the sentence: early, in the middle, or late.

Procedures

In this book you have read about several different **procedures** that psycholinguists employ to collect data from participants. Some of those procedures collect responses **off-line**, that is, after processing routines have applied. For example, in a **questionnaire task**, a participant reads or listens to a sentence and answers a comprehension question. The measure of interest is how participants respond to those questions: if there is a single correct answer, error rates can be analyzed; if the question has two or more possible answers, the distribution of responses can be analyzed.

On-line tasks are of broader interest, because they allow psycholinguists to ask sophisticated questions about how language processing takes place in real time. They measure behavior while the participant is in the middle of processing a word or a sentence. Within the class of on-line procedures, **response time methods** (also sometimes called **behavioral** methods) are very common. A number of response time procedures are used in experiments described in Chapters 6 and 7, including: phoneme monitoring, lexical decision, masked priming, word spotting, phoneme monitoring, cross-modal priming, self-paced reading, and others. The measure of interest is the time it takes participants to respond by pressing a button or making a verbal response; these methods sometimes also examine error rates in making responses.

In Chapter 3, we discussed some of the technologies available to examine language processing directly in the brain. The two most common non-invasive procedures are **electroencephalography** (**EEG**) and **functional magnetic resonance imaging** (**fMRI**). In fMRI experiments, blood flow levels in the brain are recorded, and the resulting data provide topographical information about what specific brain regions are active during language processing. In an EEG experiment, electrical activity in the brain is recorded, and the measure of interest is the timing, the direction (positive or negative), and the amplitude of the voltage, as well as the general location for observed effects. Different types of linguistic contrasts give rise to recognizable electrical responses called ERPs (for *event-related potentials*). For example, semantic anomalies provoke an N400 response (negativity about 400 milliseconds following the anomalous stimulus), while morphosyntactic violations cause LAN (left anterior negativity) or ELAN (early left anterior negativity) responses. ERPs have a very high temporal resolution; that is, they reflect brain activity, millisecond by millisecond. Given their complementary strengths, some investigations now combine EEG and fMRI within the same experiment; the resulting data provide rich information about both when and where the brain responds to linguistic stimuli.

We have also occasionally referred to experiments that record people's **eye movements** as they participate in a task that involves language processing. Somewhat counter-intuitively, when we read text or scan scenes, our eyes do not move smoothly along the observed object. Instead, our eyes move in two ways: **fixations** (stops while the eye focuses on something) and **saccades** (rapid movements from one fixation point to the next). **Eye tracking** studies fall into two broad categories: studies that track eye movements while participants are reading, and studies that track eye movements while participants are viewing scenes (and sometimes manipulating objects in those scenes). Studies that track people's eyes while reading record multiple measures of eye movements, such as time of first fixations on words inside critical regions, regressions to earlier parts of the sentence, and total time in a critical region. The resulting data can be very informative about what is called first pass versus second pass (or reanalysis) effects. Tracking people's eye movements while they are listening to spoken language and viewing a scene is a technique called the visual world paradigm. Studies using this procedure are frequently concerned with how non-linguistic context affects aspects of language processing. The visual world procedure also lends itself well to studying how aspects of the speech signal (its segmental or suprasegmental details) affect language processing. Visual world studies capture a moment-by-moment record of where the eye is fixating during language comprehension (or production). The assumption in all forms of eye tracking research is that the eye fixates, without lag, on what the mind is presently processing.

■ Analysis

When we describe a particular finding in a given experiment, bear in mind that the results we report are generally an average from the responses of many participants over many items. Remember also that calculating average responses is not enough; data from experiments are also subjected to **statistical tests** that confirm (or disconfirm) the reliability of an observed difference between two conditions. In most psycholinguistic experiments, statistical tests are performed on both participant-based and item-based data. The objective of such analyses is to test whether observed differences are **statistically significant**. If a difference is statistically significant, it is judged to be greater than we would obtain if the variable of interest really had no effect and the observed difference was due simply to chance. If the difference were only due to chance, we could conduct the same experiment again and perhaps find no difference between the groups, or the difference could be in the opposite direction. If, instead, observed differences are statistically significant, we can attribute them to the effectiveness of the variable we were testing. In this case, we judge the observed difference to be **reliable**, that is, the same differences would be observed again with a new sample of participants from the same pool, or with a new set of items constructed to meet the same criteria.

To illustrate this using the example from earlier, suppose we recorded average phoneme monitoring times of 300 and 350 milliseconds for materials in (1a) and (1b), respectively. The result is as predicted: responses are faster with the high-frequency than with the low-frequency word. A statistical analysis of the data would tell us whether that 50-millisecond difference is merely due to chance. The graphs in Figure A.1 provide two possible (idealized) outcomes. In both graphs, the means are 300 and 350 milliseconds, respectively. What differs is the standard deviation, greater in the distribution in the graph on the left than in the distribution in the graph on the right. (The standard deviation of a distribution indicates variability, that is, the amount of dispersion there is in the data.) A statistical analysis of the data would indicate that the two distributions on the left are not reliably different, while the two distributions on the right are reliably different. The graphs in Figure A.I are idealized; crucially, statistical significance depends not only on the difference between means, but also on the variability of the samples. Consequently, numerically small differences can be reliable, and numerically large differences are not necessarily reliable. Every statistical test compares the amount

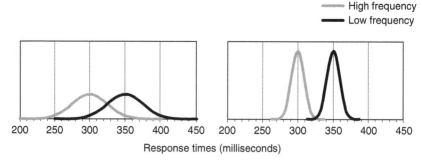

Figure A.1 Two possible but mutually exclusive outcomes for the hypothetical experiment described in this Appendix, which records phoneme monitoring times (measured in milliseconds) for phonemes carried by words in sentences containing high- or low-frequency words. The graphs display idealized data distributions. The means of the distributions are 300 and 350 milliseconds, in both graphs. What differs is the standard deviation (a measure of data dispersion): it is 25 for the two distributions in the graph on the left, 9 for the distributions on the right.

of variability attributable to the variable of interest to the variability of responses in the population. This is why we want to hold at a minimum variability due to noise.

A Bibliographical Note

This appendix should have given you a taste of how experiments are designed and carried out in psycholinguistics. Methods, experimental design, and analysis of data in psycholinguistic research are addressed by many publications, including the following:

- Carreiras and Clifton (2004): a range of methods, with a focus on sentence processing by adults;
- Grosjean and Frauenfelder (1996): paradigms involving spoken word recognition;
- Trueswell and Tanenhaus (2005): the visual world paradigm;
- McDaniel, McKee, and Cairns (1996) and Sekerina, Fernández, and Clahsen (2008): research with children; and
- Sudhoff et al. (2006): empirical research of prosody.

New Concepts

comparison
counterbalancing
electroencephalography (EEG)
experimental (target) materials
eye movements
eye tracking
filler (distracter) materials
fixations
materials
noise
off-line tasks

on-line tasks
procedures
questionnaire task
reliable
response time (behavioral)
    methods
saccades
statistical tests
statistically significant
trial
variable

References

Adams, M. J. 1990. *Beginning to Read: Thinking and Learning about Print.* Cambridge, MA: The MIT Press.

Aitchison, J. 2003. *Words in the Mind: An Introduction to the Mental Lexicon.* Malden, MA: Blackwell Publishing.

Altenberg, E. P. and Cairns, H. S. 1983. The effects of phonotactic constraints on lexical processing in bilingual and monolingual subjects. *Journal of Verbal Learning and Verbal Behavior* 22: 174–88.

Anderson, A. H. and Boyle, E. A. 1994. Forms of introduction in dialogues: Their discourse contexts and communicative consequences. *Language and Cognitive Processes* 9: 101–22.

Anderson, A. H., Clark, A., and Mullin, J. 1994. Interactive communication between children: Learning how to make language work in dialogue. *Journal of Child Language* 21: 439–63.

Anderson, R. C., Pichert, J., Goetz, E. T., Schallert, D. L., Stevens, K. V., and Trolip, S. R. 1976. Instantiation of general terms. *Journal of Verbal Learning and Verbal Behavior* 15: 667–79.

Aronoff, M. and Fudeman, K. A. 2005. *What Is Morphology?* Oxford: Blackwell Publishing.

Artésano, C., Besson, M., and Alter, K. 2004. Brain potentials during semantic and prosodic processing in French. *Cognitive Brain Research* 18: 172–84.

Aslin, R. N., Woodward, J. Z., Lamendola, N. P., and Bever, T. G. 1996. Models of word segmentation in fluent maternal speech to infants. In J. L. Morgan and K. Demuth (eds.), *Signal to Syntax*, 117–34. Hillside, NJ: Lawrence Erlbaum.

Austin, J. L. 1962. *How to Do Things with Words.* New York: Oxford Unversity Press.

Bach, E. 1974. *Syntactic Theory.* New York: Holt, Rinehart, and Winston.

Baker, M. C. 2001. *The Atoms of Language: The Mind's Hidden Rules of Grammar.* New York: Basic Books.

Baldwin, D. A. 1991. Infant contributions to the achievement of joint reference. In P. Bloom (ed.), *Language Acquisition: Core Readings*, 129–53. Cambridge, MA: The MIT Press.

Bardovi-Harlig, K. 1999. From morpheme studies to temporal semantics: Tense-aspect research in SLA. *Studies in Second Language Acquisition* 21: 341–82.

Beattie, G. 1980. The role of language production processes in the organization of behaviour in face to face interaction. In B. Butterworth (ed.), *Language Production: Vol. 1, Speech and Talk*. London: Academic.

Beattie, G. and Coughlan, J. 1999. An experimental investigation of the role of iconic gestures in lexical access using the tip-of-the-tongue phenomenon. *British Journal of Psychology* 90: 35–56.

Beauvillain, C. and Grainger, J. 1987. Accessing interlexical homographs: Some limitations of a language-selective access. *Journal of Memory and Language* 26: 658–72.

Beilock, S. L. and Lyons, I. M. 2008. Expertise and the mental simulation of action. In K. Markman, B. Klein, and J. Suhr (eds.), *The Handbook of Imagination and Mental Simulation*, 21–34. London: Psychology Press.

Beliavsky, N. 1994. The evolution of pronominal reference in children's narratives: Who are "They"? Doctoral dissertation. Northwestern University, Evanston, IL.

Ben-Dror, I., Frost, R., and Bentin, S. 1995. Orthographic representation and phonemic segmentation in skilled readers: A cross-language comparison. *Psychological Science* 6 (3): 176–81.

Best, C., McRoberts, G., and Goodell, E. 2001. Discrimination of non-native consonant contrasts varying in perceptual assimilation to the listener's native phonological system. *Journal of the Acoustical Society of America* 109: 775–94.

Bever, T. G. 1970. The cognitive basis for linguistic structures. In J. R. Hayes (ed.), *Cognition and the Development of Language*. New York: Wiley.

Bialystok, E. 2009. Bilingualism: The good, the bad, and the indifferent. *Bilingualism: Language and Cognition* 12 (1): 3–11.

Bialystok, E. and Hakuta, K. 1999. Confounded age: Linguistic and cognitive factors in age differences for second language acquisition. In D. Birdsong (ed.), *Second Language Acquisition and the Critical Period Hypothesis*, 161–81. Mahwah, NJ: Lawrence Erlbaum.

Birdsong, D. 2005. Interpreting age effects in second language acquisition. In J. F. Kroll and A. M. de Groot (eds.), *Handbook of Bilingualism: Psycholinguistic Approaches*, 109–27. Oxford: Oxford University Press.

Birdsong, D. and Molis, M. 2001. On the evidence for maturational effects in second language acquisition. *Journal of Memory and Language* 44: 235–49.

Bloom, P. 1990. Subjectless sentences in child language. *Linguistic Inquiry* 21, 491–504.

Bock, K. 1986. Syntactic persistence in language production. *Cognitive Psychology* 18: 355–87.

Bock, K. 1991. A sketchbook of production problems. *Journal of Psycholinguistic Research* 20: 141–60.

Bock, K. and Griffin, Z. 2000. The persistence of structural priming: Transient activation or implicit learning? *Journal of Experimental Psychology: General* 129: 177–92.

Bock, K. and Levelt, W. J. 1994. Language production: Grammatical encoding. In M. Gernsbacher (ed.), *Handbook of Psycholinguistics*, 945–84. New York: Academic Press.

Bock, K. and Miller, C. 1991. Broken agreement. *Cognitive Psychology* 23: 45–93.

Bock, K., Eberhard, K. M., Cutting, J. C., Meyer, A. S., and Schriefers, H. 2001. Some attractions of verb agreement. *Cognitive Psychology* 43 (2): 83–128.

Boersma, P. and Weenink, D. 2009. Praat: Doing phonetics by computer [Computer software]. Amsterdam, The Netherlands: University of Amsterdam.

Bond, Z. S. 2005. Slips of the ear. In D. Pisoni and R. Remez (eds.), *The Handbook of Speech Perception*, 290–309. Malden, MA: Blackwell.

Boomer, D. 1965. Hesitation and grammatical encoding. *Language and Speech* 8: 145–58.

Bornkessel-Schlesewsky, I. D. and Friederici, A. D. 2007. Neuroimaging studies of sentence and discourse comprehension. In M. G. Gaskell (ed.), *The Oxford Handbook of Psycholinguistics*, 407–24. Oxford: Oxford University Press.

Borsky, S., Tuller, B., and Shapiro, L. P. 1998. How to milk a coat: The effect of semantic and acoustic information on phoneme categorization. *Journal of the Acoustical Society of America* 103: 2670–6.

Bosch, L. and Sebastián-Gallés, N. 1997. Native-language recognition abilities in 4-month-old infants from monolingual and bilingual environments. *Cognition* 65: 33–69.

Bradley, D. 1980. Lexical representation of derivational relation. In M. Aronoff and M. L. Kean (eds.), *Juncture*, 37–55. Saratoga, CA: Anma Libri.

Braine, M. D. 1971. On two types of models of the internalization. In D. I. Slobin (ed.), *The Ontogenesis of Grammar*, 153–88. New York: Academic Press.

Bransford, J. D. and Franks, J. J. 1971. The abstraction of linguistic ideas. *Cognitive Psychology* 2 (4): 331–50.

Bransford, J. D., Barclay, J. R., and Franks, J. J. 1972. Sentence memory: A constructive versus interpretive approach. *Cognitive Psychology* 3: 193–209.

Brown, G. and Yule, G. 1983. *Discourse Analysis*. Cambridge: Cambridge University Press.

Brown, R. 1970. The first sentences of child and chimpanzee. In R. Brown, *Psycholinguistics: Selected Papers*, 208–31. New York: The Free Press.

Brown, R. 1973. *A First Language: The Early Stages*. Cambridge, MA: Harvard University Press.

Brown, R. and Hanlon, C. 1970. Derivational complexity and order of acquisition in child speech. In J. R. Hayes (ed.), *Cognition and the Development of Language*, 11–54. New York: Wiley.

Brown, R. and McNeill, D. 1966. The "tip of the tongue" phenomenon. *Journal of Verbal Learning and Verbal Behavior* 5: 325–37.

Butterworth, B. 1980. Some constraints on models of language production. In B. Butterworth (ed.), *Language Production: Vol. 1, Speech and Talk*. London: Academic.

Cabeza, R. and Lennartson, R. 2005. False memory across languages: Implicit associative response vs. fuzzy trace views. *Memory* 13 (1): 1–5.

Cairns, H. S. 1999. *Psycholinguistics: An Introduction*. Austin, TX: Pro-Ed.

Cairns, H. S. and Kamerman, J. 1976. Lexical information processing. *Journal of Verbal Learning and Verbal Behavior* 14: 170–9.

Cairns, H. S., Cowart, R. W., and Jablon, A. D. 1981. Effects of prior context upon the integration of lexical information during sentence processing. *Journal of Verbal Learning and Verbal Behavior* 20: 445–53.

Cairns, H. S., McDaniel, D., Hsu, J. R., and Rapp, M. 1994. A longitudinal study of principles of control and pronominal reference in child English. *Language* 70: 260–88.

Cairns, H., Schlisselberg, G., Waltzman, D., and McDaniel, D. 2006. Development of a metalinguistic skill: Judging the grammaticality of sentences. *Communication Disorders Quarterly* 27 (4): 213–20.

Cairns, H. S., Waltzman, D., and Schlisselberg, G. 2004. Detecting the ambiguity of sentences: Relationship to early reading skill. *Communication Disorders Quarterly* 25: 68–78.

Caramazza, A. and Zurif, E. 1976. Dissociation of algorithmic and heuristic processes in language comprehension: Evidence from aphasia. *Brain and Language* 3: 572–82.

Carey, S. 1978. The child as a word learner. In M. Halle, J. Bresnan, and G. A. Miller (eds.), *Linguistic Theory and Psychological Reality*, 264–93. Cambridge, MA: The MIT Press.

Carnie, A. 2006. *Syntax: A Generative Introduction* (2nd edition). Malden, MA: Wiley-Blackwell.

Carpenter, P. A., Miyake, A., and Just, M. A. 1994. Working memory constraints in comprehension: Evidence from individual differences, aphasia, and aging. In M. A. Gernsbacher (ed.), *Handbok of Psycholinguistics*, 1075–115. New York: Academic Press.

Carr, T. H. and Dagenbach, D. 1990. Semantic priming and repetition priming from masked words: Evidence for a center-surround attentional mechanism in perceptual recognition. *Journal of Experimental Psychology: Human Learning and Memory* 16 (2): 341–50.

Carreiras, M. 1992. Estrategias de análisis sintáctico en el procesamiento de frases: cierre temprano versus cierre tardío. *Cognitiva* 4 (1): 3–27.

Carreiras, M. and Clifton, C. 2004. *The On-line Study of Sentence Comprehension: Eyetracking, ERP, and Beyond*. Brighton, UK: Psychology Press.

Cheang, H. S. and Pell, M. D. 2008. The sound of sarcasm. *Speech Communication* 50: 366–81.

Chernela, J. 2004. The politics of language acquisition: Language learning as social modeling in the northwest Amazon. *Women and Language* (Spring): 13–21.

Chistovich, L. A., Klass, I. A., Kuz'min, I. I., and Holden, R. M. 1963. *The Process of Speech Sound Discrimination*. Bedford, MA: Research Translation ETR 63–10, Air Force, Cambridge Research Laboratories.

Chomsky, N. 1959. Review of Skinner's *Verbal Behavior*. *Language* 35: 16–58.

Chomsky, N. 1965. *Aspects of the Theory of Syntax*. Cambridge, MA: The MIT Press.

Chomsky, N. 1975. On cognitive capacity. In N. Chomsky, *Reflections on Language*, 3–35. New York: Pantheon.

Clahsen, H. and Felser, C. 2006. Grammatical processing in language learners. *Applied Psycholinguistics* 27: 3–42.

Clark, H. H. and Sengul, C. J. 1979. In search of referents for nouns and pronouns. *Memory and Cognition* 7: 35–41.

Clarke, C. M. and Garrett, M. F. 2004. Rapid adaptation to foreign-accented English. *Journal of the Acoustical Society of America* 116 (6): 3647–58.

Clifton, C., Carlson, K., and Frazier, L. 2006. Tracking the what and why of speakers' choices: Prosodic boundaries and the length of constituents. *Psychonomic Bulletin and Review* 13 (5): 854–61.

Cole, R. A., Jakimik, J., and Cooper, W. E. 1978. Perceptibility of phonetic features in fluent speech. *Journal of the Acoustical Society of America* 64: 44–56.

Connine, C. M. 1994. Vertical and horizontal similarity in spokenword recognition. In C. Clifton, L. Frazier, and K. Rayner (eds.), *Perspectives on Sentence Processing*, 107–22. Hillsdale, NJ: Lawrence Erlbaum.

Connine, C. M., Blasko, D. M., and Titone, D. A. 1993. Do the beginnings of spoken words have a special status in auditory word recognition? *Journal of Memory and Language* 32: 193–210.

Cowart, R. W. and Cairns, H. S. 1987. Evidence for an anaphoric mechanism within syntactic processing: Some reference relations defy semantic and pragmatic constraints. *Memory and Cognition* 15: 318–31.

Crain, S. 1991. Language acquisition in the absence of experience. *Behavioral and Brain Sciences* 14: 597–650.

Crystal, D. 2003. *The Cambridge Encyclopedia of the English Language* (2nd edition). Cambridge: Cambridge University Press.

Crystal, D. 2006. *Language and the Internet* (2nd edition). Cambridge: Cambridge University Press.

Cuetos, F. and Mitchell, D. C. 1988. Cross-linguistic differences in parsing: Restrictions on the use of the Late Closure strategy in Spanish. *Cognition* 30: 73–105.

Curtin, S., Goad, H., and Pater, J. V. 1998. Phonological transfer and levels of representation: The perceptual acquisition of Thai voice and aspiration by English and French speakers. *Second Language Research* 14 (4): 389–405.

Curtiss, S. 1977. *Genie: A Psycholinguistic Study of a Modern-day "Wild Child."* New York: Academic Press.

Curtiss, S. 1988. Abnormal language acquisition and the modularity of language. In F. J. Newmeyer (ed.), *Linguistics: The Cambridge Survey II. Linguistic Theory: Extensions and Implications*, 96–117. Cambridge: Cambridge University Press.

Curtiss, S., Fromkin, V., Krashen, S., Rigler, D., and Rigler, M. 1974. The linguistic development of Genie. *Language* 50: 528–54.

Cutler, A. and Clifton, C. 1984. The use of prosodic information in word recognition. In H. Bouma and D. G. Bouwhuis (eds.), *Attention and Performance X: Control of Language Processes*, 183–96. Hillsdale, NJ: Lawrence Erlbaum.

Cutler, A. and Norris, D. 1988. The role of strong syllables in segmentation for lexical access. *Journal of Experimental Psychology: Human Perception and Performance* 14 (1): 113–21.

Cutler, A., Mehler, J., Norris, D., and Seguí, J. 1986. The syllable's differing role in the segmentation of French and English. *Journal of Memory and Language* 25: 385–400.

Dapretto, M. and Byork, E. L. 2000. The development of word retrieval abilities in the second year and its relation to early vocabulary growth. *Child Development* 71: 635–48.

Davidson, D. and Tell, D. 2005. Monolingual and bilingual children's use of mutual exclusivity in the naming of whole objects. *Journal of Experimental Child Psychology* 92 (1): 25–45.

Davis, C. J. 2003. Factors underlying masked priming effects in competitive network models of visual word recognition. In S. Kinoshita and S. J. Lupker (eds.), *Masked Priming: The State of the Art*, 121–70. Hove, UK: Psychology Press.

De Bleser, R. 1988. Localization of aphasia: Science or fiction? In G. Denese, C. Semenza, and P. Bisiacchi (eds.), *Perspectives on Cognitive Neuropsychology*. Hove, UK: Psychology Press.

de Bot, K. 2004. The multilingual lexicon: Modeling selection and control. *The International Journal of Multilingualism* 1: 17–32.

De Vincenzi, M. and Job, R. 1993. Some observations on the universality of the Late Closure strategy. *Journal of Psycholinguistic Research* 22 (2): 189–206.

Dennett, D. 2009. Darwin's "strange inversion of reasoning." *Proceedings of the National Academy of Sciences* 106: 10061–65.

Dennis, M. and Whitaker, H. A. 1976. Language acquisition following hemidecortication: Linguistic superiority of the left over the right hemisphere. *Brain and Language* 3 (3): 404–33.

Desmet, T., Brysbaert, M., and De Baecke, C. 2002. The correspondence between sentence production and corpus frequencies in modifier attachment. *The Quarterly Journal of Experimental Psychology* 55A (3): 879–96.

Desmet, T., De Baecke, C., Drieghe, D., Brysbaert, M., and Vonk, W. 2006. Relative clause attachment in Dutch: On-line comprehension corresponds to corpus frequencies when lexical variables are taken into account. *Language and Cognitive Processes* 21 (4): 453–85.

Deuchar, M. and Quay, S. 2000. *Bilingual Acquisition: Theoretical Implications of a Case Study*. Oxford: Oxford University Press.

Dijkstra, T. 2005. Bilingual visual word recognition and lexical access. In J. F. Kroll, and A. M. de Groot (eds.), *Handbook of Bilingualism: Psycholinguistic Approaches*, 179–201. Oxford: Oxford University Press.

Dingwall, W. O. 1993. The biological basis of human communicative behavior. In J. B. Gleason and N. B. Ratner (eds.), *Psycholinguistics*, 41–88. New York: Harcourt Brace.

Dussias, P. E. 2003. Syntactic ambiguity resolution in L2 learners. *Studies in Second Language Acquisition* 25: 529–57.

Ehrlich, K. and Rayner, K. 1983. Pronoun assignment and semantic integration during reading: Eye-movements and immediacy of processing. *Journal of Verbal Learning and Verbal Behavior* 22: 75–87.

Entus, A. K. 1975. Hemisphere asymmetry in processing of dichotically presented speech and nonspeech stimuli by infants. Paper presented at the biennial meeting of the Society for Research in Child Development. Denver, CO.

Ervin-Tripp, S. 1993. Conversational discourse. In J. B. Gleason and N. B. Ratner (eds.), *Psycholinguistics*, 238–71. New York: Harcourt Brace.

Evans, N. 1998. Myth 19: Aborigines speak a primitive language. In L. Bauer and P. Trudgill (eds.), *Language Myths*, 159–68. London: Penguin Books.

Everett, D. L. 2005. Cultural constraints on grammar and cognition in Pirahã. *Current Anthropology* 46 (4): 621–46.

Fassold, R. 1984. *The Sociolinguistics of Society*. New York: Blackwell.

Fernald, A. 1994. Human maternal vocalizations to infants as biologically relevant signals: An evolutionary perspective. In P. Bloom (ed.), *Language Acquisition: Core Readings*, 51–94. Cambridge, MA: The MIT Press.

Fernández, E. M. 2003. *Bilingual Sentence Processing: Relative Clause Attachment in English and Spanish*. Amsterdam, The Netherlands: John Benjamins.

Fernández, E. M. 2007. How might a rapid serial visual presentation of text affect the prosody projected implicitly during silent reading? *Conferências do V Congresso Internacional da Associação Brasiliera de Lingüística* 5: 117–54.

Fernson, L., Pethick, S., Renda, C., Cox, J., Dale, P. S., and Reznick, J. S. 1994. *Technical Manual and User's Guide for MacArthur Communicative Development Inventories: Short Form Versions*. San Diego, CA: Department of Psychology, San Diego State University.

Ferreira, F. 1991. Effects of length and syntactic complexity on initiation times for prepared utterances. *Journal of Memory and Language* 30 (2): 210–33.

Ferreira, F. and Patson, N. D. 2007. The 'good enough' approach to language comprehension. *Language and Linguistics Compass* 1 (1–2): 71–83.

Ferreira, F., Christianson, K., and Hollingworth, A. 2001. Misinterpretations of garden-path sentences: Implications for models of reanalysis. *Journal of Psycholinguistic Research* 30: 3–20.

Fitch, W. T. 2005. The evolution of language: A comparative perspective. In M. G. Gaskell (ed.), *The Oxford Handbook of Psycholinguistics*, 787–804. Oxford: Oxford University Press.

Flege, J. E. 2003. Assessing constraints on second-language segmental production and perception. In A. Meyer and N. Schiller (eds.), *Phonetics and Phonology in Language Comprehension and Production, Differences and Similarities*, 319–55. Berlin, Germany: Mouton de Gruyter.

Flege, J. E., Munro, M. J., and MacKay, I. R. 1995. Factors affecting strength of perceived foreign accent in a second language. *Journal of the Acoustical Society of America* 97, 3125–34.

Fodor, J. A. 1975. *Language of Thought*. New York: Crowell.

Fodor, J. A. and Bever, T. G. 1965. The psychological reality of linguistic segments. *Journal of Verbal Learning and Verbal Behavior* 4: 414–20.

Fodor, J. A., Bever, T., and Garrett, M. 1974. *The Psychology of Language*. New York: McGraw-Hill.

Fodor, J. D. 1978. Parsing strategies and constraints on transformations. *Linguistic Inquiry* 9 (3): 427–73.

Ford, M. 1978. Planning units and syntax in sentence production. Doctoral dissertation. University of Melbourne, Australia.

Forster, K. I. 1981. Frequency blocking and lexical access: One mental lexicon or two? *Journal of Verbal Learning and Verbal Behavior* 20: 190–203.

Forster, K. I. and Chambers, S. M. 1973. Lexical access and naming time. *Journal of Verbal Learning and Verbal Behavior* 12 (6): 627–35.

Forster, K. I. and Davis, C. 1984. Repetition priming and frequency attenuation in lexical access. *Journal of Experimental Psychology: Learning, Memory, and Cognition* 10: 680–98.

Foss, D. J. 1969. Decision processes during sentence comprehension: Effects of lexical item difficulty and position upon decision times. *Journal of Verbal Learning and Verbal Behavior* 8: 457–62.

Foss, D. J. and Cairns, H. S. 1970. Some effects of memory limitation upon sentence comprehension. *Journal of Verbal Learning and Verbal Behavior* 9: 541–7.

Foulke, E. and Sticht, T. G. 1969. Review of research on the intelligibility and comprehension of accelerated speech. *Psychological Bulletin* 72 (1): 50–62.

Fox, R. A. and Unkefer, J. 1985. The effect of lexical status on the perception of tone. *Journal of Chinese Linguistics* 13: 69–90.

Francis, W. N. and Kucera, H. 1982. *Frequency Analysis of English Usage: Lexicon and Grammar*. Boston, MA: Houghton Mifflin.

Frazier, L. 1987. Sentence processing: A tutorial review. In M. Coltheart (ed.), *Attention and Performance XII: The Psychology of Reading*, 554–86. Hillsdale, NJ: Lawrence Erlbaum.

Frazier, L. and Clifton, C. 1989. Successive cyclicity in the grammar and the parser. *Language and Cognitive Processes* 4: 93–126.

Frazier, L. and Clifton, C. 1996. *Construal*. Cambridge, MA: The MIT Press.

Frazier, L. and Fodor, J. D. 1978. The sausage machine: A new two-stage parsing model. *Cognition* 6: 291–325.

Frazier, L. and Rayner, K. 1982. Making and correcting errors during sentence comprehension: Eye movements in the analysis of structurally ambiguous sentences. *Cognitive Psychology* 14 (2): 178–210.

Fremgen, A. and Fay, D. 1980. Overextensions in production and comprehension: A methodological clarification. *Journal of Child Language* 7: 205–11.

Frenck-Mestre, C. 1999. Examining second language reading: an on-line look. In A. Sorace, C. Heycock, and R. Shillcock (eds.), *Language Acquisition, Knowledge Representation, and Processing*, 474–8. Amsterdam: North-Holland.

Friederici, A. D. 2002. Towards a neural basis of auditory sentence processing. *Trends in Cognitive Sciences* 6 (2): 78–84.

Friederici, A. D., Meyer, M., and Cramon, D. Y. 2000. Auditory language comprehension: An event-related fMRI study on the processing of syntactic and lexical information. *Brain and Language* 74: 289–300.

Fromkin, V. A. 1971. The non-anomalous nature of anomalous utterances. *Language* 47: 27–52.

Fromkin, V. 1973. Slips of the tongue. *Scientific American* 229 (6): 110–17.

Fromkin, V. A. 1980. *Errors in Linguistic Performance: Slips of the Tongue, Ear, Pen, and Hand*. New York: Academic Press.

Fromkin, V. A. 1988. Grammatical aspects of speech errors. In F. J. Newmeyer (ed.), *Linguistics: The Cambridge Survey, Vol. II. Linguistic Theory: Extensions and Implications*, 117–38. Cambridge: Cambridge University Press.

Frost, R. and Ziegler, J. C. 2007. Speech and spelling interaction: The interdependence of visual and auditory word recognition. In M. G. Gaskell (ed.), *The Oxford Handbook of Psycholinguistics*, 107–18. Oxford: Oxford University Press.

Gardner, R. A. and Gardner, B. T. 1969. Teaching sign language to a chimpanzee. *Science* 165: 664–72.

Gardner, R. C. 1985. *Social Psychology and Second Language Learning: The Role of Attitudes and Motivation*. London: Edward Arnold.

Garnes, S. and Bond, Z. S. 1976. The relationship between semantic expectation and acoustic information. In W. Dressler, and O. Pfeiffer (eds.), *Proceedings of The Third International Phonology Meeting*. Innsbrück, Austria: Phonologische Tagung.

Garnsey, S. M., Pearlmutter, N. J., Myers, E., and Lotocky, M. A. 1997. The contributions of verb bias and plausibility to the comprehension of temporarily ambiguous sentences. *Journal of Memory and Language* 37: 58–93.

Garnsey, S. M., Tanenhaus, M. K., and Chapman, R. M. 1989. Evoked potentials in the study of sentence comprehension. *Journal of Memory and Language* 29: 181–200.

Garrett, M. F. 1980a. Levels of processing in sentence production. In B. Butterworth (ed.), *Language Production: Vol. 1. Speech and Talk*, 170–220. London: Academic Press.

Garrett, M. F. 1980b. The limits of accommodation: Arguments for independent processing levels in sentence production. In V. A. Fromkin (ed.), *Errors in Linguistic Performance*, 263–72. London: Academic Press.

Garrett, M. F. 1988. Processes in language production. In F. Newmeyer (ed.), *Linguistics: The Cambridge Survey: Vol. III. Language: Psychological and Biological Aspects*, 69–96. Cambridge: Cambridge University Press.

Garrett, M. F., Bever, T. G., and Fodor, J. A. 1966. The active use of grammar in speech perception. *Perception and Psychophysics* 1: 30–2.

Garrod, S. C. and Sanford, A. J. 1994. Resolving sentences in a discourse context: How discourse representation affects language understanding. In M. A. Gernsbacher (ed.), *Handbook of Psycholinguistics*, 675–98. New York: Academic Press.

Gazzaniga, M. 1970. *The Bisected Brain*. New York: Appleton-Century Crofts.

Gazzaniga, M. and Hillyard, S. A. 1971. Language and speech capacity of the right hemisphere. *Neuropsychologia* 90: 273–80.

Gee, J. P. 2003. *What Video Games Have to Teach Us about Learning and Literacy*. New York: Palgrave Macmillan.

Gerken, L. A. and McIntosh, B. J. 1993. The interplay of function morphemes and prosody in early language. *Developmental Psychology* 29: 448–57.

Gibbs, R. W. 1986. On the psycholinguistics of sarcasm. *Journal of Experimental Psychology: General* 15 (1): 3–15.

Gibson, E., Pearlmutter, N., Canseco-Gonzalez, E., and Hickok, G. 1996. Recency preference in the human sentence processing mechanism. *Cognition*, 59 (1): 23–59.

Gleason, J. B. and Ratner, N. B. (eds.) 1993. *Psycholinguistics*. New York: Harcourt Brace.

Gleitman, L. R. 2000. The structural sources of verb meaning. *Language Acquisition: A Journal of Developmental Linguistics* 1: 3–56.

Gleitman, L. R., Newport, E. L., and Gleitman, H. 1984. The current status of the motherese hypothesis. *Journal of Child Language* 11: 43–79.

Golinkoff, R. M., Mervis, C. B., and Hirsch-Pasek, K. 1994. Early object labels: The case for a developmental lexical principles framework. *Journal of Child Language* 21: 125–56.

Gopnik, M. 1990. Genetic basis of grammar defect. *Nature* 344: 6268.

Gopnik, M. 1997. *The Inheritance and Innateness of Grammars*. Oxford: Oxford University Press.

Gordon, R. G. (ed.) 2005. *Ethnologue: Languages of the World* (15th edition). Dallas, TX: SIL International.

Green, D. W. 1986. Control, activation, and resource: A framework and a model for the control of speech in bilinguals. *Brain and Language* 27 (2): 210–23.

Green, D. W. 2005. The neurocognition of recovery patterns in bilingual aphasics. In J. F. Kroll and A. M. de Groot (eds.), *Handbook of Bilingualism: Psycholinguistic Approaches*, 516–30. Oxford: Oxford University Press.

Grice, H. P. 1975. Logic and conversation. In P. Cole and J. Morgan (eds.), *Syntax and Semantics, Vol. 3: Speech Acts*. New York: Academic Press.

Grodzinsky, Y. 1990. *Theoretical Perspectives on Language Deficits*. Cambridge, MA: The MIT Press.

Grosjean, F. 2001. The bilingual's language modes. In J. Nicol (ed.), *One Mind, Two Languages: Bilingual Language Processing*, 1–22. Oxford: Blackwell.

Grosjean, F. and Frauenfelder, U. H. (eds.) 1996. *Spoken Word Recognition Paradigms. Special Issue of Language and Cognitive Processes* 11 (6).

Hahne, A. and Jescheniak, J. D. 2001. What's left if the Jabberwock gets the semantics? An ERP investigation into semantic and syntactic processes during auditory sentence comprehension. *Cognitive Brain Research* 11: 199–212.

Hakes, D. T. 1972. Effects of reducing complement constructions on sentence comprehension. *Journal of Verbal Learning and Verbal Behavior* 11: 278–86.

Halle, P. A., Chereau, C., and Seguí, J. 2000. Where is the /b/ in "absurde" [apsyrd]? It is in French listeners' minds. *Journal of Memory and Language* 43 (4): 618–39.

Han, Z. 2009. Interlanguage and fossilization: Towards an analytic model. In V. Cook and L. Wei (eds.), *Contemporary Applied Linguistics (Vol. I: Language Teaching and Learning)*, 137–62. London: Continuum.

Hartsuiker, R. J., Pickering, M. J., and Veltkamp, E. 2004. Is syntax separate or shared between languages? *Psychological Science* 15 (6): 409–14.

Hauser, M. D., Chomsky, N., and Fitch, W. T. 2002. The faculty of language: What is it, who has it, and how did it evolve? *Science* 298 (22): 1569–79.

Haviland, S. E. and Clark, H. H. 1974. What's new? Acquiring new information as a process in comprehension. *Journal of Verbal Learning and Verbal Behavior* 13: 512–21.

Hayes, B. 2009. *Introductory Phonology*. Malden, MA: Blackwell.

Hess, D. J., Foss, D. J., and Caroll, P. 1995. Effects of global and local context on lexical processing during language comprehension. *Journal of Experimental Psychology: General* 124: 62–82.

Hillenbrand, J., Getty, L. A., Clark, M. J., and Wheeler, K. 1995. Acoustic characteristics of American English vowels. *Journal of the Acoustical Society of America* 97: 3099–111.

Hirsch-Pasek, K., Gleitman, L. R., and Gleitman, H. 1978. What did the brain say to the mind? A study of the detection and report of ambiguity by young children. In A. Sinclair, R. J. Jervella, and W. J. Levelt (eds.), *The Child's Conception of Language*, 97–132. Berlin: Springer.

Hirsh-Pasek, K., Golinkoff, R., Fletcher, A., DeGaspe Beaubien, F., and Caley, K. 1978. In the beginning: One-word speakers comprehend word order. Paper presented at Boston Language Conference. Boston, MA.

Hirsh-Pasek, K., Treiman, R., and Schneiderman, M. 1984. Brown and Hanlon revisited: Mothers' sensitivity to ungrammatical forms. *Journal of Child Language* 11: 81–8.

Hockett, C. F. 1955. *A Manual of Phonology* (Publications in Anthropology and Linguistics, no. 11). Bloomington, IN: Indiana University.

Holcomb, P. J. and Neville, H. J. 1991. The electrophysiology of spoken sentence processing. *Psychobiology* 19: 286–300.

Hudson, S. B., Tanenhaus, M., and Dell, G. S. 1986. The effect of discourse center on the local coherence of a discourse. In *Proceedings of the Eighth Annual Conference of the Cognitive Science Society*, 96–101. Mahwah, NJ: Lawrence Erlbaum.

Hyams, N. 1986. *Language Acquisition and the Theory of Parameters*. Boston, MA: Reidel.

Jackendoff, R. 2002. *Foundations of Language: Brain, Meaning, Grammar, Evolution*. Oxford: Oxford University Press.

Jacobson, P. F., and Cairns, H. S. 2009. Exceptional rule learning in a longitudinal case study of Williams syndrome: Acquisition of past tense. *Communication Disorders Quarterly*, prepublished June 5, 2009.

Jarmulowicz, L. 2006. School-aged children's phonological production of derived English words. *Journal of Speech, Language, and Hearing Research* 49 (2): 294–308.

Jenkins, C. M. 1971. Memory and linguistic information: A study of sentence memory, linguistic form, and inferred information. Unpublished doctoral dissertation. The University of Texas at Austin.

Johnson, M. K., Bransford, J. D., and Solomon, S. K. 1973. Memory for tacit implications of sentences. *Journal of Experimental Psychology* 98: 203–5.

Juffs, A. 1998. Main verb versus reduced relative clause ambiguity resolution in L2 sentence processing. *Language Learning* 48 (1): 107–47.

Just, M. A. and Carpenter, P. A. 1992. A capacity theory of comprehension: Individual differences in working memory. *Psychological Review* 99: 122–49.

Katz, W. F. and Assmann, P. F. 2001. Identification of children's and adults' vowels: Intrinsic fundamental frequency, fundamental frequency dynamics, and presence of voicing. *Journal of Phonetics* 29 (1): 23–51.

KayPENTAX. 2008. Computerized Speech Lab (CSL) [Computer software]. Lincoln Park, NJ.

Keenan, J. M., MacWhinney, B., and Mayhew, D. 1977. Pragmatics in memory: A study of natural conversation. *Journal of Verbal Learning and Verbal Behavior* 16: 549–60.

Kegl, J. 1994. The Nicaraguan Sign Language project: An overview. *Signpost* 7 (1) (Spring): 24–31.

Kegl, J., Senghas, A., and Coppola, M. 1999. Creation through contact: Sign language emergence and sign language change in Nicaragua. In *Language Creation and Language Change: Creolization, Diachrony, and Development*, 179–237. Cambridge, MA: The MIT Press.

Kent, R. D. 1997. *The Speech Sciences*. San Diego, CA: Singular Publishing Group.

Kess, J. F. 1992. *Psycholinguistics*. Philadelphia, PA: John Benjamins.

Kidd, E., Stewart, A., and Serratrice, L. 2006. Can children overcome lexical biases? The role of the referential scene. Paper presented at the Workshop on On-Line Methods in Children's Language Processing, CUNY. New York: Graduate Center, City University of New York.

Kimura, D. 1961. Cerebral dominance and the perception of verbal stimuli. *Canadian Journal of Psychology* 15: 166–71.

Kimura, D. 1964. Left–right differences in the perception of melodies. *Quarterly Journal of Experimental Psychology* 16: 355–8.

Kimura, D. 1973. The asymmetry of the human brain. *Scientific American* 228: 70–8.

Kisilevsky, B. S., Hains, S. M., Lee, K., Xie, X., Huang, H., Ye, H. H., et al. 2003. Effects of experience on fetal voice recognition. *Psychological Science* 14 (3): 220–4.

Kroll, J. F. and Dijkstra, A. 2002. The bilingual lexicon. In R. Kaplan (ed.), *Handbook of Applied Linguistics*, 301–21. Oxford: Oxford University Press.

Kroll, J. F. and Sunderman, G. 2003. Cognitive processes in second language learners and bilinguals: The development of lexical and conceptual representations. In C. Doughty and M. Long (eds.), *Handbook of Second Language Acquisition*, 104–29. Cambridge, MA: Blackwell.

Kuhl, P. K., Tsao, F., and Liu, H. 2003. Foreign-language experience in infancy: Effects of short-term exposure and social interaction on phonetic learning. *Proceedings of the National Academy of Sciences of the United States of America*, 100 (15), 9096–101.

Kutas, M. and Van Petten, C. 1988. Event-related brain potential studies of language. In P. K. Ackles, J. R. Jennings, and M. G. Coles (eds.), *Advances in Psychophysiology*, 139–87. Greenwich, CT: JAI Press.

Ladefoged, P. 2005. *Vowels and Consonants: An Introduction to the Sounds of Languages* (2nd edition). Oxford: Blackwell.

Ladefoged, P., Ladefoged, J., and Everett, D. 1997. Phonetic structures of Banawa, an endangered language. *Phonetica* 54: 94–111.

Lai, C. S., Fischer, S. E., Hurst, J. A., Vargha-Khadem, F., and Monaco, A. P. 2001. A forkhead-domain gene is mutated in a severe speech and language disorder. *Nature* 413: 519–23.

Lashley, K. K. 1951. The problem of serial order in behavior. In L. A. Jefress (ed.), *Cerebral Mechanisms in Behavior*, 112–36. New York: Wiley.

Lenhoff, H. M., Wang, P. P., Greenberg, E., and Bellugi, U. 1997. Williams syndrome and the brain. *Scientific American* 277: 68–73.

Lenneberg, E. H. 1964. A biological perspective of language. In E. H. Lennenberg (ed.), *New Directions in the Study of Language*, 65–88. Cambridge, MA: The MIT Press.

Lenneberg, E. H. 1967. *Biological Foundations of Language*. New York: Wiley.

Leonard, L. B. 1998. *Children with Specific Language Impairment*. Cambridge, MA: The MIT Press.

Levelt, W. J. 1983. Monitoring and self-repair in speech. *Cognition* 14: 41–104.

Levelt, W. J. 1989. *Speaking: From Intention to Articulation*. Cambridge, MA: The MIT Press.

Levelt, W. J. and Kelter, S. 1982. Surface form and memory in question answering. *Cognitive Psychology* 14: 78–106.

Liberman, A. M. 1970. The grammars of speech and language. *Cognitive Psychology* 1: 301–23.

Liberman, A. M. and Mattingly, I. G. 1985. The motor theory of speech perception revised. *Cognition* 21: 1–36.

Liberman, A. M., Cooper, F. S., Shankweiler, D. P., and Studdert-Kennedy, M. 1967. Perception of the speech code. *Psychological Review* 74: 431–61.

Liberman, A. M., Harris, K. S., Hoffman, H. S., and Griffith, B. C. 1957. The discrimination of speech sounds within and across phoneme boundaries. *Journal of Experimental Psychology* 54: 358–68.

Liberman, I. Y., Shankweiler, D. P., Liberman, A. M., Fowler, C., and Fischer, F. W. 1977. Phonetic segmentation and recoding in the beginning reader. In A. S. Reber and D. Scarborough (eds.), *Toward a Psychology of Reading*, 207–26. Hillsdale, NJ: Lawrence Erlbaum.

Limber, J. 1973. The genesis of complex sentences. In T. Moore (ed.), *Cognitive Development and the Acquisition of Language*, 169–86. New York: Academic Press.

Linebarger, M. C., Schwartz, M. F., and Saffran, E. M. 1983. Sensitivity to grammatical structure in so-called agrammatic aphasics. *Cognition* 13: 361–92.

Lipski, J. M. 2005. Code-switching or borrowing? No sé so no puedo decir, you know. In L. Sayahi and M. Westmoreland (eds.), *Selected Proceedings of the Second Workshop on Spanish Sociolinguistics*, 1–15. Somerville, MA: Cascadilla Proceedings Project.

Lisker, L. and Abramson, A. S. 1964. A cross-language study of voicing in initial stops: acoustic measurements. *Word* 20: 384–422.

Loebell, H. and Bock, K. 2003. Structural priming across languages. *Linguistics* 41–5: 791–824.

Loftus, E. F. 2003. Our changeable memories: Legal and practical implications. *Nature Reviews: Neuroscience* 4: 231–4.

Loftus, E. F. and Palmer, J. C. 1974. Reconstruction of automobile destruction: An example of the interaction between language and memory. *Journal of Verbal Learning and Verbal Behavior* 13: 585–9.

Lombardi, L. and Potter, M. C. 1992. The regeneration of syntax in short-term memory. *Journal of Memory and Language* 31: 713–33.

MacDonald, M. C., Pearlmutter, N. J., and Seidenberg, M. S. 1994. Syntactic ambiguity resolution as lexical ambiguity resolution. In C. L. Clifton, L. Frazier, and K. Rayner (eds.), *Perspectives on Sentence Processing*, 123–53. Hillsdale, NJ: Lawrence Erlbaum.

Macleod, A. and Summerfield, Q. 1987. Quantifying the contribution of vision to speech perception in noise. *British Journal of Audiology* 21 (2): 131–41.

Männel, C. and Friederici, A. D. 2008. Event-related brain potentials as a window to children's language processing: From syllables to sentences. In I. A. Sekerina, E. M. Fernández, and H. Clahsen (eds.), *Developmental Psycholinguistics: On-line Methods in Children's Language Processing*, 30–72. Amsterdam, The Netherlands: John Benjamins.

Marchman, V. A. and Fernald, A. 2008. Speed of word recognition and vocabulary knowledge in infancy predict cognitive and language outcomes in later childhood. *Developmental Science* 11 (3): F9–F16.

Marcus, G. F. and Fisher, S. E. 2003. FOXP2 in focus: What can genes tell us about speech and language? *Trends in Cognitive Sciences* 7 (6): 257–62.

Marian, V. and Kaushanskaya, M. 2004. Self-construal and emotion in bicultural bilinguals. *Journal of Memory and Language* 51: 190–201.

Markman, E. M. 1992. The whole object, taxonomic, and mutual exclusivity assumptions as initial constraints on word meanings. In J. P. Byrnes and S. A. Gelman (eds.), *Perspectives on Language and Cognition: Interrelations in Development*, 72–106. Cambridge: Cambridge University Press.

Markman, E. M. 1994. Constraints children place on word meanings. In P. Bloom (ed.), *Language Acquisition: Core Readings*, 154–73. Cambridge, MA: The MIT Press.

Markman, E. M. and Hutchinson, J. E. 1984. Children's sensitivity to constraints on word meaning: Taxonomic vs. thematic relations. *Cognitive Psychology* 16: 1–27.

Markman, E. M. and Wachtel, G. F. 1988. Children's use of mutual exclusivity to constrain the meanings of words. *Cognitive Psychology* 20: 121–57.

Marslen-Wilson, W. D. 1987. Functional parallelism in spoken word recognition. *Cognition* 25: 71–102.

Marslen-Wilson, W. D. 2005. Morphological processes in language comprehension. In M. G. Gaskell (ed.), *The Oxford Handbook of Psycholinguistics*, 175–93. Oxford: Oxford University Press.

Marslen-Wilson, W. D. and Tyler, L. K. 1980. The temporal structure of spoken word recognition. *Cognition* 8: 1–71.

Marslen-Wilson, W. D. and Welsh, A. 1978. Processing interactions and lexical access during word recognition in continuous speech. *Cognitive Psychology* 10: 29–63.

Matthews, A. and Chodorow, M. S. 1988. Pronoun resolution in two-clause sentences: Effects of ambiguity, antecedent location, and depth of embedding. *Journal of Memory and Language* 27 (3): 245–60.

Mayo, L. H., Florentine, M., and Buus, S. 1997. Age of second-language acquisition and perception of speech in noise. *Journal of Speech, Language, and Hearing Research* 40, 686–93.

McDaniel, D., Cairns, H. S., and Hsu, J. R. 1990. Control principles in the grammars of young children. *Language Acquisition: A Journal of Developmental Linguistics* 1 (4): 297–336.

McDaniel, D., McKee, C., and Cairns, H. S. (eds.) 1996. *Methods for Assessing Children's Syntax*. Cambridge, MA: The MIT Press.

McDaniel, D., McKee, C., and Garrett, M. F. 2010. Children's sentence planning: Syntactic correlates of fluency variations. *Journal of Child Language* 37 (1): 59–94.

McGurk, H. and MacDonald, J. 1978. Hearing lips and seeing voices. *Nature* 264: 746–8.

McKain, K. S., Studdert-Kennedy, M., Speiker, S., and Stern, D. 1983. Infant inter-modal speech perception is a left-hemisphere function. *Science* 219: 1347–9.

McKee, C., McDaniel, D., and Snedeker, J. 1998. Relatives children say. *Journal of Psycholinguistic Research* 27 (5): 573–96.

McNeill, D. 1966. Developmental psycholinguistics. In F. Smith and G. A. Miller (eds.), *The Genesis of Language*. Cambridge, MA: The MIT Press.

McQueen, J. M., Otake, T., and Cutler, A. 2001. Rhythmic cues and possible-word constraints in Japanese speech segmentation. *Journal of Memory and Language* 45: 103–32.

Mehler, J., Jusczyk, P. W., Lambertz, G., Halsted, G., Bertoncini, J., and Amiel-Tison, C. 1988. A precursor of language acquisition in young infants. *Cognition* 29: 143–78.

Meisel, J. 1989. Early differentiation of languages in bilingual children. In K. Hyltenstam and L. Obler (eds.), *Bilingualism across the Lifespan. Aspects of*

Acquisition, Maturity and Loss, 13–40. Cambridge: Cambridge University Press.

Menyuk, P., Chesnick, M., Liebergott, J. W., Korngold, B., D'Agostino, R., and Belanger, A. 1991. Predicting reading problems in at-risk children. *Journal of Speech and Hearing Research* 34: 893–903.

Meyer, D. E. and Schvaneveldt, R. W. 1971. Facilitation in recognizing words: Evidence of a dependence upon retrieval operations. *Journal of Experimental Psychology* 90: 227–34.

Miller, G. A. 1956. The magical number seven, plus or minus two: some limits on our capacity for processing information. *Psychological Review* 63: 81–97.

Miller, G. A. 1965. Some preliminaries to psycholinguistics. *American Psychologist* 20: 15–20.

Miller, G. A. and Gildea, P. M. 1987. How children learn words. *Scientific American* 257, 94–9.

Miller, G. A. and Selfridge, J. A. 1950. Verbal context and the recall of meaningful material. *American Journal of Psychology* 63: 176–85.

Mitchell, D. C. and Cuetos, F. 1991. The origins of parsing strategies. In C. Smith (ed.), *Current Issues in Natural Language Processing*, 1–12. Austin, TX: Center for Cognitive Science, University of Austin.

Molfese, D. L. 1973. Cerebral asymmetry in infants, children, and adults: Auditory evoked responses to speech and noise stimuli. *Journal of the Acoustical Society of America* 53: 363.

Morais, J., Cary, L., Alegria, J., and Bertelson, P. 1979. Does awareness of speech as a sequence of phones arise spontaneously? *Cognition* 7 (4): 323–31.

Müller-Lyer, F. C. 1889. Optische Urteilstäuschungen. *Achiv für Physiologie* Suppl. 263–70.

Myers-Scotton, C. 1988. Code-switching as indexical of social negotiations. In M. Heller (ed.), *Codeswitching*, 151–186. Berlin: Mouton de Gruyter.

Myers-Scotton, C. 1993. *Duelling Languages: Grammatical Structure in Codeswitching*. Oxford: Clarendon Press.

Naigles, L. G. 1990. Children use syntax to learn verb meanings. *Journal of Child Language* 17: 357–74.

National Endowment for the Arts. 2004. *Reading at Risk: A Survey of Literary Reading in America*. Research division report no. 46, Washington, DC.

Neville, H., Nicol, J. L., Barss, A., Forster, K. I., and Garrett, M. F. 1991. Syntactically based sentence processing classes: Evidence from event-related brain potentials. *Journal of Cognitive Neuroscience* 3 (2): 151–65.

Nevins, A. I., Pesetsky, D., and Rodrigues, C. 2009. Pirahã exceptionality: A reassessment. *Language* 85 (2): 355–404.

Newport, E. L. 1990. Maturational constraints on language acquisition. *Cognitive Science* 14: 11–28.

Nicol, J. L. 1988. Coreference processing during sentence comprehension. Doctoral dissertation. Massachusetts Institute of Technology, Cambridge, MA.

Ojemann, G. 1983. Brain organization for language from the perspective of electrical stimulation mapping. *Behavioral and Brain Sciences* 6: 189–230.

REFERENCES

Osgood, C. E. and Sebeok, L. A. 1954. *Psycholinguistics: A Survey of Theory and Research Problems.* Bloomington, IN: Indiana University.

Osterhout, L. 1994. Event-related brain potentials as tools for comprehending language comprehension. In J. C. Clifton, L. Frazier, and K. Rayner (eds.), *Perspectives on Sentence Processing,* 15–44. Hillsdale, NJ: Lawrence Erlbaum.

Osterhout, L. and Holcomb, P. J. 1992. Event-related potentials elicited by syntactic anomaly. *Journal of Memory and Language* 31: 785–806.

Osterhout, L. and Holcomb, P. J. 1993. Event-related potentials and syntactic anomaly: Evidence of anomaly detection during the perception of continuous speech. *Language and Cognitive Processes* 8: 413–38.

Osterhout, L. and Mobley, L. A. 1995. Event-related brain potentials elicited by failure to agree. *Journal of Memory and Language* 34: 739–73.

Osterhout, L. and Nicol, J. 1999. On the distinctiveness, independence, and time course of the brain responses to syntactic and semantic anomalies. *Language and Cognitive Processes* 14 (3): 283–317.

Owens, R. E. 2001. *Language Development: An Introduction* (5th edition). Needham Heights, MA: Allyn and Bacon.

Paradis, J. and Genesee, F. 1996. Syntactic acquisition in bilingual children: Autonomous or interdependent? *Studies in Second Language Acquisition* 18: 1–25.

Paradis, J., Nicoladis, E., and Genesee, F. 2000. Early emergence of structural constraints on code-mixing: Evidence from French–English bilingual children. *Bilingualism: Language and Cognition* 3: 245–62.

Park, B. 1992. *Junie B. Jones and the Stupid Smelly Bus.* New York: Random House.

Pearson, B. Z. 1998. Assessing lexical development in bilingual babies and toddlers. *The International Journal of Bilingualism* 2 (3): 347–72.

Pearson, B. Z., Fernández, S. C., Lewedag, V., and Oller, D. K. 1997. Input factors in lexical learning of bilingual infants (ages 10 to 30 months). *Applied Psycholinguistics* 18: 41–58.

Pearson, B. Z., Fernández, S. C., and Oller, D. K. 1993. Lexical development in bilingual infants and toddlers: Comparison to monolingual norms. *Language Learning* 43: 93–120.

Penfield, W. and Roberts, L. 1959. *Speech and Brain Mechanisms.* Princeton, NJ: Princeton University Press.

Pepperberg, I. 2007. Grey parrots do not always "parrot": The roles of imitation and phonological awareness in the creation of new labels from existing vocalizations. *Language Sciences* 29: 1–13.

Perfetti, C. A., Liu, Y., and Tan, L. H. 2005. Lexical constituency model: Some implications of research on Chinese for general theories of reading. *Psychological Review* 112 (1): 43–59.

Peters, A. M. and Zaidel, E. 1980. The acquisition of homonymy. *Cognition* 8: 187–207.

Petersen, S. E., Fox, P. T., Snyder, A. Z., and Raichle, M. E. 1990. Activation of extrastriate and frontal cortical areas by visual words and word-like stimuli. *Science* 249: 1041–4.

Petitto, L. A., Holowka, S., Sergio, L. E., Levy, B., and Ostry, D. J. 2004. Baby hands that move to the rhythm of language: Hearing babies acquiring sign languages babble silently on the hands. *Cognition* 93: 43–73.

Piaget, J. 1962. *Play, Dreams, and Imitation in Childhood*, trans. C. Gattegno and F. M. Hodgson. New York: Norton.

Pickering, M. J. and Garrod, S. 2004. Toward a mechanistic psychology of dialogue. *Behavioral and Brain Sciences* 27: 169–226.

Pienemann, M., Di Biase, B., Kawaguchi, S., and Håkansson, G. 2005. Processing constraints on L1 transfer. In J. F. Kroll and A. M. de Groot (eds.), *Handbook of Bilingualism: Psycholinguistic Approaches*, 128–53. Oxford: Oxford University Press.

Pierce, A. 1992. *Language Acquisition and Syntactic Theory: A Comparative Analysis of French and English Child Grammars*. Dordrecht, The Netherlands: Kluwer.

Poizner, H., Klima, E., and Bellugi, U. 1987. *What the Hands Reveal about the Brain*. Cambridge, MA: The MIT Press.

Polka, L. and Werker, J. F. 1994. Developmental changes in perception of non-native vowel contrasts. *Journal of Experimental Psychology: Human Perception and Performance* 20: 421–35.

Pollack, I. and Pickett, J. M. 1964. The intelligibility of excerpts from conversation. *Language and Speech* 6 (3): 165–71.

Poplack, S. 1980. Sometimes I'll start a sentence in Spanish y termino en español. *Linguistics* 18: 581–618.

Potter, M. C. and Lombardi, L. 1990. Regeneration in the short-term recall of sentences. *Journal of Memory and Language* 29: 633–54.

Premack, D. 1971. Language in chimpanzee? *Science* 172: 808–22.

Premack, D. 1976. *Intelligence in Ape and Man*. Hillsdale, NJ: Lawrence Erlbaum.

Preston, D. R. 1998. They speak really bad English down South and in New York City. In L. Bauer and P. Trudgill (eds.), *Language Myths*, 139–49. London: Penguin.

Ramus, F., Nespor, M., and Mehler, J. 1999. Correlates of linguistic rhythm in the speech signal. *Cognition* 73 (3): 265–92.

Raphael, L. J., Borden, G. J., and Harris, K. S. 2006. *Speech Science Primer* (5th edition). Philadelphia: Lippincott Williams & Wilkins.

Rasmussen, T. and Milner, B. 1977. The role of early left-brain injury in determining lateralization of cerebral speech functions. *Annals of the New York Academy of Sciences* 299: 355–69.

Rayner, K., Carlson, M., and Frazier, L. 1983. The interaction of syntax and semantics during sentence processing. *Journal of Verbal Learning and Verbal Behavior* 22: 358–74.

Rayner, K., Garrod, S., and Perfetti, C. A. 1992. Discourse influences during parsing are delayed. *Cognition* 45: 109–39.

Roca, I. and Johnson, W. 1999. *A Course in Phonology*. Oxford: Blackwell Publishing.

Rodd, J., Gaskell, G., and Marslen-Wilson, W. 2002. Making sense of semantic ambiguity: Semantic competition in lexical access. *Journal of Memory and Language* 46: 245–66.

Romaine, S. 1995. *Bilingualism* (2nd edition). Oxford: Blackwell Publishing.

Rowe, M. and Goldin-Meadow, S. 2009. Early gestures selectively predict later language learning. *Developmental Science* 12: 182–7.

Rumbaugh, D. M. and Gill, T. V. 1976. Language and the acquisition of language-type skills by a chimpanzee. *Annals of the New York Academy of Sciences* 270: 90–135.

Sachs, J. 1967. Recognition memory for syntactic and semantic aspects of connected discourse. *Perception and Psychophysics* 2: 437–42.

Sachs, J., Bard, B., and Johnson, M. L. 1981. Language learning with restricted input: Case studies of two hearing children of deaf parents. *Journal of Applied Psycholinguistics* 2: 33–54.

Saffran, J. R. 2003. Statistical language learning: Mechanisms and constraints. *Current Directions in Psychological Science* 12 (4): 110–14.

Saffran, J. R., Aslin, R. N., and Newport, E. L. 1996. Statistical learning by 8-month-old infants. *Science* 274 (5294): 1926–28.

Salverda, A. P., Dahan, D., and McQueen, J. M. 2003. The role of prosodic boundaries in the resolution of lexical embedding in speech comprehension. *Cognition* 90: 51–89.

Sampson, G. 1985. *Writing Systems: A Linguistic Introduction.* Stanford, CA: Stanford University Press.

Samuel, A. G. 1981. Phonemic restoration: Insights from a new methodology. *Journal of Experimental Psychology: General* 110: 474–94.

Sánchez-Casas, R. and García-Albea, J. E. 2005. The representation of cognate and noncognate words in bilingual memory. In J. F. Kroll and A. M. de Groot (eds.), *Handbook of Bilingualism: Psycholinguistic Approaches*, 226–50. Oxford: Oxford University Press.

Sánchez-Casas, R., Davis, C. W., and García-Albea, J. E. 1992. Bilingual lexical processing: Exploring the cognate/non-cognate distinction. *European Journal of Cognitive Psychology* 4: 311–22.

Sanford, A. J., Moar, K., and Garrod, S. C. 1988. Proper names as controllers of discourse focus. *Language and Speech* 31 (1): 43–56.

Sapir, E. 1949. The psychological reality of phonemes. In D. G. Mandelbaum (ed.), *Selected Writings of Edward Sapir*, 46–60. Berkeley, CA: University of California Press.

Saporta, S. (ed.) 1961. *Psycholinguistics: A Book of Readings.* New York: Holt, Rinehart, and Winston.

Savage-Rumbaugh, S. and Lewin, R. 1994. *Kanzi: The Ape at the Brink of the Human Mind.* New York: Wiley.

Schank, R. C. 1976. The role of memory in language processing. In C. Cofer (ed.), *The Nature of Human Memory.* San Francisco, CA: Freeman.

Schank, R. C. and Abelson, R. 1977. *Scripts, Plans, Goals, and Understanding.* Hillsdale, NJ: Lawrence Erlbaum.

Schlisselberg, G. 1988. Development of selected conversation skills and the ability to judge sentential well-formedness in young children. Doctoral dissertation. City University of New York, New York.

Schrauf, R. W. and Durazo-Arvizu, R. 2006. Bilingual autobiographical memory and emotion: Theory and methods. In A. Pavlenko (ed.), *Bilingual Minds: Emotional Experience, Expression and Representation*, 284–311. Clevedon, UK: Multilingual Matters Ltd.

Schumann, J. H. 1975. Affective factors and the problem of age in second language acquisition. *Language Learning* 25 (2): 209–35.

Searle, J. R. 1969. *Speech Acts*. London: Cambridge University Press.

Sekerina, I. A., Fernández, E. M., and Clahsen H. (eds.) 2008. *Developmental Psycholinguistics: On-line Methods in Children's Language Processing*. Amsterdam, The Netherlands: John Benjamins.

Senghas, A., Kita, S., and Özyürek, A. 2004. Children creating core properties of language: Evidence from an emerging sign language in Nicaragua. *Science* 305 (5691): 1779–82.

Shakibai, M. 2007. The efficacy of a training program to teach kindergarteners to detect lexical ambiguities. Doctoral dissertation. City University of New York, New York.

Shin, N. L. 2006. The development of null vs. overt subject pronoun expression in monolingual Spanish-speaking children: The influence of continuity of reference. Doctoral dissertation. City University of New York, New York.

Shockley, K., Sabadini, L., and Fowler, C. A. 2004. Imitation in shadowing words. *Perception and Psychophysics* 66 (3): 422–9.

SIL International. 2007. Speech Analyzer (Version 3.0.1) [Computer software]. Dallas, TX: Available from www.sil.org/computing/sa/index.htm.

Singer, M. 1994. Discourse inference processes. In M. A. Gernsbacher (ed.), *Handbook of Psycholinguistics*, 479–515. New York: Academic Press.

Slobin, D. I. 1972. Children and language: They learn the same way all around the world. *Psychology Today* 6 (2): 71–4.

Slobin, D. I. 1973. Cognitive prerequisites for the development of grammar. In C. A. Ferguson and D. I. Slobin (eds.), *Studies of Child Language Development*, 175–276. New York: Holt, Rinehart and Winston.

Slobin, D. I. 1985. Crosslinguistic evidence for the language-making capacity. In D. I. Slobin (ed.), *The Crosslinguistic Study of Language Acquisition: Vol. 2. Theoretical Issues*, 1157–256. Hillsdale, NY: Lawrence Erlbaum.

Slowiaczek, M. L. and Clifton, C. 1980. Subvocalization and reading for meaning. *Journal of Verbal Learning and Verbal Behavior* 19: 573–82.

Smith, M. C. and Wheeldon, L. R. 2001. Syntactic priming in spoken sentence production: An online study. *Cognition* 78: 123–64.

Smith, N. V., Tsimpli, I.-M., and Ouhalla, J. 1993. Learning the impossible: The acquisition of possible and impossible languages by a polyglot savant. *Lingua* 91: 279–347.

Spelke, E. and Cortelyou, A. 1981. In M. E. Lamb and L. R. Sherrod (eds.), *Infant Social Cognition: Empirical and Theoretical Considerations*. Hillsdale, NJ: Lawrence Erlbaum.

Sperry, R. W. 1968. Hemisphere deconnection and unity in conscious awareness. *American Psychologist* 23: 723–33.

Spivey, M. J., Tanenhaus, M. K., Eberhard, K. M., and Sedivy, J. C. 2002. Eye movements and spoken language comprehension: Effects of visual context on syntactic ambiguity resolution. *Cognitive Psychology* 45: 447–81.

Staub, A. and Rayner, K. 2007. Eye movements and on-line comprehension processes. In M. G. Gaskell (ed.), *The Oxford Handbook of Psycholinguistics*, 327–42. Oxford: Oxford University Press.

Steinhauer, K., Alter, K., and Friederici, A. D. 1999. Brain potentials indicate immediate use of prosodic cues in natural speech processing. *Nature Neuroscience* 2 (2): 191–6.

Stevenson, R. J. and Vitkovitch, M. 1986. The comprehension of anaphoric relations. *Language and Speech* 29: 335–60.

Stivers, T., Enfield, N. J., Brown, P., Englert, C., Hayashi, M., Heinemann, T., et al. 2009. Universals and cultural variation in turn-taking in conversation. *Proceedings of the National Academy of Sciences of the United States of America* 106 (26): 10587–92.

Stoyneshka, I., Fodor, J. and Fernández, E. M. 2010. Phoneme restoration methods for investigating prosodic influences on syntactic processing. *Language and Cognitive Processes*, prepublished April 7, 2010.

Sudhoff, S., Lenertova, D., Meyer, R., Pappert, S., and Augurzky, P. (eds.) 2006. *Methods in Empirical Prosody Research*. Berlin, Germany: Walter de Gruyter.

Swinney, D. A. 1979. Lexical access during sentence comprehension: (Re)consideration of context effects. *Journal of Verbal Learning and Verbal Behavior* 18, 645–59.

Swinney, D., Ford, M., Frauenfelder, U., and Bresnan, J. 1988. On the temporal course of gap-filling and antecedent assignment during sentence comprehension. In B. Grosz, R. Kaplan, M. Macken, and I. Sag (eds.), *Language Structure and Processing*. Stanford, CA: CSLI.

Taft, M. 1981. Prefix stripping revisited. *Journal of Verbal Learning and Verbal Behavior* 20: 284–97.

Tash, J. and Pisoni, D. B. 1973. Auditory and phonetic levels of processing as revealed by reaction time. *Journal of the Acoustical Society of America* 54 (1): 299.

Teira, C. and Igoa, J. M. 2007. The prosody–syntax relationship in sentence processing. *Anuario de Psicología* 38 (1): 45–69.

Thordardottir, E. T. and Ellis Weismer, S. 1998. Mean length of utterance and other language sample measures in early Icelandic. *First Language* 18: 1–32.

Traxler, M. J., Pickering, M. J., and Clifton, C. 1998. Adjunct attachment is not a form of lexical ambiguity resolution. *Journal of Memory and Language* 39: 558–92.

Trueswell, J. C. 2008. Using eye movements as a developmental measure within psycholinguistics. In I. A. Sekerina, E. M. Fernández, and H. Clahsen (eds.), *Developmental Psycholinguistics: On-line Methods in Children's Language Processing*, 73–96. Amsterdam, The Netherlands: John Benjamins.

Trueswell, J. C. and Tanenhaus, M. K. (eds.) 2005. *Approaches to Studying World-Situated Language Use: Bridging the Language-as-Product and Language-as-Action Traditions*. Cambridge, MA: The MIT Press.

Trueswell, J. C., Sekerina, I., Hill, N. M., and Logrip, M. L. 1999. The kindergarten-path effect: Studying on-line sentence processing in young children. *Cognition* 73: 89–134.

Trueswell, J. C., Tanenhaus, M. K., and Garnsey, S. M. 1994. Semantic influences on parsing: Use of thematic role information in syntactic ambiguity resolution. *Journal of Memory and Language* 33: 285–318.

Tsiamtsiouris, J., and Cairns, H. S. 2009. Effects of syntactic complexity and sentence-structure priming on speech initiation time in adults who stutter. *Journal of Speech, Language, and Hearing Research*, 52 (6), 1623–39.

Tsiamtsiouris, J., Cairns, H. S., and Frank, C. M. 2007. *Sentence Structure Production and Processing Time in Adults Who Stutter*. Boston, MA: American Speech Language Hearing Association.

Tunmer, W. E. and Hoover, W. A. 1992. Cognitive and linguistic factors in learning to read. In P. B. Gough, L. C. Ehri, and R. Treiman (eds.), *Reading Acquisition*. Hillsdale, NJ: Lawrence Erlbaum.

Valian, V. 1990. Syntactic subjects in the early speech of American and Italian children. *Cognition* 40: 21–81.

Van Gompel, R. P. and Pickering, M. J. 2005. Syntactic parsing. In M. G. Gaskell (ed.), *The Oxford Handbook of Psycholinguistics*, 289–307. Oxford: Oxford University Press.

Van Heuven, W. J., Dijkstra, A., and Grainger, J. 1998. Orthographic neighborhood effects in bilingual word recognition. *Journal of Memory and Language* 39: 458–83.

VanPatten, B. 1987. On babies and bathwater: Input in foreign language learning. *The Modern Language Journal* 71 (2): 156–64.

Vigliocco, G., Hartsuiker, R. J., Jarema, G., and Kolk, H. H. 1996. One or more labels on the bottles? Notional concord in Dutch and French. *Language and Cognitive Processes* 11 (4): 407–42.

Vonk, W. and Noordman, L. G. 1990. Control of inferences in text understanding. In D. A. Balota, F. d'Arcais, and K. Rayner (eds.), *Comprehension Processes in Reading*, 447–64. Hillsdale. NJ: Lawrence Erlbaum.

Wankoff, L. and Cairns, H. 2009. Why ambiguity detection is a predictor of reading skill. *Communication Disorders Quarterly* 30 (3): 183–92.

Wanner, E. and Maratsos, M. 1978. An ATN approach to comprehension. In M. Halle, J. Bresnan, and G. A. Miller (eds.), *Linguistic Theory and Psychological Reality*. Cambridge, MA: The MIT Press.

Warren, R. M. 1970. Perceptual restoration of missing speech sounds. *Science* 176: 392–3.

Watkins, K. E., Dronkers, N. F., and Vargha-Khadem, F. 2002. Behavioural analysis of an inherited speech and language disorder: Comparison with acquired aphasia. *Brain* 125: 452–64.

Weikum, W. M., Vouloumanos, A., Navarra, J., Soto-Faraco, S., Sebastián-Gallés, N., and Werker, J. F. 2007. Visual language discrimination in infancy. *Science* 316: 1159.

Weinberg, A. 1990. Markedness versus maturation: The case subject–auxiliary inversion. *Language Acquisition: A Journal of Developmental Linguistics* 1: 165–95.

Werker, J. F. and Byers-Heinlein, K. 2008. Bilingualism in infancy: First steps in perception and comprehension. *Trends in Cognitive Science* 12 (4): 144–51.

Werker, J. F. and Lalonde, C. E. 1988. The development of speech perception: Initial capabilities and the emergence of phonemic categories. *Developmental Psychology* 24: 672–83.

Werker, J. F. and Tees, R. C. 2002. Cross-language speech perception: Evidence for perceptual reorganization during the first year of life. *Infant Behavior and Development* 25: 121–33.

Wexler, K. 2002. Very early parameter setting and the unique checking constraint: A new explanation of the optional infinitive stage. *Lingua* 106: 23–79.

Whalen, D. H. and Levitt, A. G. 1995. The universality of intrinsic F_0 of vowels. *Journal of Phonetics* 23 (3): 349–66.

Wilkes-Gibbs, D. and Clark, H. H. 1992. Coordinating beliefs in conversation. *Journal of Memory and Language* 31, 183–94.

Willmes, K. and Poeck, K. 1993. To what extent can aphasic syndromes be localized? *Brain* 116: 1527–40.

Wolf, M. 2007. *Proust and the Squid: The Story and Science of the Reading Brain.* New York: Harper Collins.

Yuan, J., Liberman, M., and Cieri, C. 2006. Towards an integrated understanding of speech rate in conversation. *Interspeech* 2006: 541–4.

Zipke, M., Ehri, L., and Cairns, H. 2009. Using semantic ambiguity instruction to improve third graders' metalinguistic awareness and reading comprehension. *Reading Research Quarterly* 44 (3): 300–321.

Zurif, E. B., Swinney, D., Prather, P., Solomon, J., and Bushell, C. 1993. An on-line analysis of syntactic processing in Broca's and Wernicke's aphasia. *Brain and Language* 45: 448–64.

Name Index

Note: Page numbers after 276 are in the References section.

Subject Index

Page numbers in **bold** indicate the page on which a New Concept is introduced.

CPSIA information can be obtained
at www.ICGtesting.com
Printed in the USA
BVHW09s0912200818
524651BV00030B/65/P

9 781405 191470